The Patchwork PATTERN BOOK

TRIP AROUND THE WORLD

or Grandmother's Dream

Cot Quilt

Alternate squares of light and dark patches radiating from a centre square. Stitched in diagonal strips across the quilt.

You will need:
Dressweight cotton (see page 64)
2. 10 m of 90 cm wide cotton lining
2.10 m of 90 cm wide lightweight terylene wadding
White cotton thread
Finished size: 102 cm square

To make up

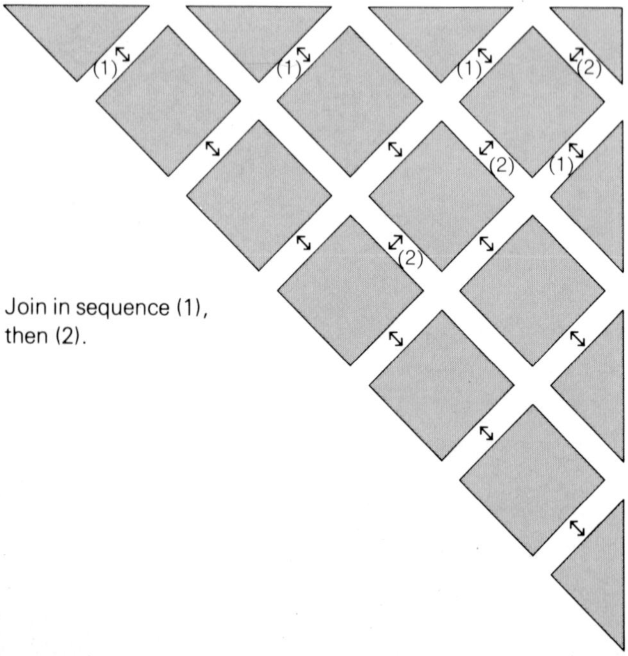

Join in sequence (1), then (2).

Patterns of the patches used (actual size)
Add 7 mm seam allowance.

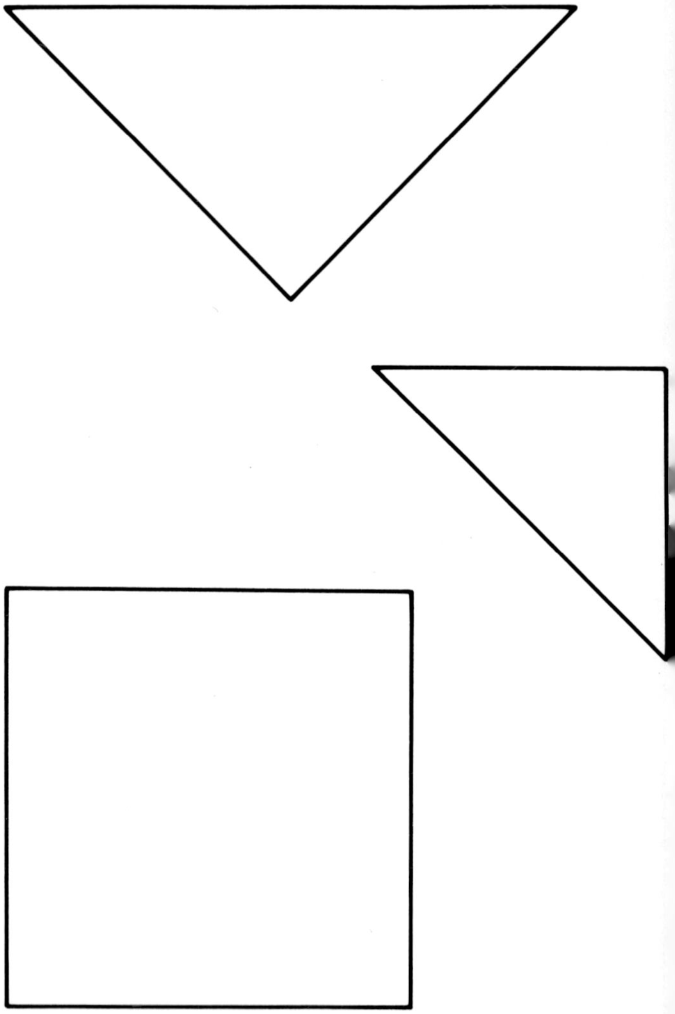

Continued on page 64.

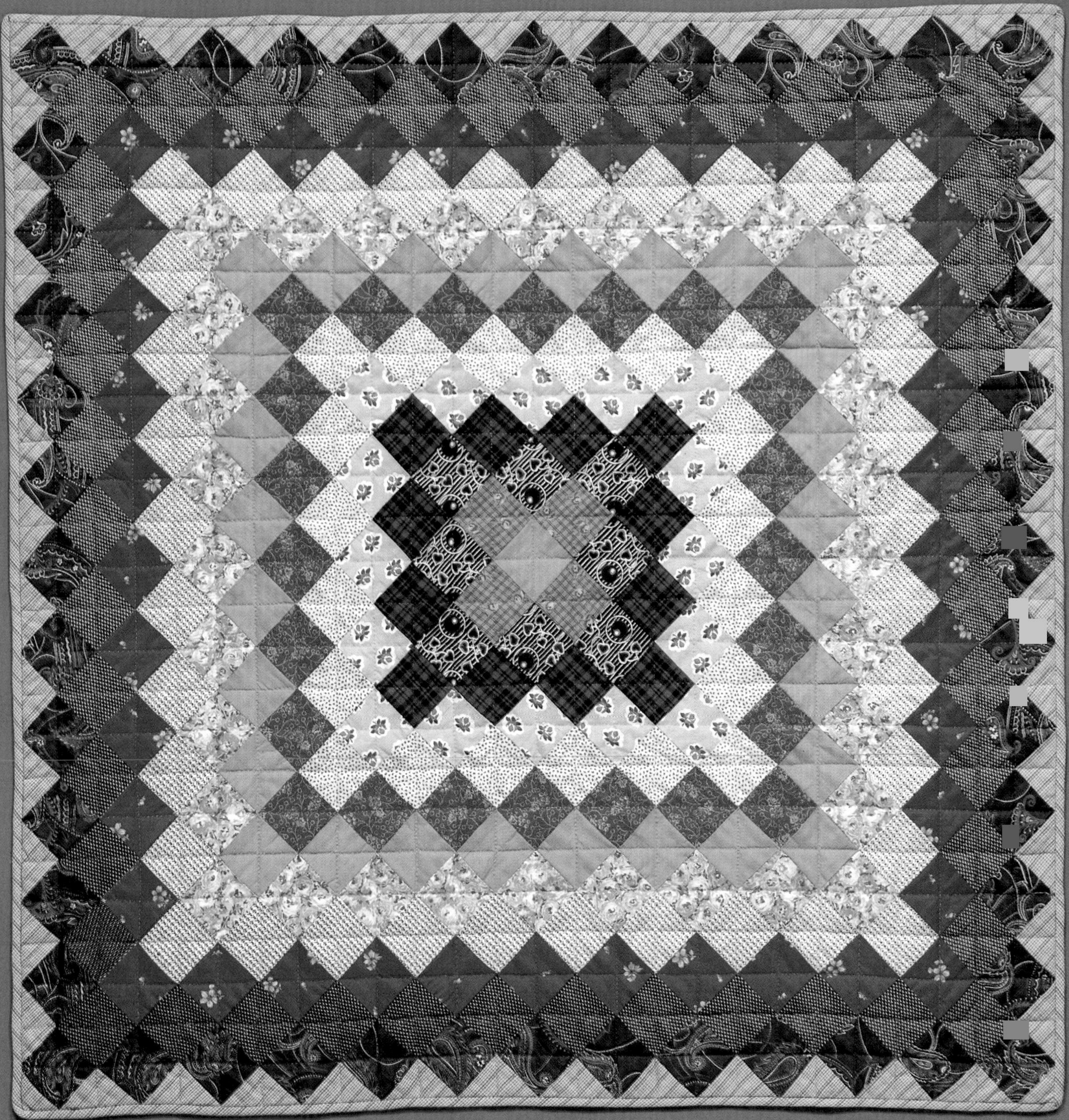

DOUBLE IRISH CHAIN
Cot Quilt

Alternate plain and patchwork blocks. The plain blocks are quilted with a traditional design once the quilt is made up (see page 67).

You will need:
2.10m of 90cm wide olive green dressweight cotton
1.10m of 90cm wide unbleached calico
40cm of 90cm wide cotton print (a)
20cm of 90cm wide cotton print (b)
2.10m of 90cm wide lightweight terylene wadding
Olive green cotton thread
Finished size: 101cm square

Patterns of the patches used (actual size)
Add 7mm seam allowance.

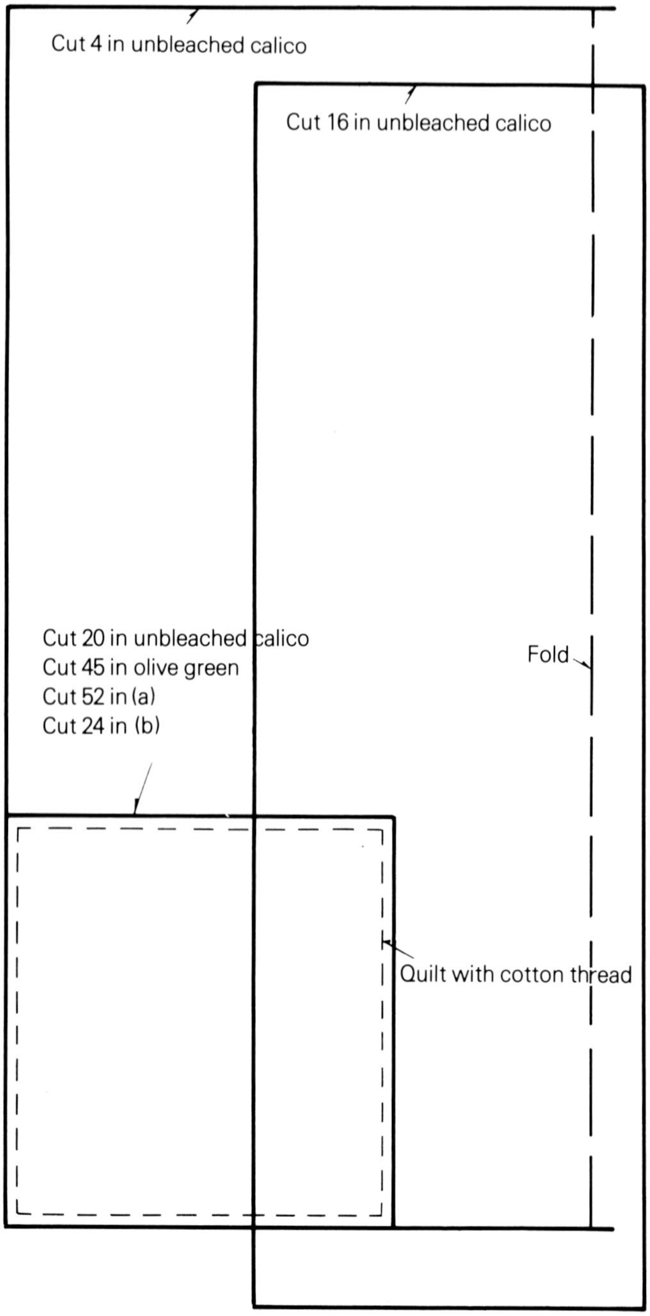

Cut 4 in unbleached calico
Cut 16 in unbleached calico
Cut 20 in unbleached calico
Cut 45 in olive green
Cut 52 in (a)
Cut 24 in (b)
Fold
Quilt with cotton thread

To make up

Join in sequences (1)-(5).

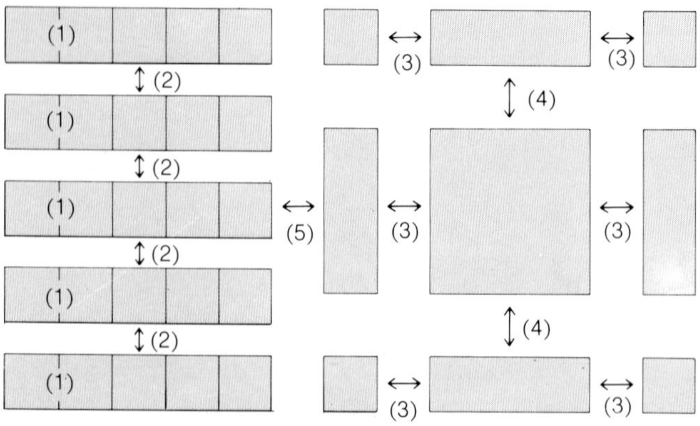

Continued on page 66.

DOUBLE IRISH CHAIN
Bedspread

You will need:
4 m of 90 cm wide unbleached calico
30 cm x 190 cm of navy blue dressweight cotton
2 m (total) of 90 cm wide cotton print and indigo cotton
3.80 m of 90 cm wide cotton lining
3.90 cm of 90 cm wide lightweight terylene wadding
Navy blue cotton thread
Finished size: 156 cm x 192 cm

Quilting Design (actual size)

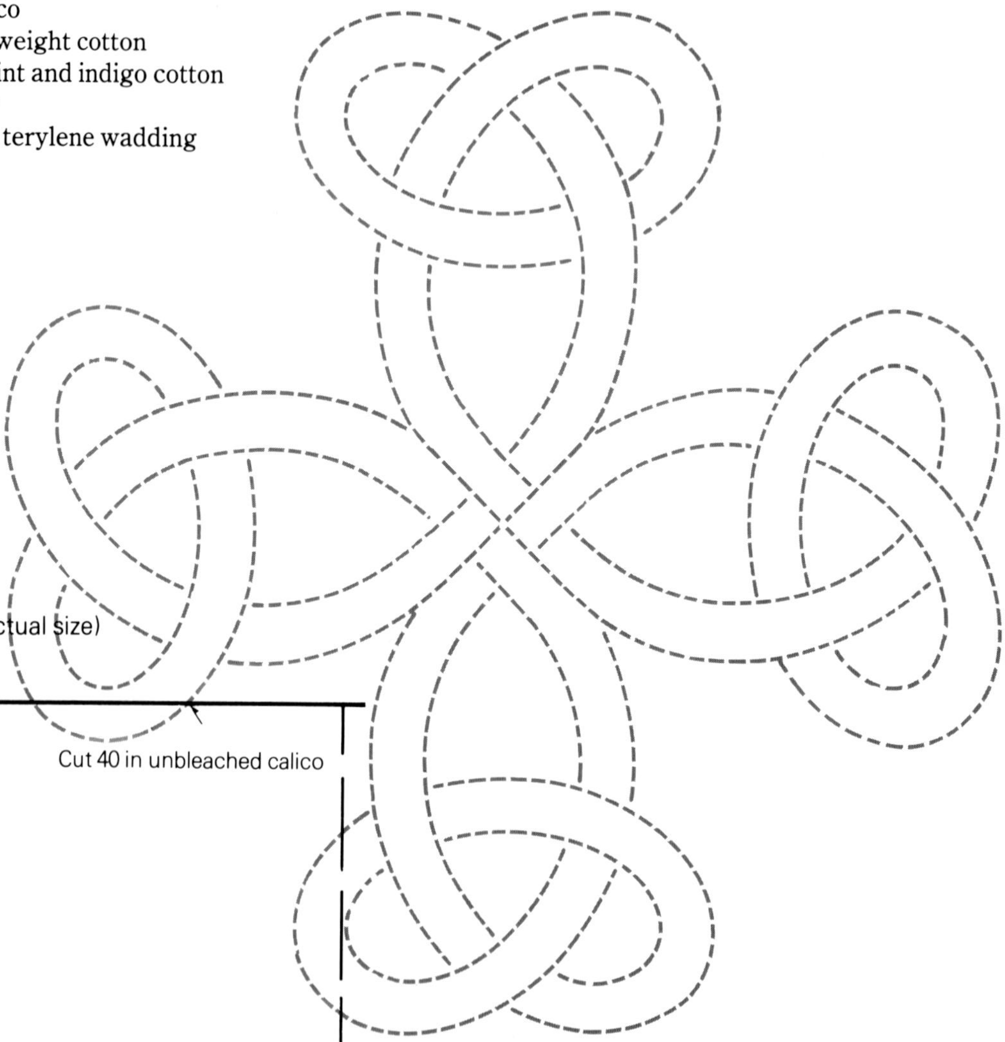

Patterns of the patches used (actual size)
Add 7 mm seam allowance.

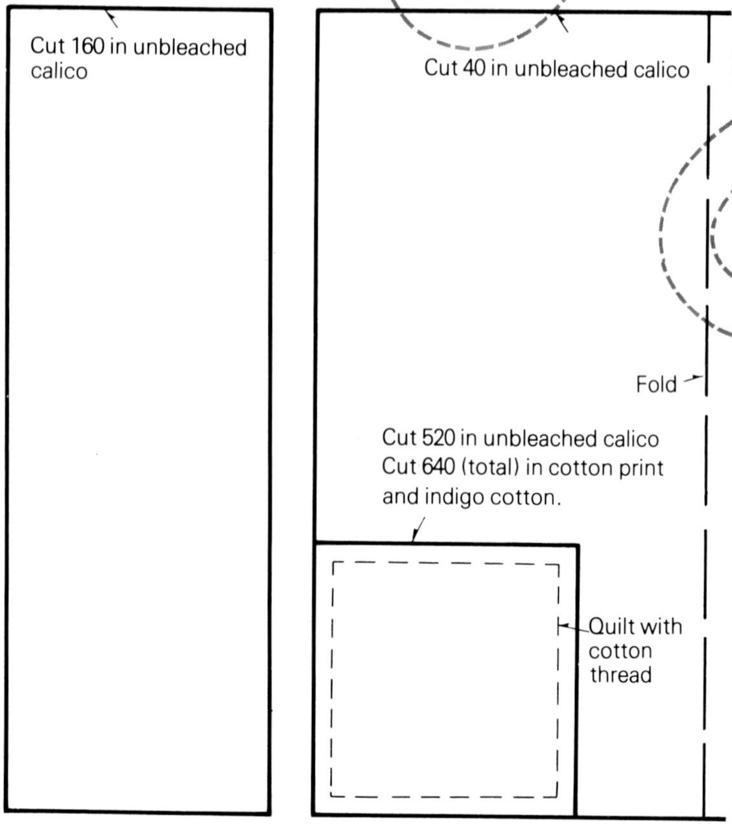
Cut 160 in unbleached calico
Cut 40 in unbleached calico
Fold
Cut 520 in unbleached calico
Cut 640 (total) in cotton print and indigo cotton.
Quilt with cotton thread

To make up see page 2

Continued on page 65.

LOG CABIN
Top Quilt for a Single Bed

The narrow strips of fabric represent the overlapping logs of a log cabin.

You will need:
Dressweight cotton (see page 68)
2.40 m of 90 cm wide cotton lining
2.40 m of 90 cm wide lightweight terylene wadding
5.10 m of 1.8 cm wide navy blue bias strip
Finished size: 127 cm square

To make up
Join in sequences (1)-(16).

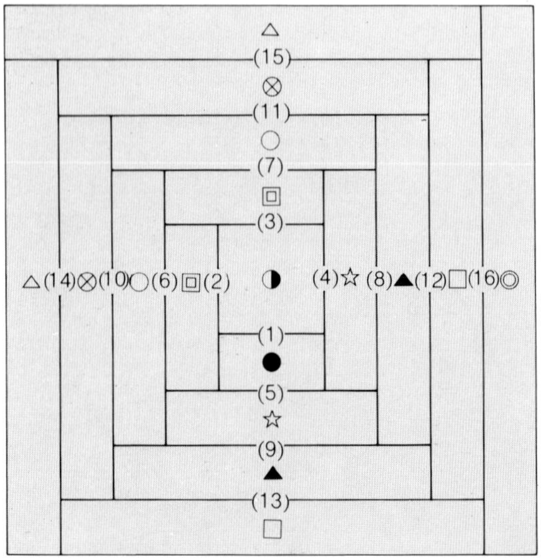

Patterns of the patches used
(actual size)
Add 7 mm seam allowance.

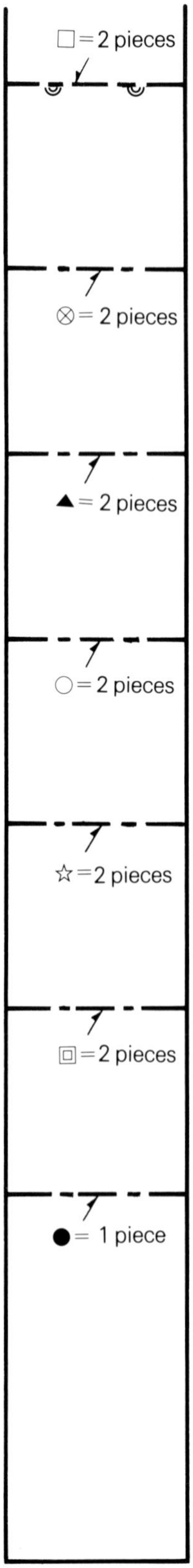

□ = 2 pieces
⊗ = 2 pieces
▲ = 2 pieces
○ = 2 pieces
☆ = 2 pieces
= 2 pieces
● = 1 piece

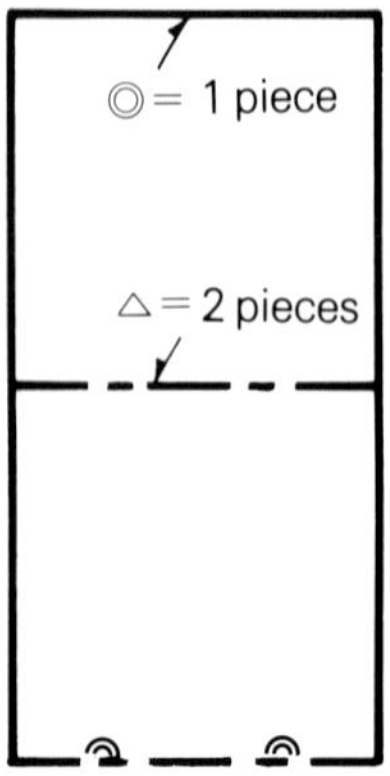

◎ = 1 piece
△ = 2 pieces

Match pieces at balance marks ( ).

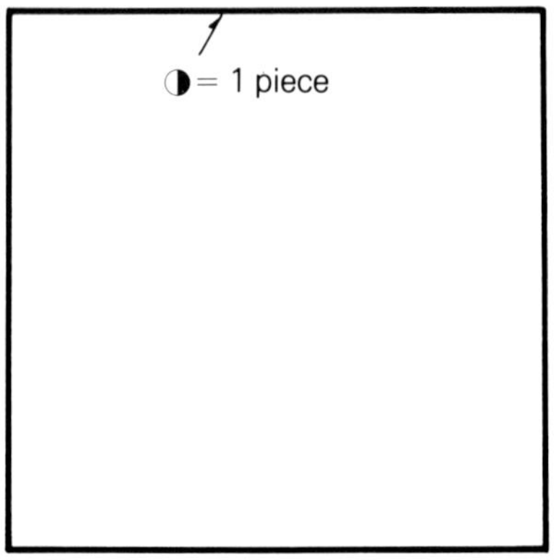

◑ = 1 piece

This pattern gives the increasing lengths for the fabric strips worked around the centre square (see left).

Continued on page 68.

MOSAIC STAR

Top Quilt for a Single Bed

This design is composed of hexagons and pentagons and can only be made using the hand-stitched method (see page 101).

You will need:
2 m of 90 cm wide navy blue dressweight cotton
30 cm of 90 cm wide yellow dressweight cotton
60 cm x 60 cm of navy blue-based polka dot print
40 sets of dressweight cotton print 50 cm x 8 cm, to make 40 sets of 6 patches
2.30 m of 90 cm wide cotton lining
2.30 m of 90 cm wide lightweight terylene wadding
Navy blue and yellow cotton thread
Finished size: 159.5 cm x 111 cm

Patterns of the patches used (actual size)
Add 7 mm seam allowance.

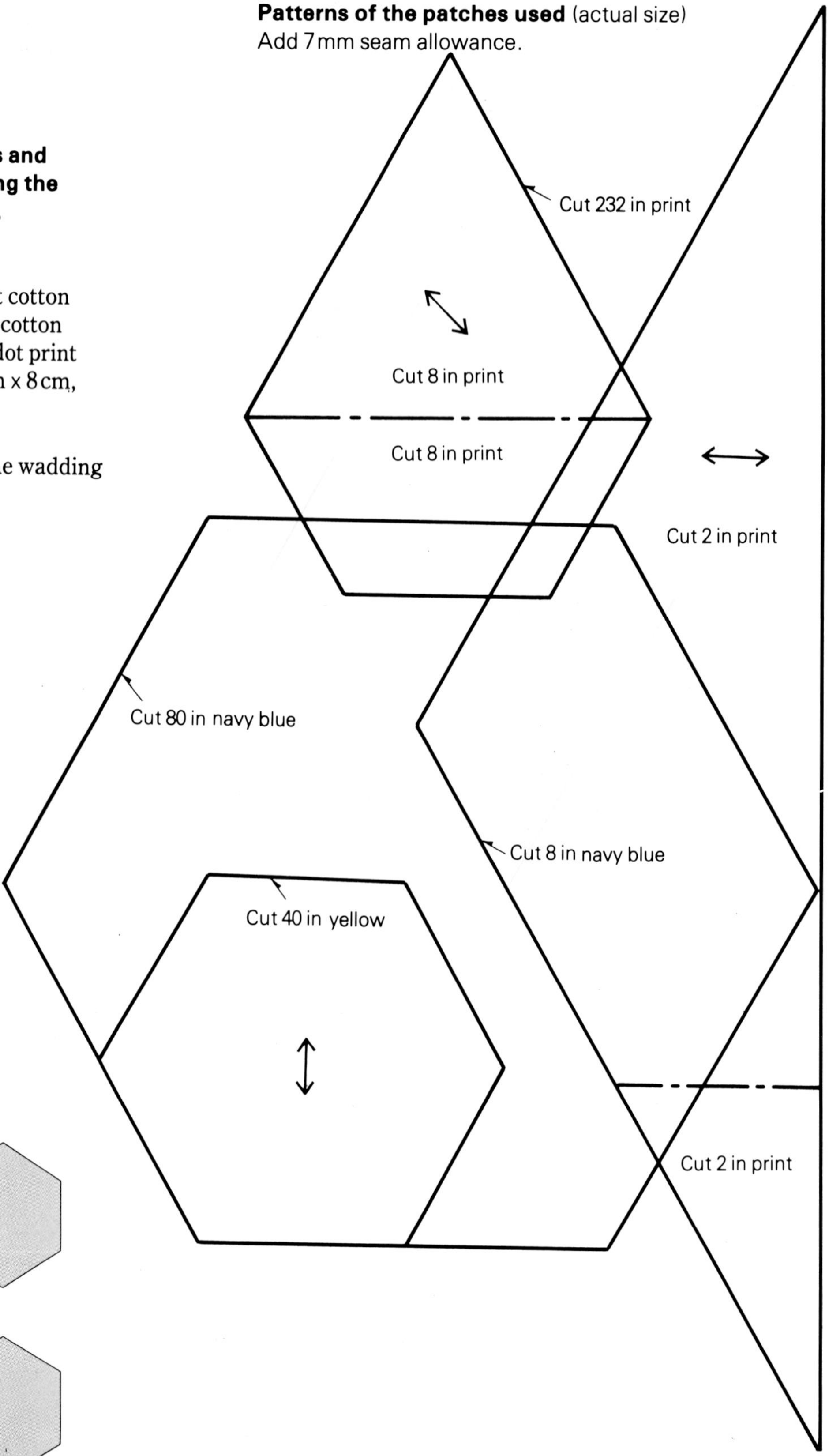
Cut 232 in print
Cut 8 in print
Cut 8 in print
Cut 2 in print
Cut 80 in navy blue
Cut 8 in navy blue
Cut 40 in yellow
Cut 2 in print

To make up
Join in sequences (1)-(8).

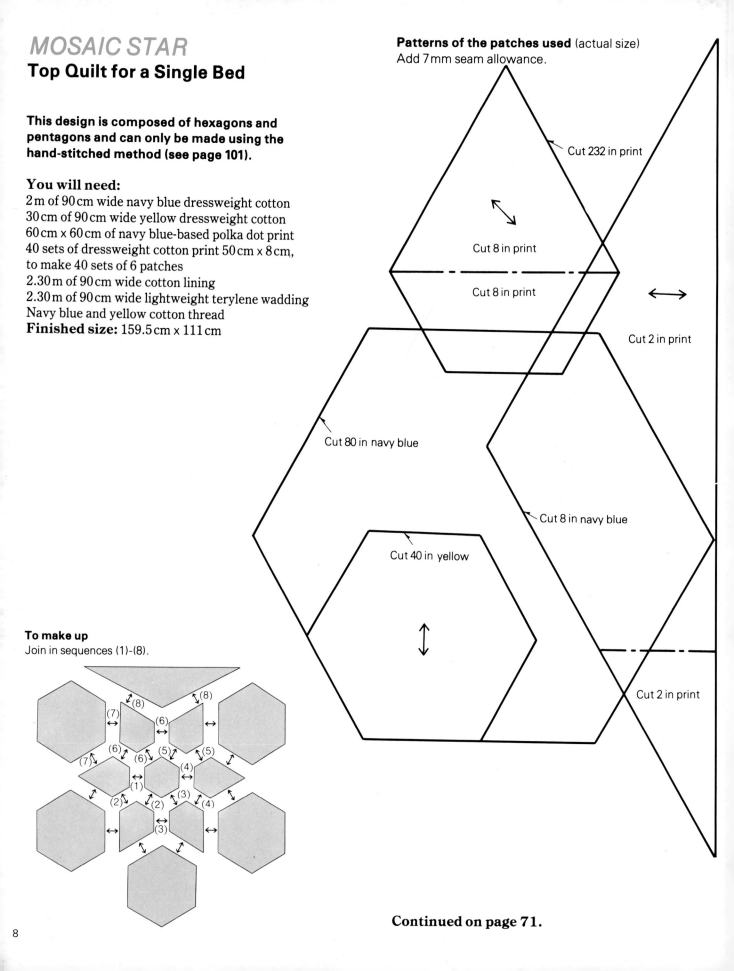

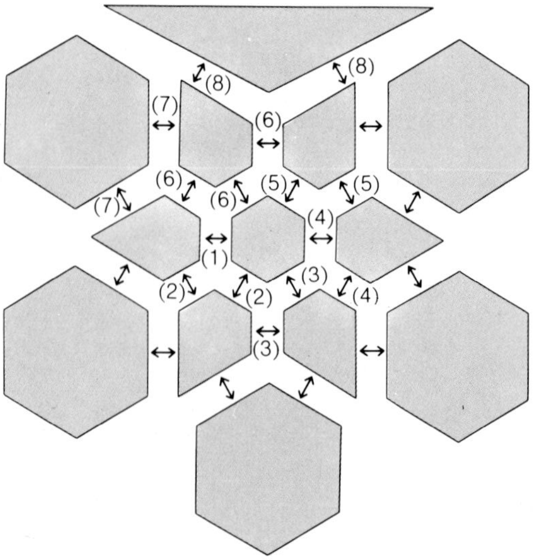

Continued on page 71.

STAR OF BETHLEHEM
Tablecloth

Six lozenges linked together in the centre are extended to a six-point star, called "star of Bethlehem".

You will need:

3 m of 90 cm wide aqua blue dressweight cotton
80 cm of 90 cm wide red dressweight cotton
80 cm of 90 cm wide pale blue dressweight cotton
50 cm of 90 cm wide white dressweight cotton
50 cm of 90 cm wide blue-and-white polka dot print
3.10 m of 90 cm wide cotton lining
Matching cotton thread
Finished size: 152 cm x 170.5 cm

Patterns of the patches used (actual size)
Add 7 mm seam allowance.

Cut 104 in red
98 in pale blue
54 in print
48 in white

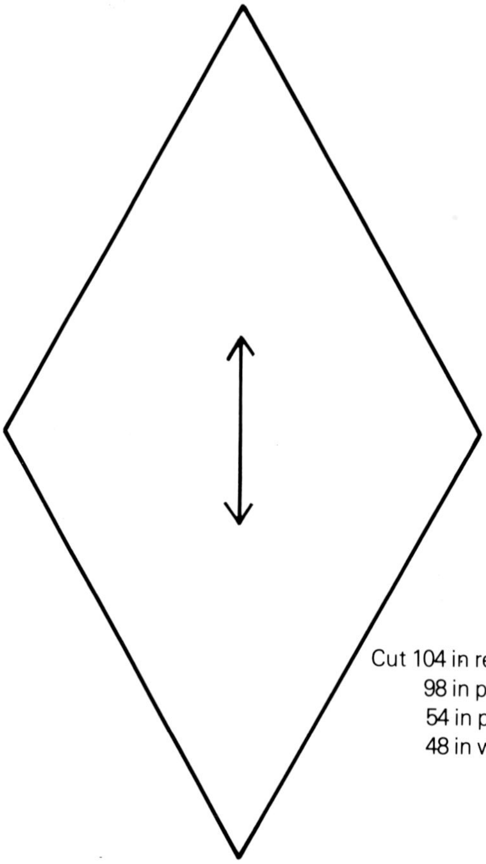

To make up
Join in sequences (1)-(3)

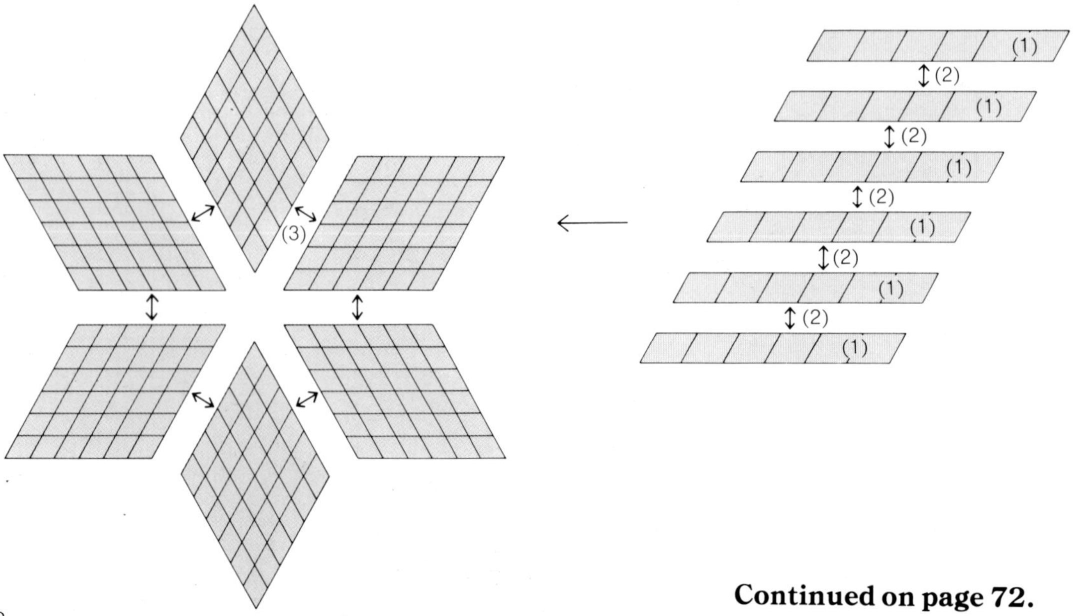

Continued on page 72.

Chronicles of Avonlea

A THOUSAND PYRAMIDS
Bed Linen & Matching Picture

This design is composed of isosceles triangles in two contrasting fabrics.

Patchwork Picture
You will need:
20 cm x 80 cm of pink dressweight cotton print
20 cm x 40 cm of pink dressweight cotton
10 cm x 50 cm of green dressweight cotton
40 cm x 30 cm of cotton lining
40 cm x 30 cm of lightweight terylene wadding
Frame with inside measurement of 20 cm x 29 cm
White cotton thread
Finished size: size of frame

Bed Linen
For the patchwork border, you will need:
1.20 m of 90 cm wide blue-and-white floral print
60 cm of 90 cm wide light blue dressweight cotton
60 cm of 90 cm wide dark blue dressweight cotton
1.20 m of 90 cm wide cotton lining
White cotton thread
Finished size: 127 cm x 55 cm

For the pillow case, you will need:
80 cm of 90 cm wide light blue dressweight cotton
70 cm x 30 cm dark blue dressweight cotton
50 cm of 90 cm wide blue-and-white floral print
50 cm x 70 cm of cotton lining
White cotton thread
Finished size 63.5 cm x 44 cm

Patterns of the patches used (actual size)
Add 7 mm seam allowance.

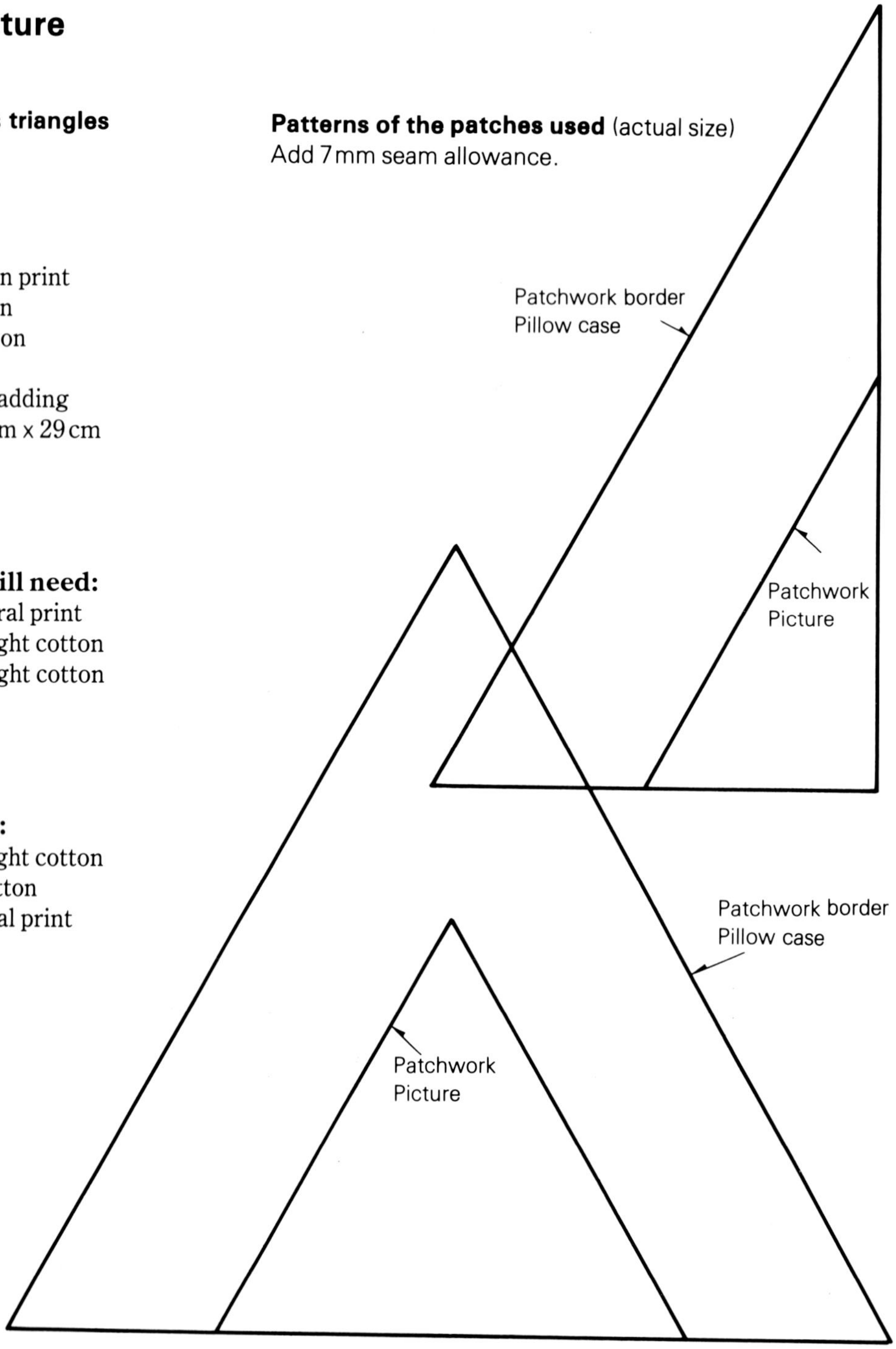

Patchwork border
Pillow case
Patchwork
Picture
Patchwork border
Pillow case
Patchwork
Picture

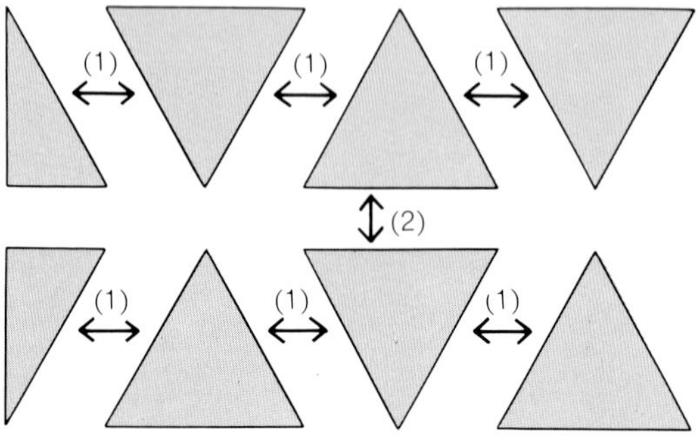

To make up
Join in sequences (1) and (2).

Continued on page 69.

milk
milk
milk

MOUNTAIN CHAIN
Placemats and Pincushions

A design which combines half-square triangles is finished in a striking colour sheme.

Placemat
You will need:
30 cm x 50 cm of dressweight cotton print (a)
30 cm x 50 cm of contrasting dressweight cotton print (b)
30 cm x 50 cm of cotton lining
30 cm x 50 cm of lightweight terylene wadding
1.50 m of 12 mm wide bias tape to match (a)
White cotton thread
Finished size: 43 cm x 29 cm

Pincushions A, B and C
You will need:
20 cm x 20 cm of blue-and-red floral print
20 cm x 10 cm of blue dressweight cotton
20 cm x 20 cm of red dressweight cotton
20 cm x 10 cm of red-and-white floral print
40 cm x 20 cm of green dressweight cotton
30 cm x 10 cm of pink-and-beige floral print
Cotton wool or kapok
Finished size of each: 9 cm square

Patterns of the patches used (actual size)
Add 7 mm seam allowance.

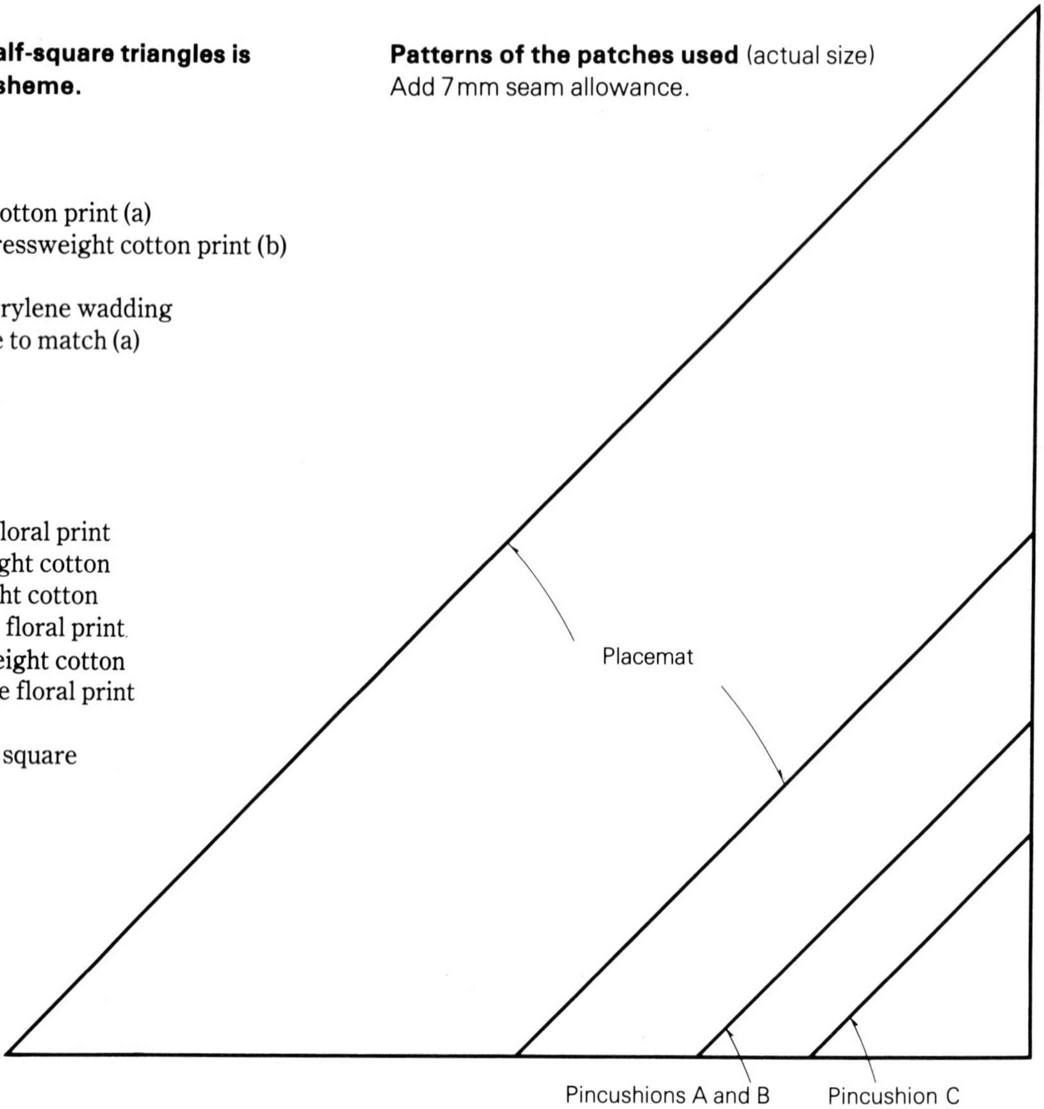

To make up
Join in sequences (1)-(3).

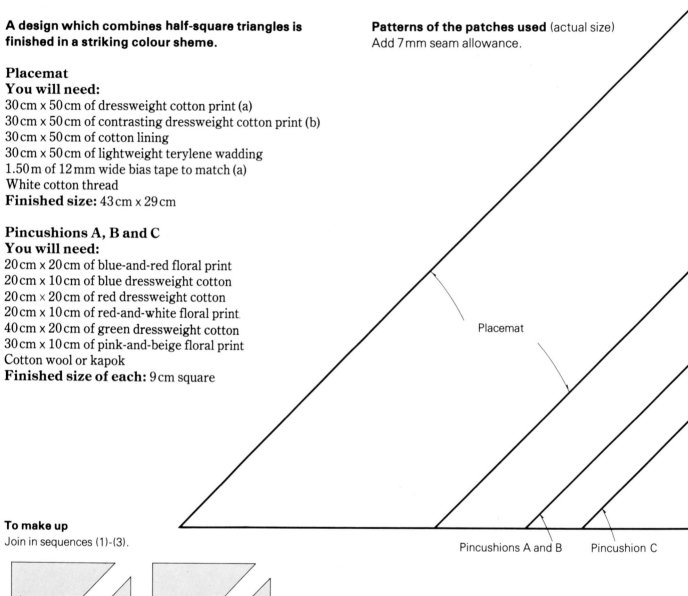

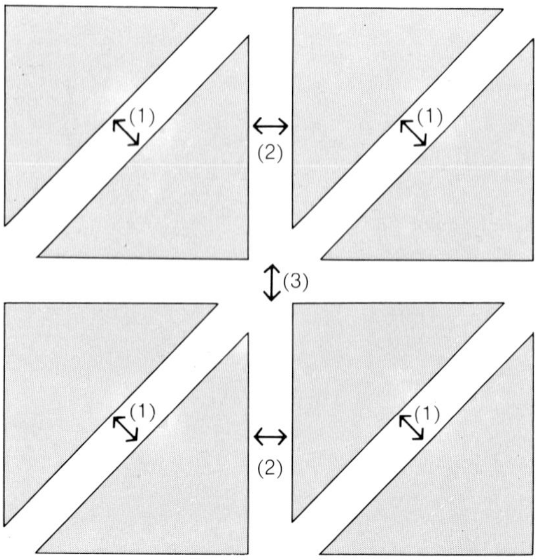

Continued on page 73.

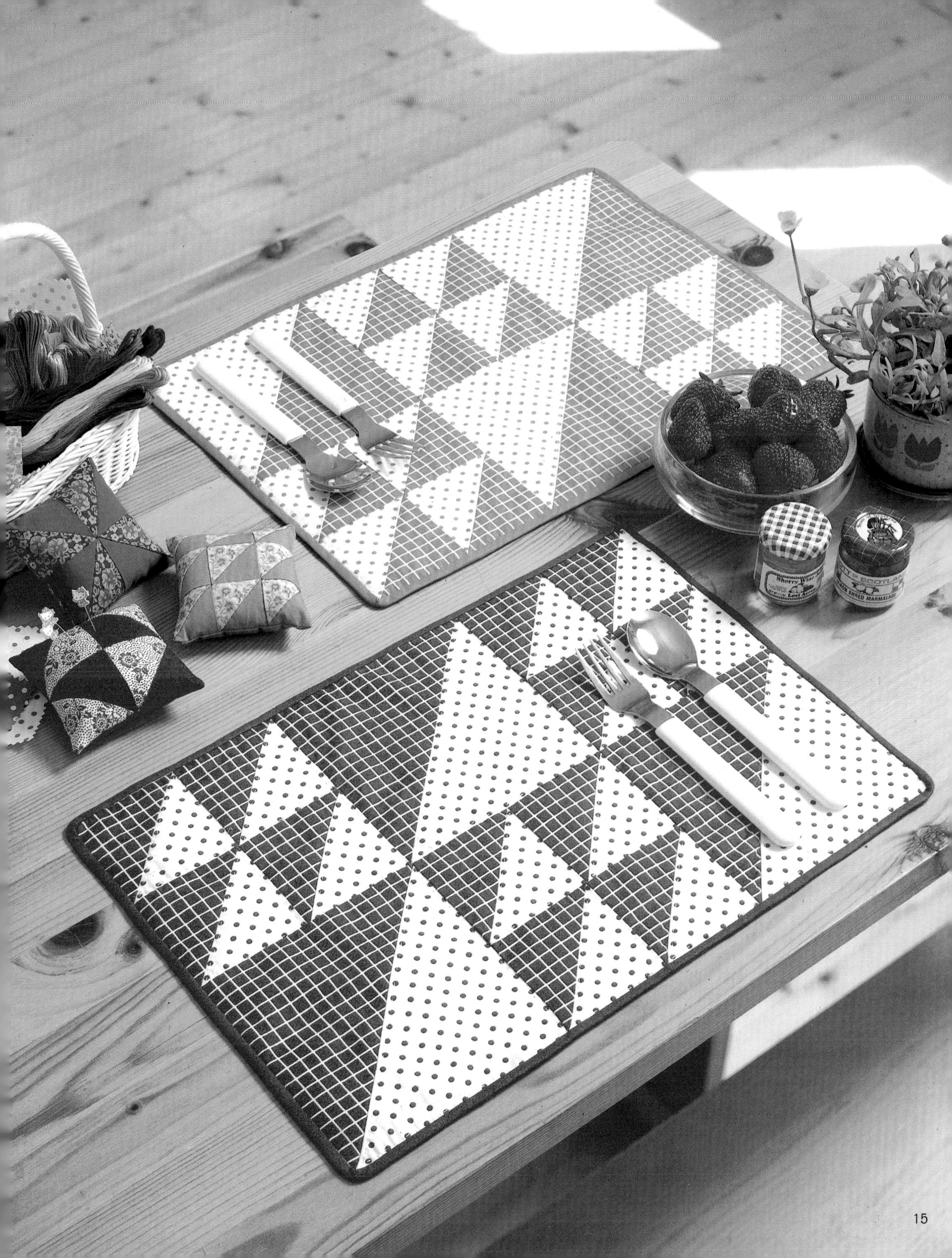
Sherry Wine
SHRED MARMALADE

FRENCH BOUQUET
Tablecloth

Hexagons form the basis of this design which can only be made using the hand-stitched method (see page 101). Each brown centre patch is surrounded by 6 patches to make a flower.

You will need:
2.20 m of 90 cm wide brown dressweight cotton
60 cm of 90 cm wide dressweight cotton print (a)
80 cm x 60 cm of both cotton prints (b) and (c)
Brown cotton thread
Finished size: see page 75

Patterns of the patches used (actual size)
Add 7 mm seam allowance.

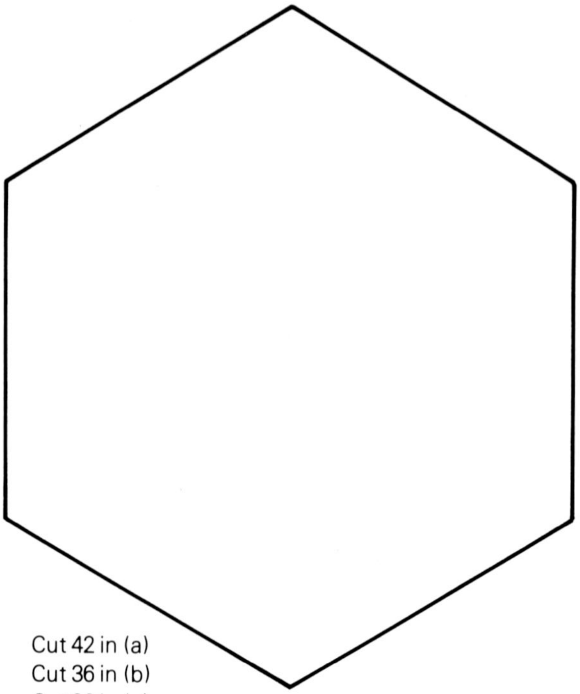

Cut 42 in (a)
Cut 36 in (b)
Cut 36 in (c)
Cut 12 in brown

To make up
Join in sequences (1)-(3)

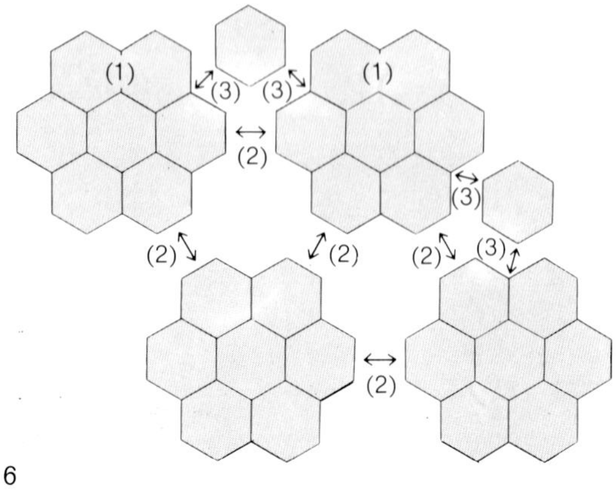

Stage 3:

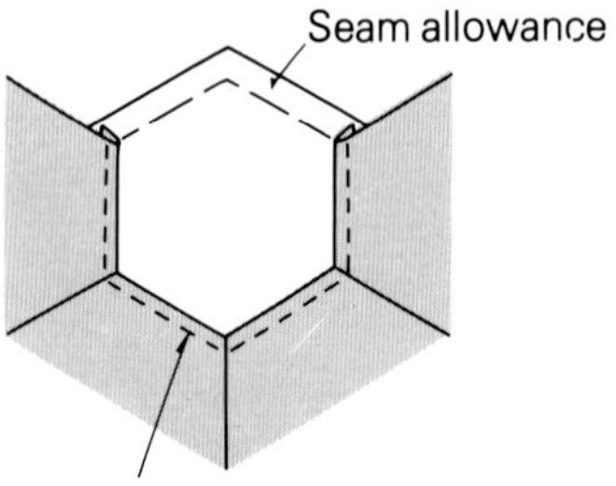

Quilt top to lining, stitching round the edges of print patches so that lining forms the central patch.

Continued on page 75.

DRUNKARD'S PATH
Bed Linen & Tray Cloth

The scalloped edges in this design form imaginative lines amongst a variety of prints.

Tray Cloth
You will need:
30 cm x 80 cm of cotton print (a)
10 cm x 90 cm of cotton print (b)
10 cm x 70 cm of both cotton prints (c) and (d)
1.40 m of 18 mm wide pink bias tape
White and pink embroidery cotton
Finished size: 36.5 cm x 29.5 cm

Bed Linen
For the patchwork border, you will need:
50 cm x 90 cm of both cotton prints (a) and (b)
30 cm x 90 cm of both cotton prints (c) and (d)
110 cm x 50 cm of cotton lining
3.50 m of 8 cm wide white cotton lace
Pink and blue embroidery cotton
Finished size: 117.5 cm x 61.5 cm

For the pillow case, you will need:
30 cm x 90 cm of cotton print (a)
80 cm x 90 cm of cotton print (b)
15 cm x 90 cm of both cotton prints (c) and (d)
3.20 m of 8 cm wide white cotton lace
Blue embroidery cotton
4.5 cm of 2.5 cm wide Velcro
Finished size: 64 cm x 48 cm

To make up
Join in sequences (1)-(3).

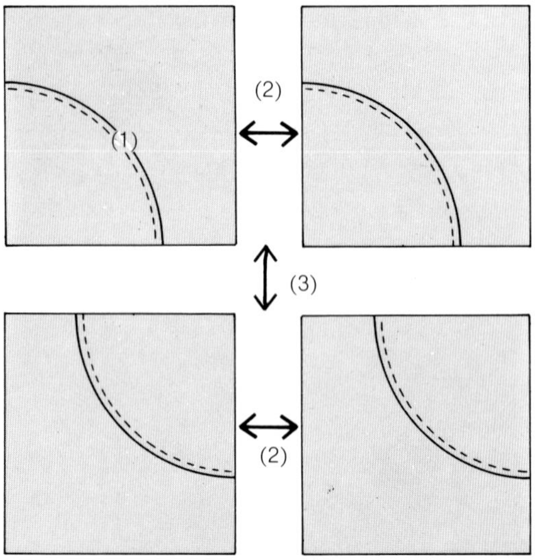

Turn under edges of curved patch and, using 2 strands of a matching cotton, topstitch to square patch.

Patterns of the patches used (actual size)
Add 7 mm seam allowance.

Tray Cloth

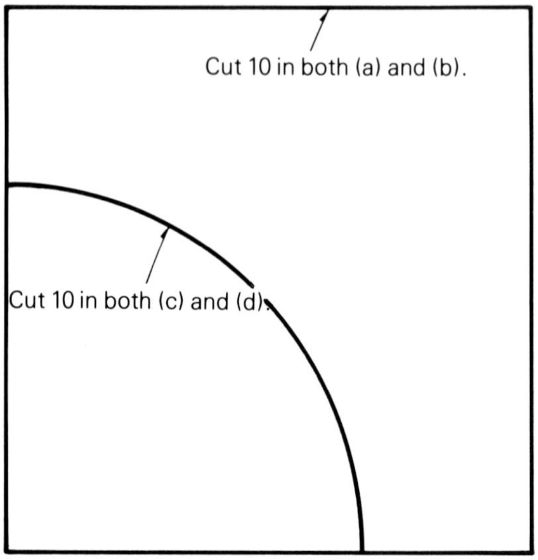

Cut 10 in both (a) and (b).
Cut 10 in both (c) and (d).

Patchwork border, Pillow case

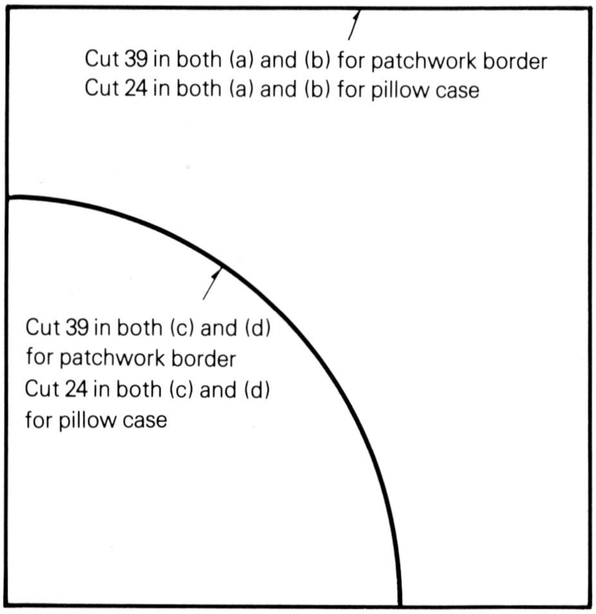

Cut 39 in both (a) and (b) for patchwork border
Cut 24 in both (a) and (b) for pillow case
Cut 39 in both (c) and (d) for patchwork border
Cut 24 in both (c) and (d) for pillow case

Continued on page 73.

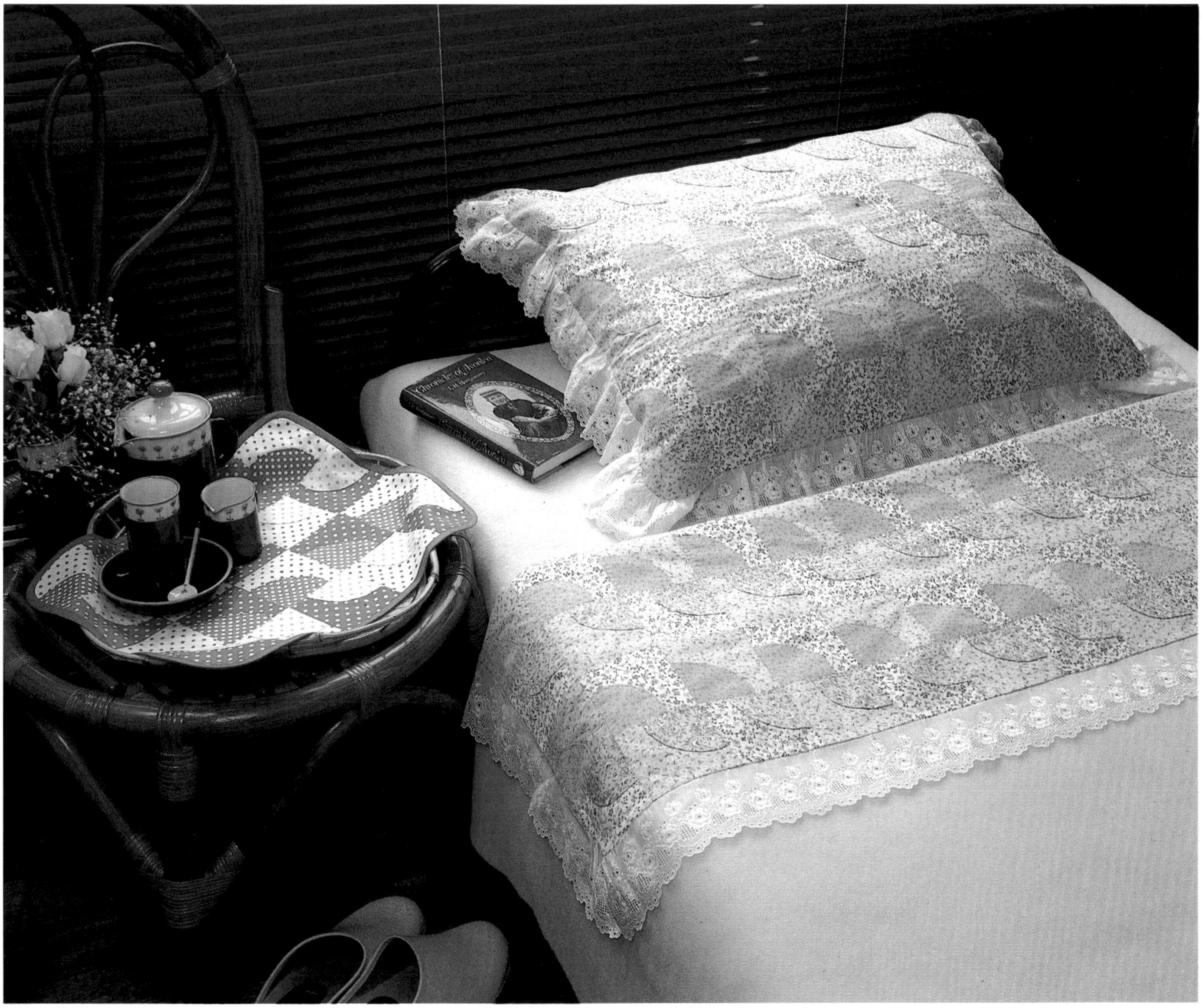

GRANDMOTHER'S FAN
Panel

Colourful fans in a variety of prints against a plain background make an attractive panel.

You will need:
1.30 m of 90 cm wide beige dressweight cotton
70 cm of 90 cm wide botton print (a)
30 cm x 90 cm of both cotton prints (b) and (c)
40 cm x 90 cm of both cotton prints (d) and (e)
170 cm x 80 cm of cotton lining
Finished size: 162.5 cm x 70.5 cm

SHOO FLY
Wall Hanging & Phone Set

The shoo fly design is the simplest variation of a nine-patch block.

Phone Set
For the phone cover, you will need:
80 cm x 30 cm of brown sheeting
20 cm x 40 cm of both cotton prints (a) and (b)
20 cm x 60 cm of cotton print (c)
20 cm x 20 cm of cotton print (d)
40 cm x 40 cm of cotton lining
Finished size: 39 cm x 39 cm

For the mat, you will need:
30 cm x 30 cm of cotton print (a) and lining
20 cm x 60 cm of brown sheeting
40 cm x 40 cm of lightweight terylene wadding
Finished size: 31 cm x 31 cm

Wall Hanging
You will need:
40 cm x 70 cm of moss green sheeting
20 cm x 30 cm of both cotton prints (a) and (b)
50 cm x 50 cm of cotton print (c)
30 cm x 30 cm of cotton print (d)
40 cm of 90 cm wide cotton lining
40 cm of 90 cm wide lightweight terylene wadding
4 cm of 2.5 cm wide Velcro
Finished size: 36 cm x 66.5 cm

Patterns of the patches used
(actual size)
Add 7 mm seam allowance.

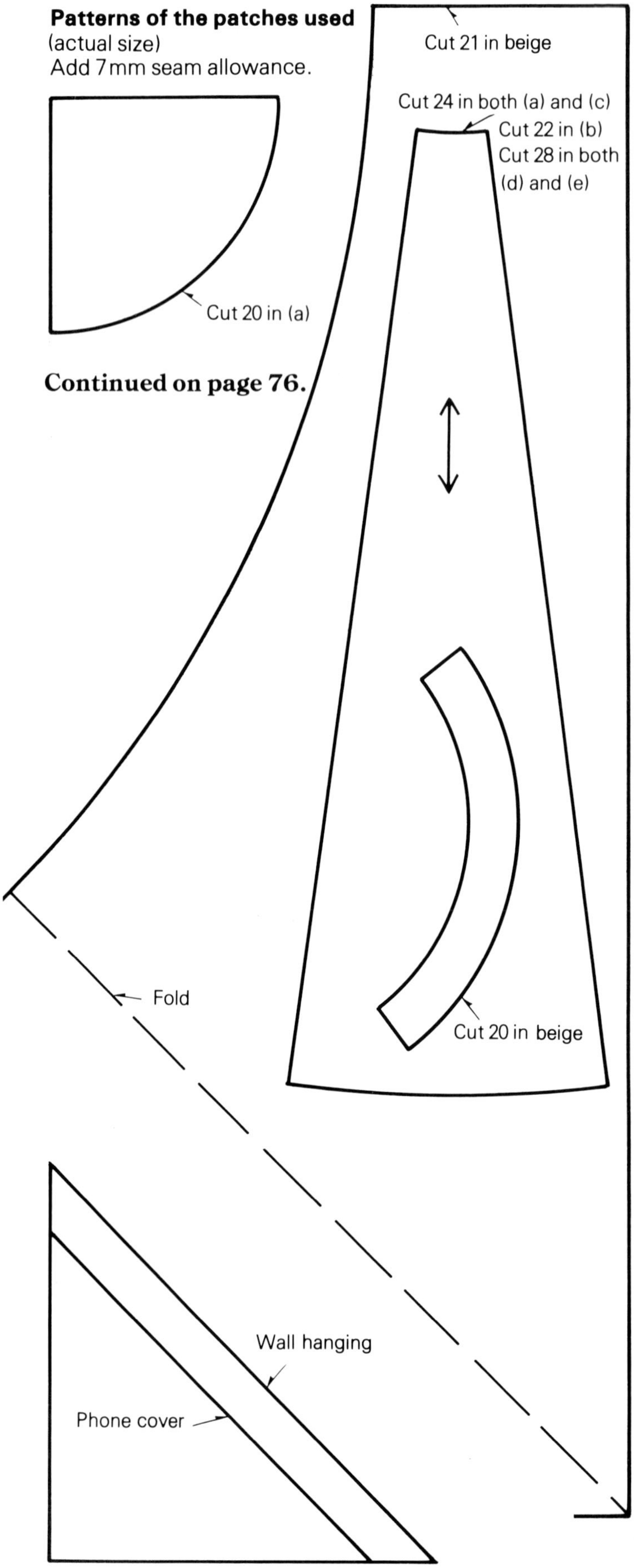
Cut 21 in beige
Cut 24 in both (a) and (c)
Cut 22 in (b)
Cut 28 in both (d) and (e)
Cut 20 in (a)
Fold
Cut 20 in beige
Wall hanging
Phone cover

Continued on page 76.

To make up

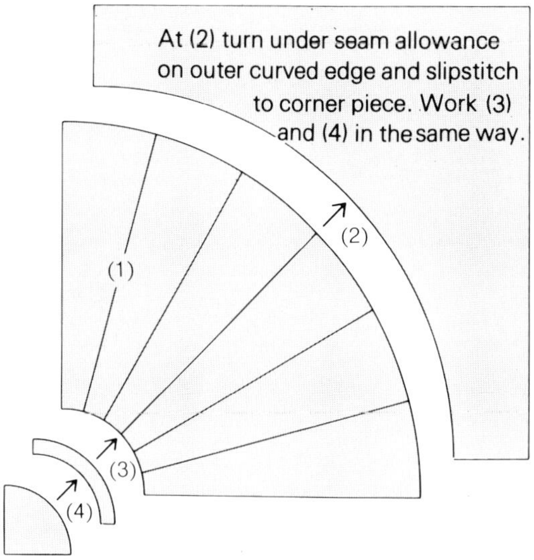
At (2) turn under seam allowance on outer curved edge and slipstitch to corner piece. Work (3) and (4) in the same way.
(1)
(2)
(3)
(4)

Join in sequences (1)-(3).

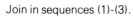

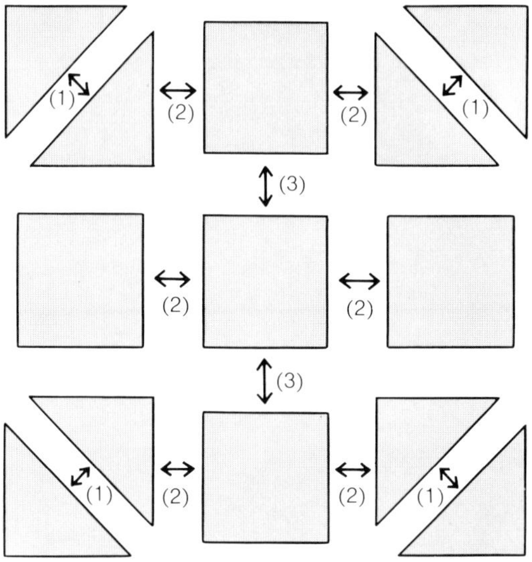

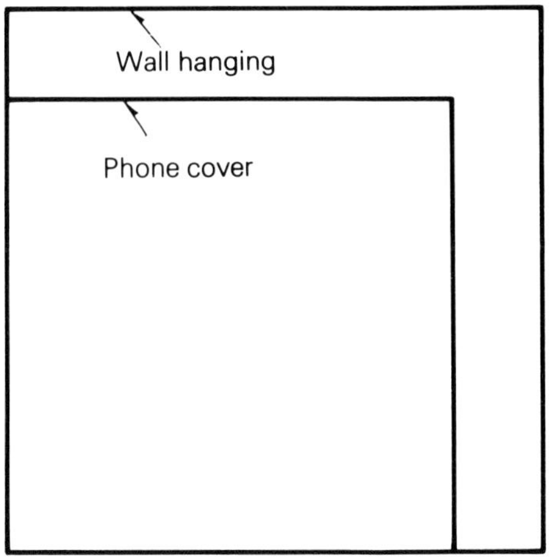
Wall hanging
Phone cover

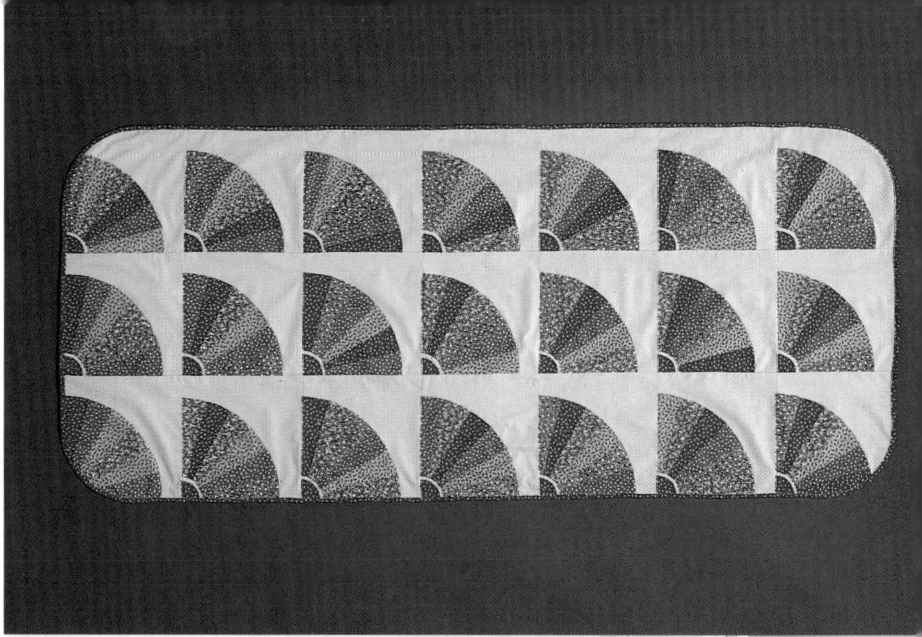

MAPLE LEAF
Table Mat & Pot Holders

Nine-patch blocks, pieced from a combination of squares and half-square triangles, make up the maple leaf design.

Table Mat
You will need:
50cm of 90cm wide unbleached calico
50cm x 50cm of cotton print (a)
50cm x 10cm of cotton print (b)
40cm x 10cm of cotton print (c)
50cm x 50cm of lightweight terylene wadding
Matching cotton thread
Finished size: 46cm square

Pot Holder
You will need:
20cm x 20cm of both cotton prints (a) and (b)
30cm x 20cm of cotton print (c)
20cm x 20cm of lightweight terylene wadding
80cm of 1.8cm wide bias tape
Cotton thread to match (b)
Finished size: 16.8cm square

To make up
Join in sequences (1)-(3).

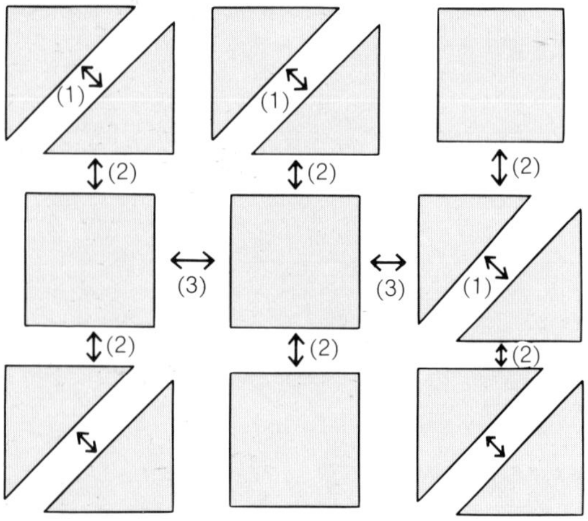

Patterns of the patches used (actual size)
Add 7mm seam allowance.

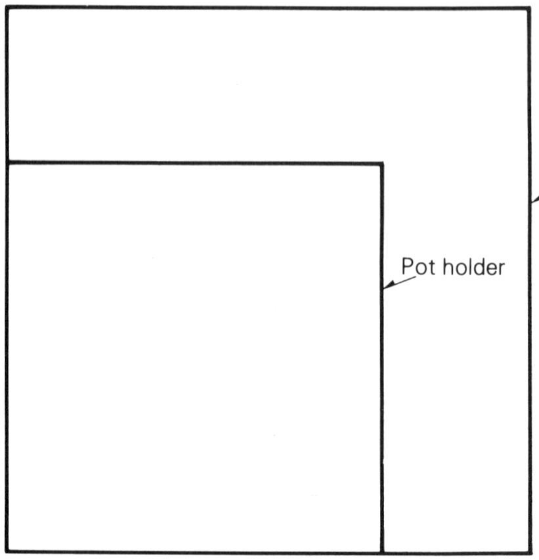

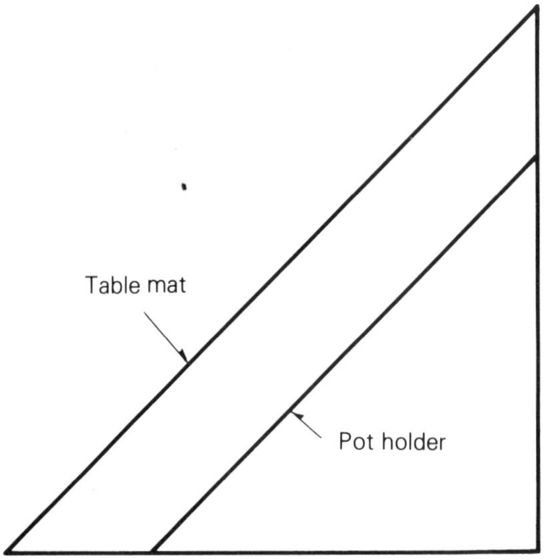

Continued on page 77.

CLAY'S CHOICE & DOUBLE BUTTERFLY

Bags & Pen Cases Vanity Bags & Spectacle Cases

A design from Mrs Clay's creations accompanied by a double butterfly. Composed of nine squares.

Bag
For each bag, you will need:
40 cm of 90 cm wide pre-quilted fabric
90 cm of 90 cm wide cotton print (a)
30 cm x 20 cm of cotton print (b)
15 cm square of lightweight terylene wadding
Finished size: see page 78

Pen Case
For each pen case, you will need:
20 cm x 10 cm of cotton print (a)
30 cm x 30 cm of cotton print (b)
30 cm x 20 cm of lining
30 cm x 20 cm of lightweight terylene wadding
70 cm of 12 mm wide bias tape to match (b)
Press studs
Cotton thread to match (b)
Finished size: see page 79

Vanity Case
For each vanity case, you will need:
50 cm x 20 cm of cotton print (a)
60 cm x 20 cm of cotton print (b)
20 cm x 10 cm of cotton print (c)
30 cm x 20 cm of lining
30 cm x 20 cm of lightweight terylene wadding
17.5 cm long zip fastener
70 cm of 18 mm wide matching bias tape
Matching cotton thread
Finished size: see page 79

Spectacle Case
For each spectacle case, you will need:
30 cm x 20 cm of both cotton prints (a) and (b)
20 cm x 20 cm of lining
20 cm x 20 cm of lightweight terylene wadding
80 cm of 12 mm wide bias tape
2 pairs of press studs
Ivory cotton thread
Finished size: see page 80

To make up
Join in sequences (1)-(3)

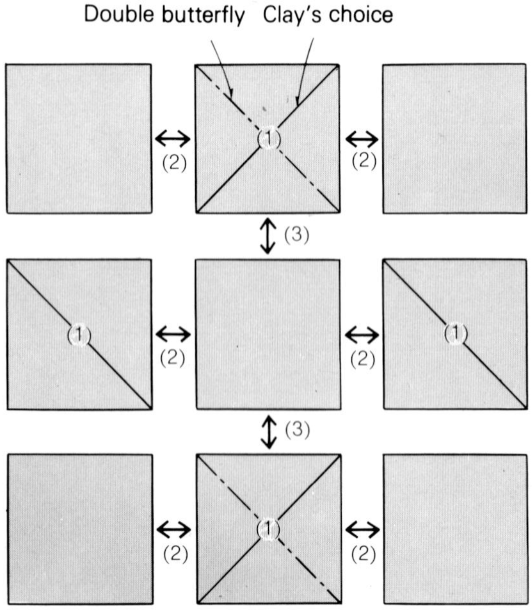

Patterns of the patches used (actual size)
Add 7 mm seam allowance.

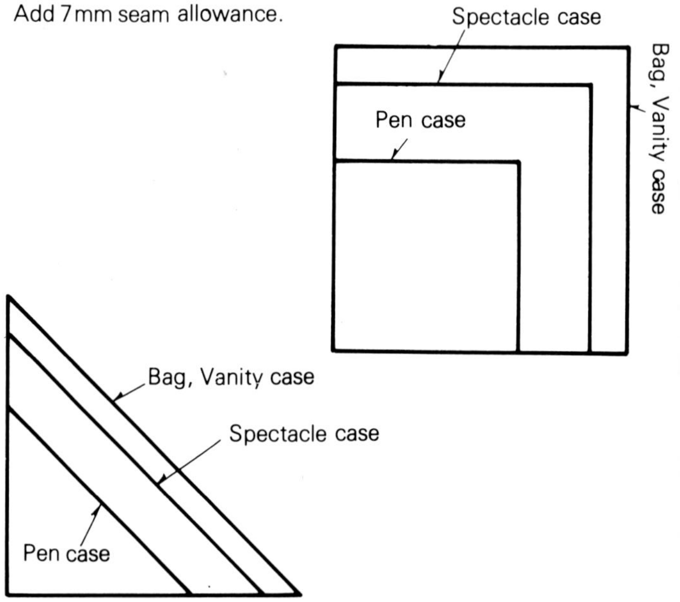

Continued on page 78.

Huntley & Palmers
Lemon Puff

PADDED PATCHWORK
Cot Quilt

Chart of Measurements
Add 7mm seam allowance.

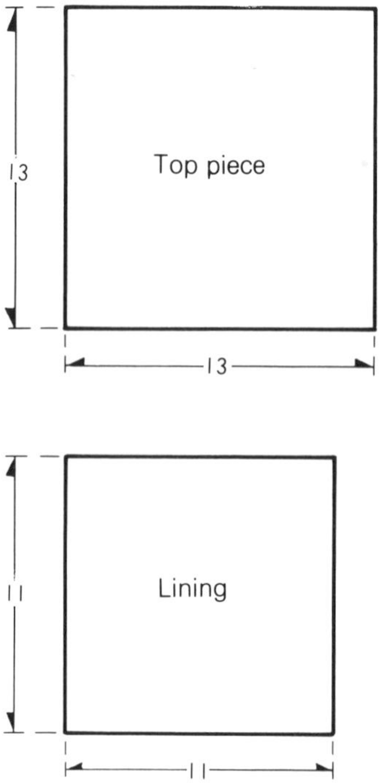

Baby's quilt made from soft, stuffed squares in pastel colours.

You will need:
2.90m of 90cm wide grey-green dressweight cotton
2.60m of 90cm wide pink dressweight cotton
90cm of 90cm wide pink cotton print
80cm of 90cm wide pink-and-white cotton print
Synthetic stuffing
Matching cotton thread
Finished size: 129cm x 107cm

Continued on page 80.

To make up

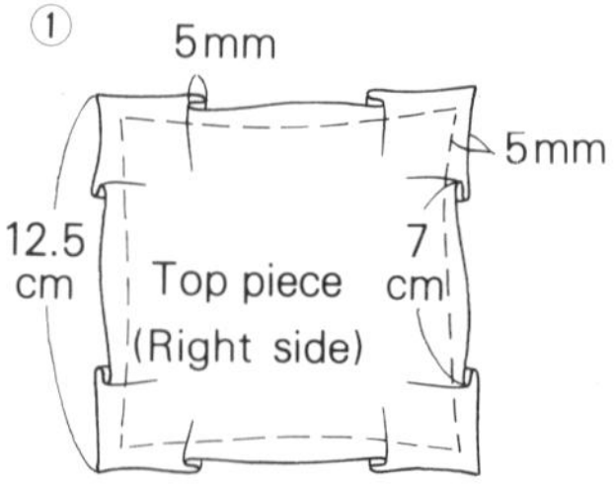

Make tucks on top piece. Tack in place.

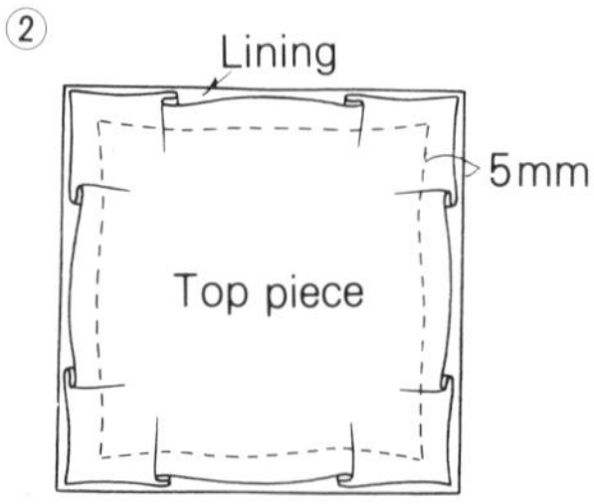

Wrong sides together, sew top pieces to lining. Remove tacking.

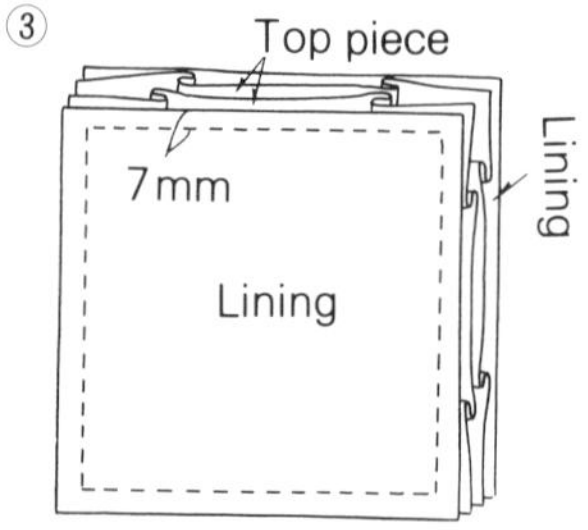

Right sides facing, hand sew patches together, allowing for a 7mm seam.

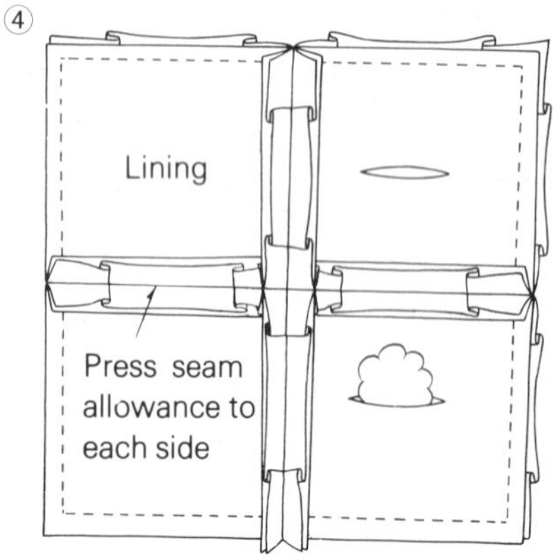

Make a slash in the lining and stuff each square.

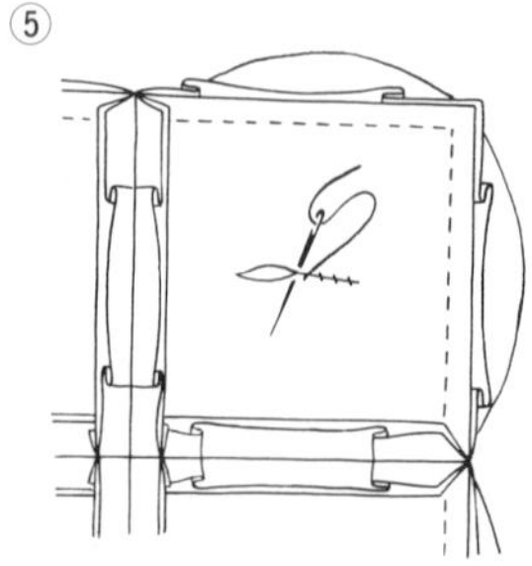

Close the slash with whip stitch.

DOUBLE WEDDING RING
Quilt

A beautiful patchwork of rings completed with diamonds of plain fabric.

You will need:
2.30 m of 90 cm wide cotton print (a)
90 cm of 90 cm wide cotton print (b)
20 cm of 90 cm wide cotton prints (c), (d), (e) and (f)
1.10 m of 90 cm wide lightweight terylene wadding
Rose pink embroidery cotton
Mauve cotton thread
Finished size: 109 cm x 89 cm

Patterns of the patches used (actual size)
Add 7 mm seam allowance.

To make up
Join in sequences (1)-(3).

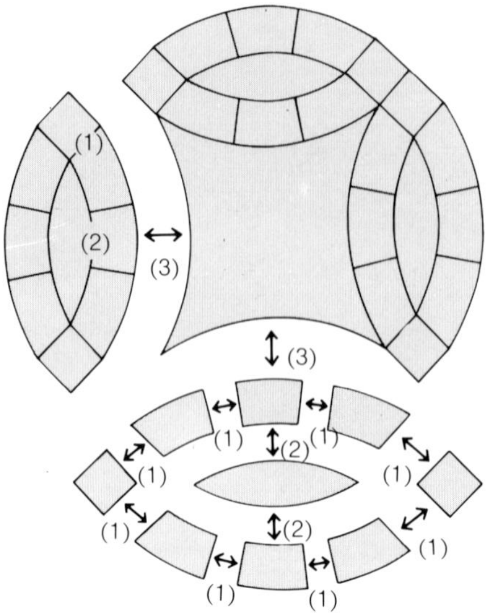

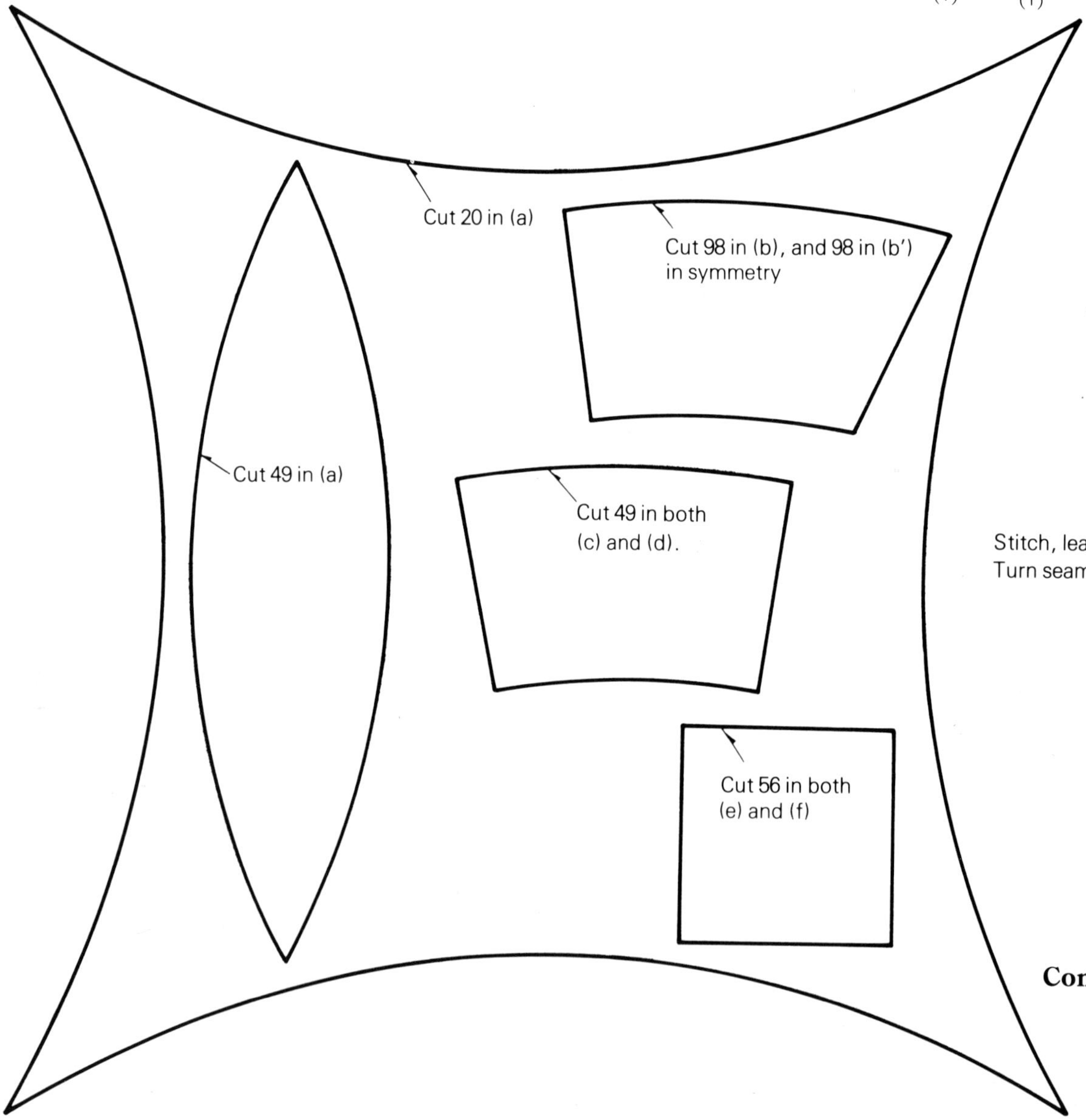
Cut 20 in (a)
Cut 98 in (b), and 98 in (b')
in symmetry
Cut 49 in (a)
Cut 49 in both
(c) and (d).
Cut 56 in both
(e) and (f)

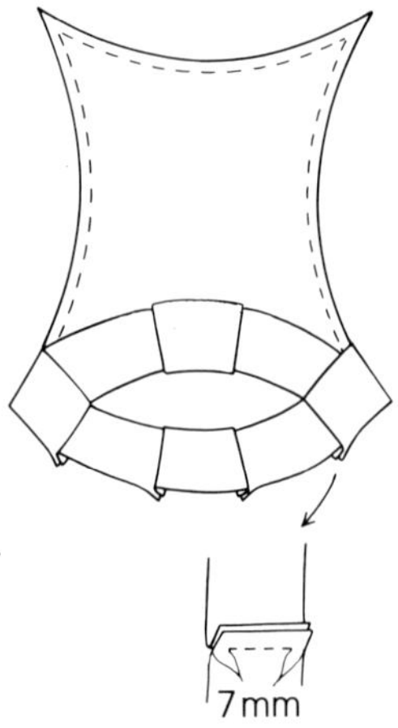
7 mm

Stitch, leaving a 7 mm allowance.
Turn seam to one side.

Continued on page 82.

Little
Grey Rabbit's
Christmas
by Alison Uttley
Pictures by Margaret Tempest

CATHEDRAL WINDOW
Cushion & Pincushions

In this modern American design plain fabric is inset with print squares to give a lovely "cathedral window" effect.

Cushion
You will need:
1.70 m of 90 cm wide bleached calico
20 cm of 90 cm wide red floral print
45 cm square inner cushion
34 cm long zip fastener
Finished size: 44 cm square

Pincushions
For each pincushion you will need:
40 cm x 30 cm of foundation fabric (70 cm x 30 cm if trimmed)
15 cm x 10 cm of fabric for decoration
Cotton wool
Finished size: 9.5 cm square (10.5 cm square if trimmed)

Continued on page 81.

Patterns of the patches used
Cushion Foundation fabric
Cut 25 in bleached calico

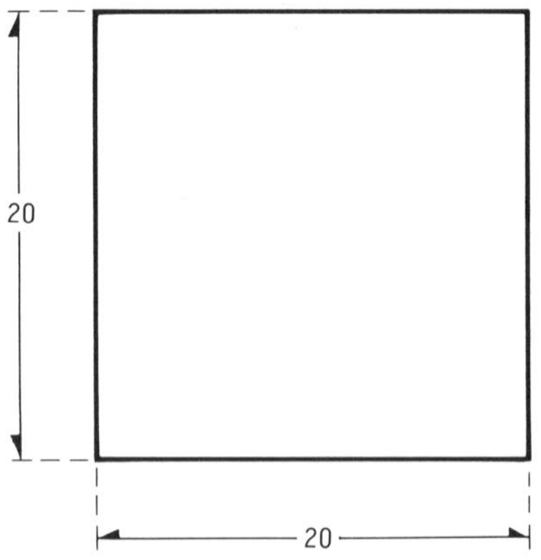

Decorative square
Cut 40 in print

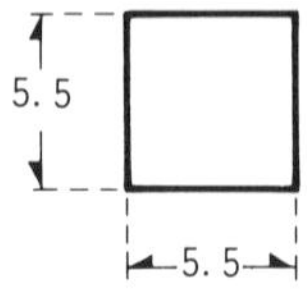

Pincushion
Cut 4 in foundation fabric

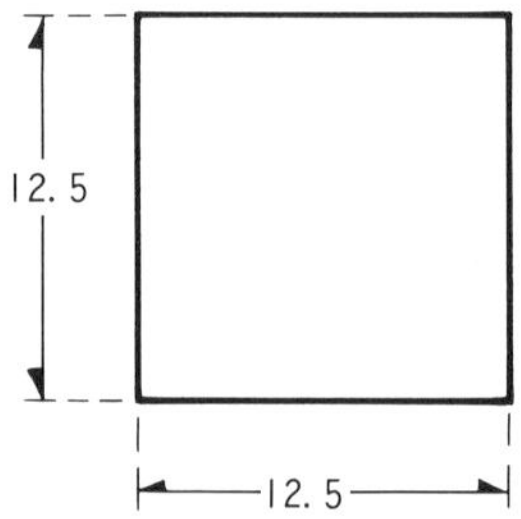

Decorative squares

Cut 4 in print

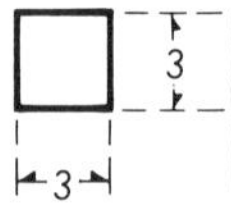

Cut 8 in print

To make up

①
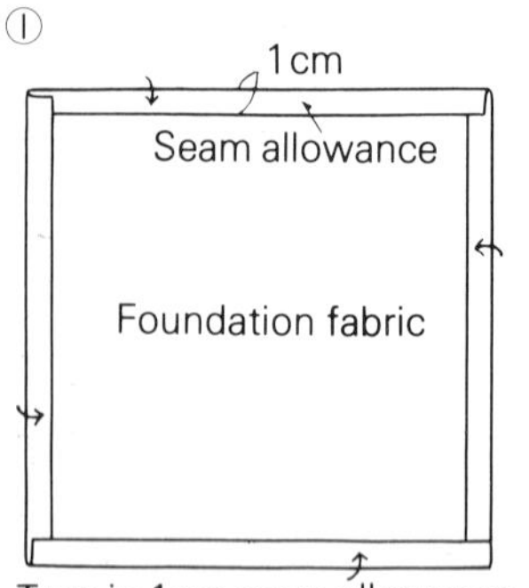

Turn in 1cm seam allowance

②
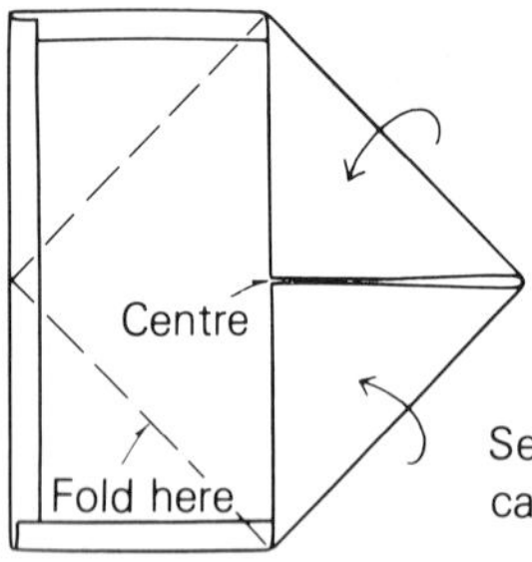

③
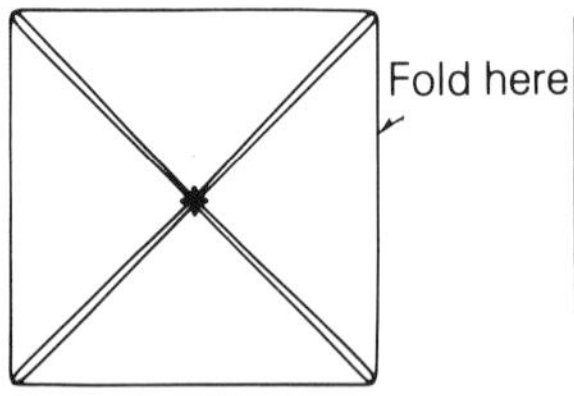

Sew centres together, without catching wrong side beneath.

④
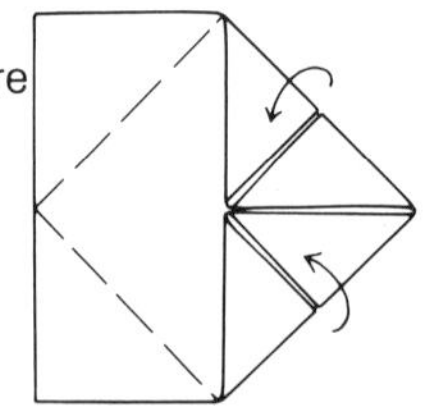

Turn (3) over, fold as before.

⑤
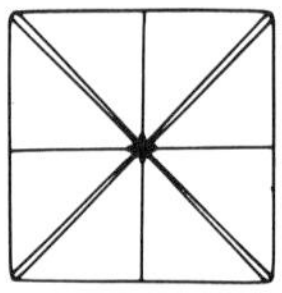

Secure the centre with cross stitch.

⑥
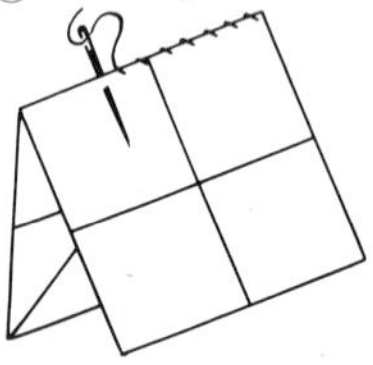

⑦
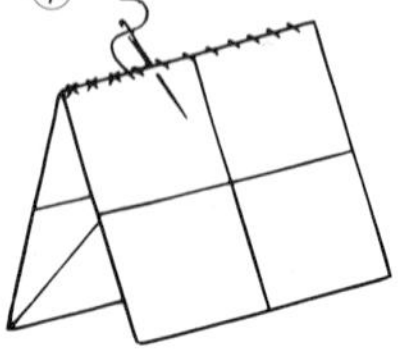

With right sides together, oversew 2 pieces to join.

⑧
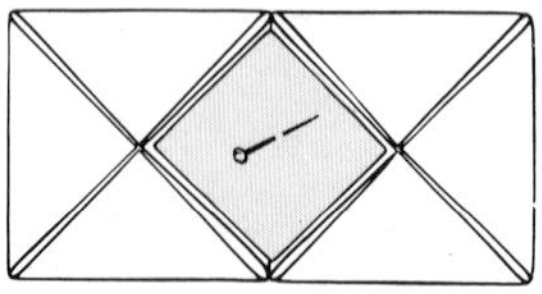

Lay print over the join.

⑨
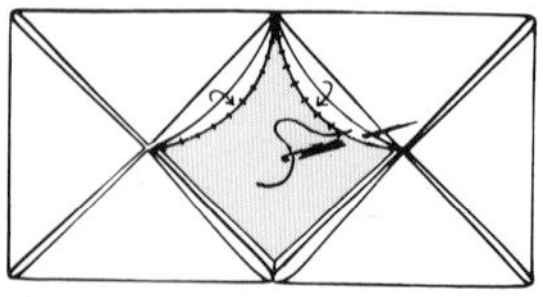

⑩
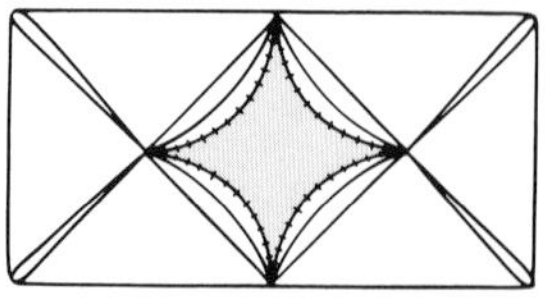

Turn edges of foundation fabric over the print shape. Secure with slipstitch.

SCHOOL HOUSE
Bags

These bags, decorated with school house patchwork are fun for children.

For each bag, you will need:
50 cm of 90 cm wide pre-quilted fabric
60 cm x 20 cm of cotton print (a)
30 cm x 10 cm of cotton print (b)
20 cm x 20 cm of both cotton prints (c) and (e)
30 cm x 20 cm of cotton print (d)
90 cm of 3 cm wide unbleached cotton tape
70 cm of 2 cm wide tape to match (a)
Finished size: see page 82

Patterns of the patches used
Add 7 mm seam allowance.

To make up
Join in sequences (1)-(5). At stage (1) appliqué using slipstitch.

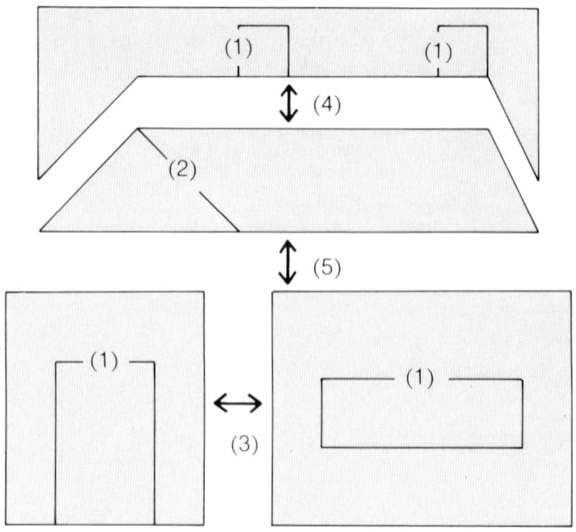

Continued on page 82.

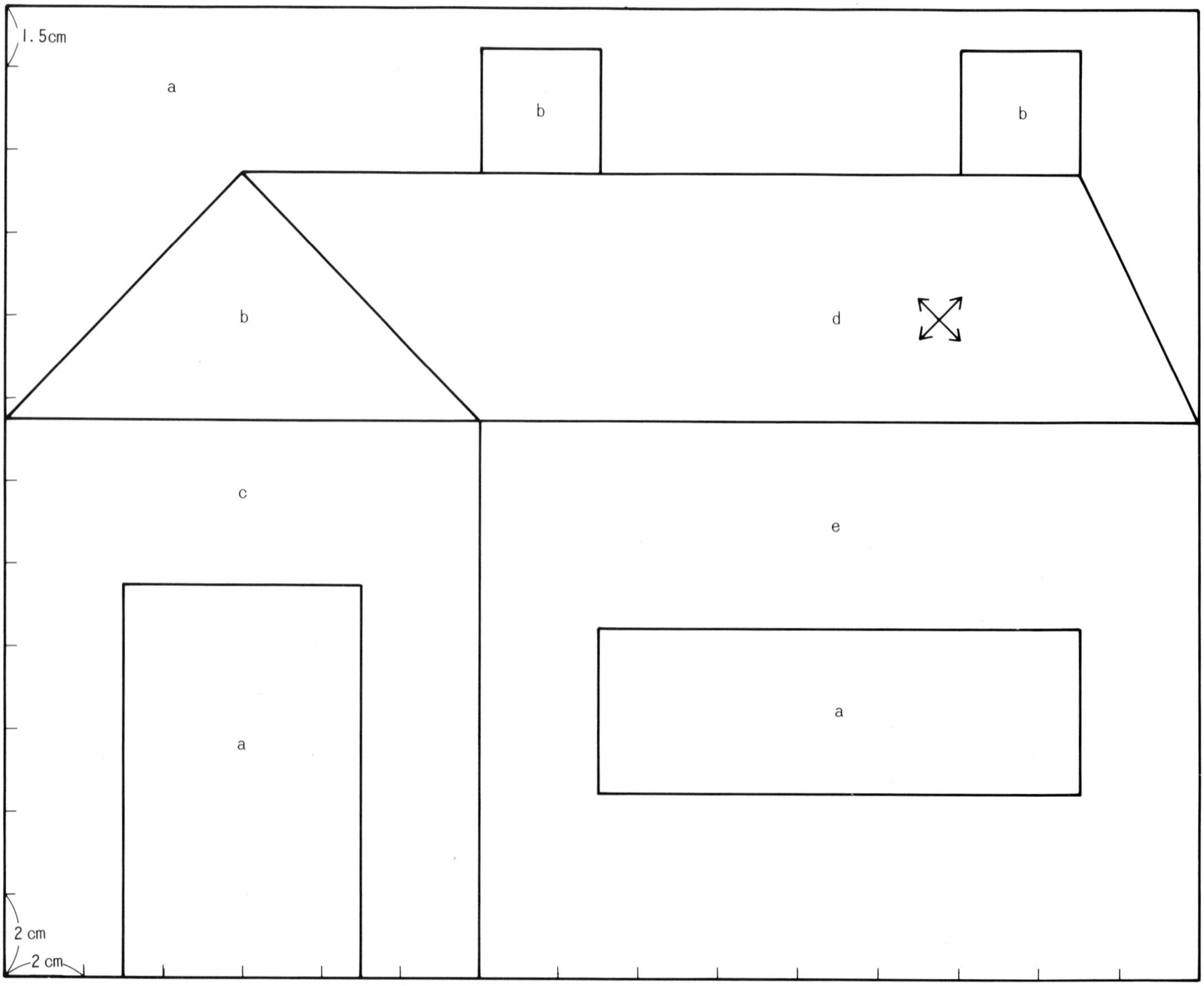

Little Grey Rabbit's Christmas

TULIP
Cushions

A triangle and lozenges make a geometrical tulip, popular in Holland.

For each cushion you will need:
50 cm x 30 cm of pale green sheeting
30 cm x 30 cm of unbleached cotton
20 cm x 20 cm of contrasting cotton (a)
50 cm x 30 cm of cotton for inner case
50 gr of kapok
Finished size: 20 cm square

To make up
Join in sequences (1) and (2).

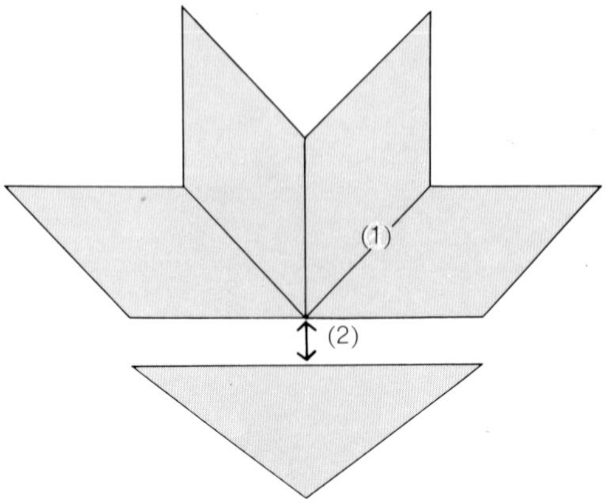

Patterns of the patches used (actual size)
Add 7 mm seam allowance.

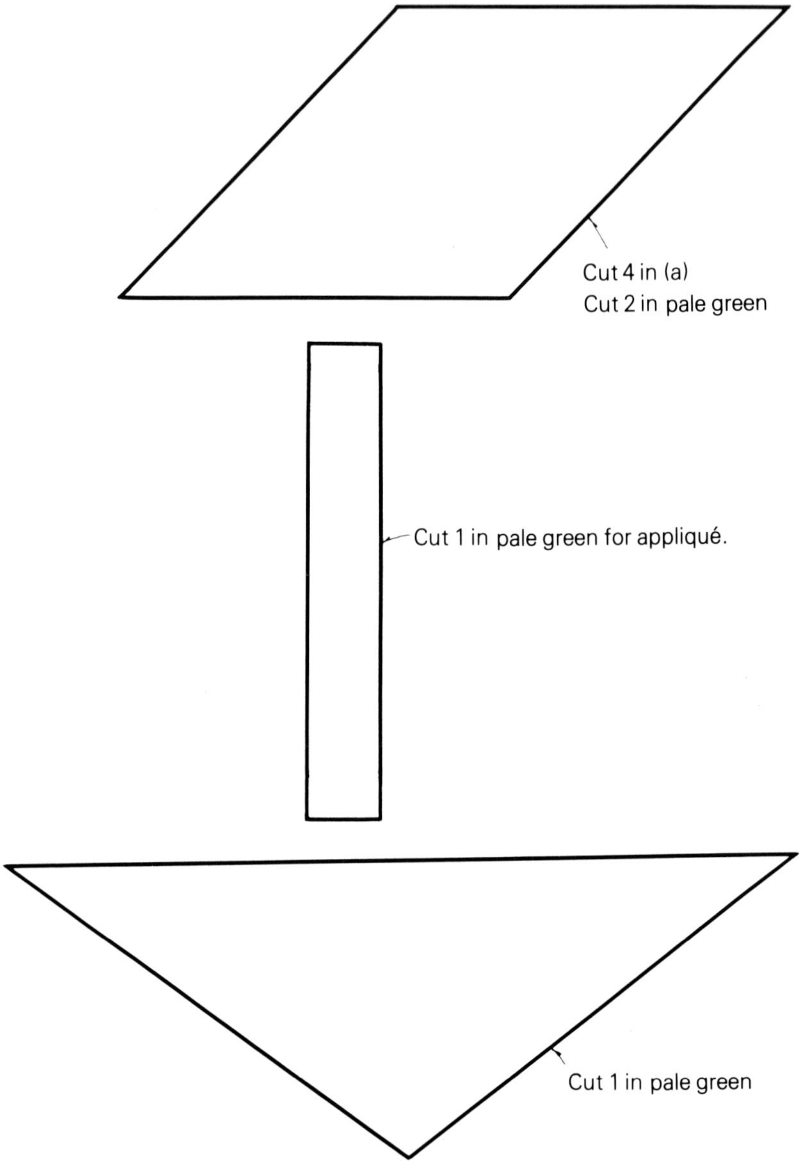

Continued on page 75.

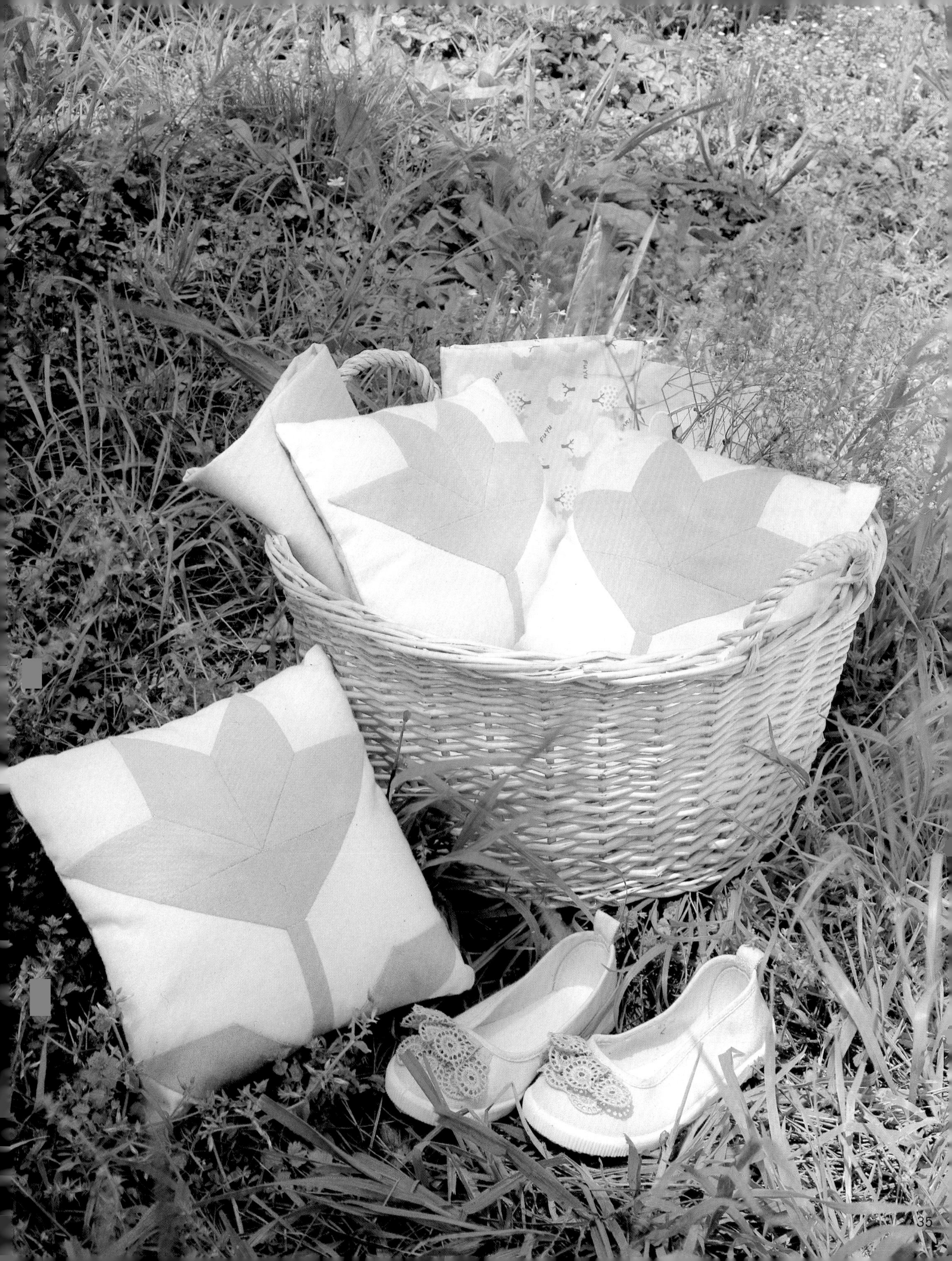

BOY AND GIRL

Toaster Cover, Tea Cosy & Cushions

These designs could brighten up a dining table or a child's room.

Toaster Cover
You will need:
70 cm x 40 cm of lime green dressweight cotton
Small amounts of yellow and navy blue dressweight cotton and cotton prints (a), (b) and (c)
70 cm x 40 cm of lining
70 cm x 40 cm of iron-on interlining
2.40 m of green tape and fine piping cord
90 cm of 12 mm wide bias tape
Brown, red, green, pink and aqua blue embroidery cottons
Finished size: see page 84

Tea Cosy
You will need:
80 cm x 30 cm of lime green dressweight cotton
Small amounts of yellow, white, moss green, red and orange dressweight cotton and cotton prints (a) and (b)
80 cm x 30 cm of lining
Stuffing
Brown, red, orange, yellow and white embroidery cottons
Finished size: see page 84

Cushions
For each cushion, you will need:
(Materials apply to both cushions, except where brackets indicate alternative for girl)
50 cm x 90 cm of blue (red) dressweight cotton print
30 cm x 30 cm of white dressweight cotton
Small amounts of yellow, navy blue (red polka dot) dressweight cotton
90 cm of 7 mm wide grosgrain ribbon in blue (red)
20 cm long zip fastener
3 cm thick foam cushion
Brown, red, blue (green, yellow) embroidery cottons
Finished size: see page 85

Appliqué Design Add 7 mm seam allowance.

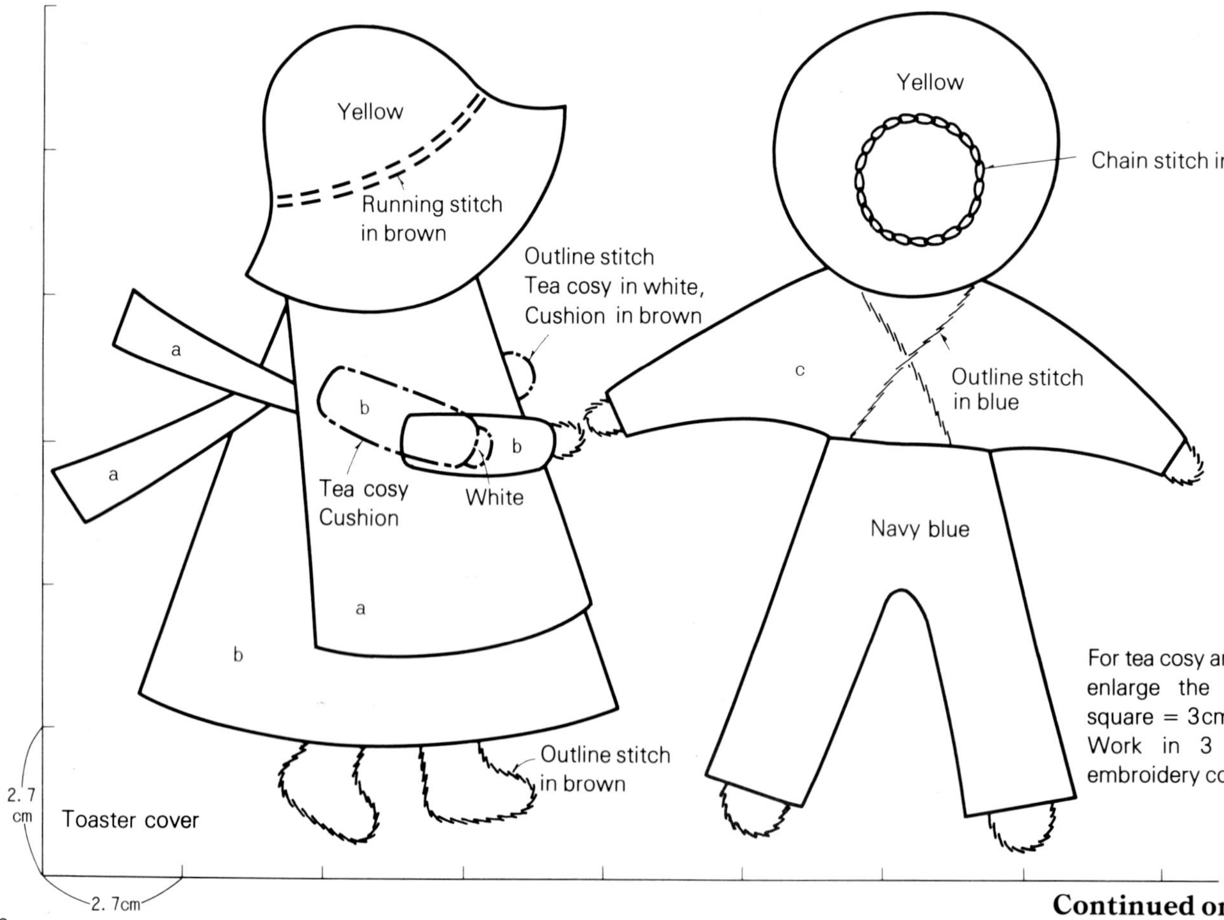

For tea cosy and cushion enlarge the scale to 1 square = 3 cm.
Work in 3 strands of embroidery cotton.

Continued on page 83.

CAROLINA LILY
Cushion

A lovely lily composed of lozenges and triangles, very popular in Germany. The striking colour scheme is impressive.

You will need:
80 cm x 50 cm of black-and-white polka dot print
70 cm x 30 cm of black dressweight cotton
30 cm x 30 cm of green dressweight cotton
90 cm x 10 cm of red dressweight cotton
30 cm x 10 cm of red-and-white polka dot print
50 cm x 50 cm of lightweight terylene wadding
36 cm long zip fastener
45 cm square inner cushion
Black, red and green cotton thread
Finished size: 42 cm square

To make up
Join in sequences (1)-(10).
At stages (7) and (8) iron green bias to shape, tack and slipstitch to patchwork.

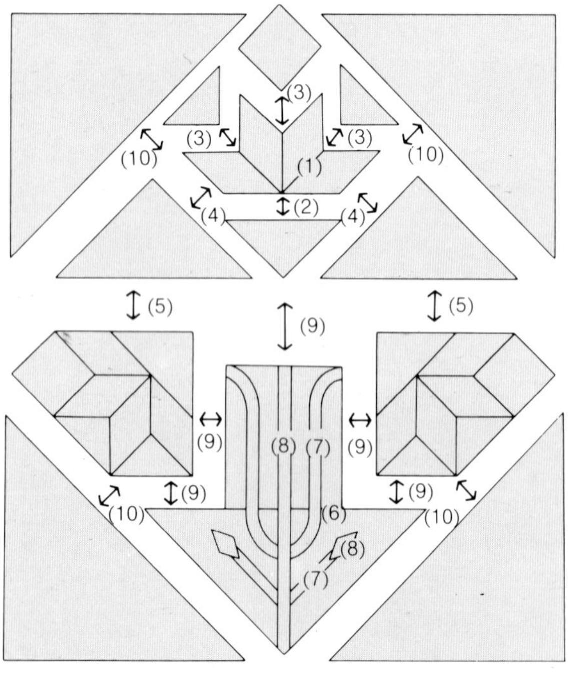

(1)
(2)
(3)
(4)
(5)
(6)
(7)
(8)
(9)
(10)

Patterns of the patches used (actual size)
Add 7 mm seam allowance.

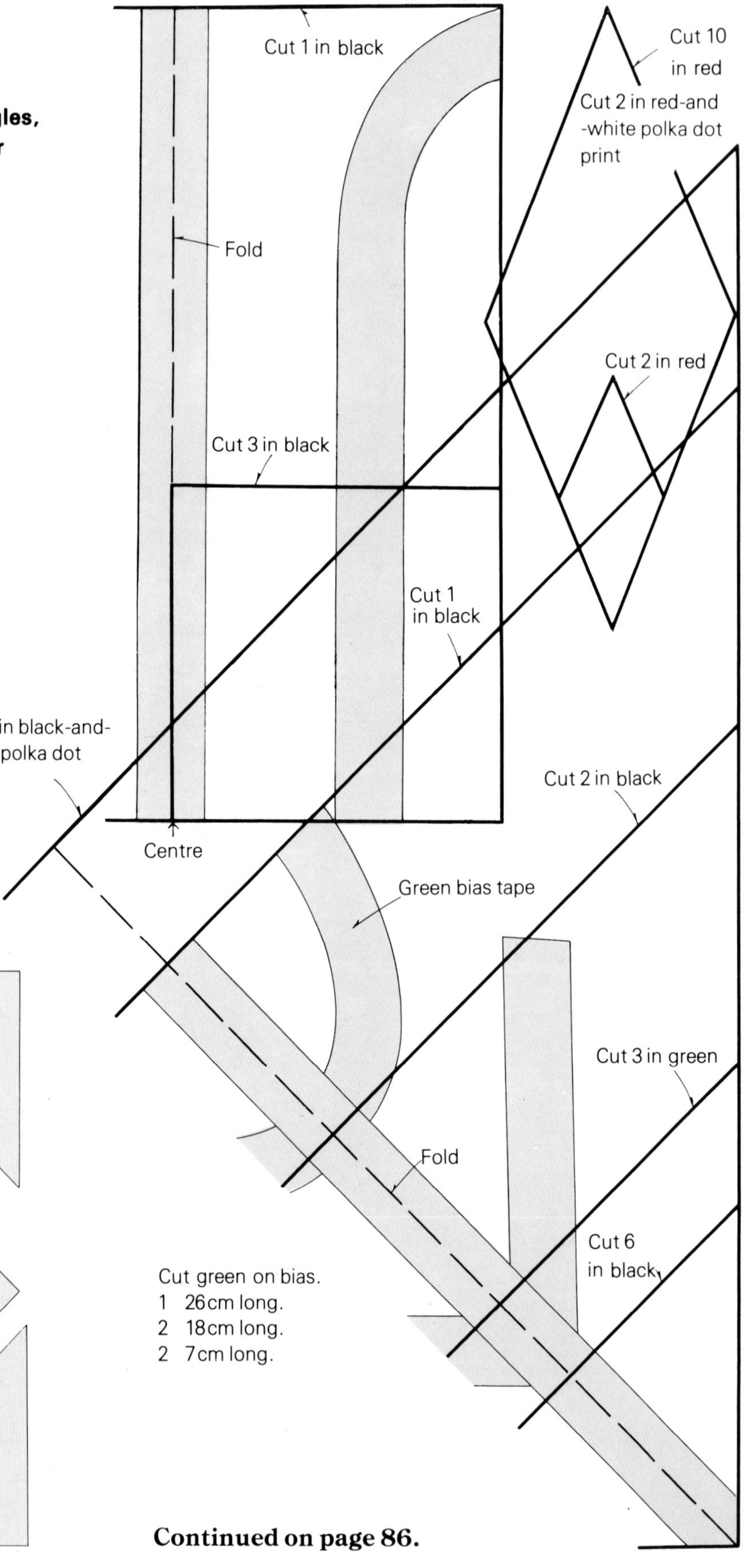

Cut 1 in black
Fold
Cut 3 in black
Cut 1 in black
Cut 10 in red
Cut 2 in red-and -white polka dot print
Cut 2 in red
Cut 4 in black-and-white polka dot print
Centre
Cut 2 in black
Green bias tape
Cut 3 in green
Fold
Cut 6 in black
Cut green on bias.
1 26cm long.
2 18cm long.
2 7cm long.

Continued on page 86.

POMPADOUR

TWO FLOWER BASKET DESIGNS
Patchwork Picture & Cushion

The baskets are composed of triangular patches. The appliquéd handle completes the picture.

Patchwork Picture
You will need:
40 cm x 20 cm of blue dressweight cotton
30 cm x 10 cm of moss green cotton print
30 cm x 30 cm of lining
30 cm x 30 cm of lightweight terylene wadding
Blue cotton thread
Frame with inside measurement of 19 cm
Finished size: size of frame

Cushion
You will need:
90 cm x 70 cm of cotton print (a)
20 cm x 10 cm of cotton print (b)
30 cm x 30 cm of both cotton prints (c) and (d)
25 cm long zip fastener
3.5 cm thick foam cushion
Matching cotton thread
Finished size: see page 86

To make up
Join in sequences (1)-(7).
Turn under seam allowance on (6) and slipstitch.

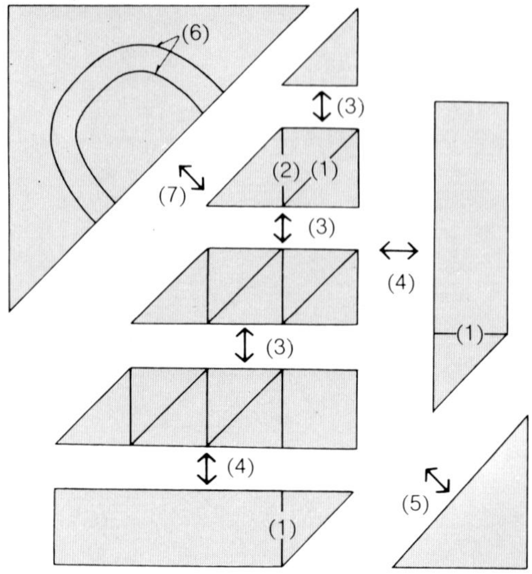

Patterns of the patches used (actual size)
Add 7 mm seam allowance.

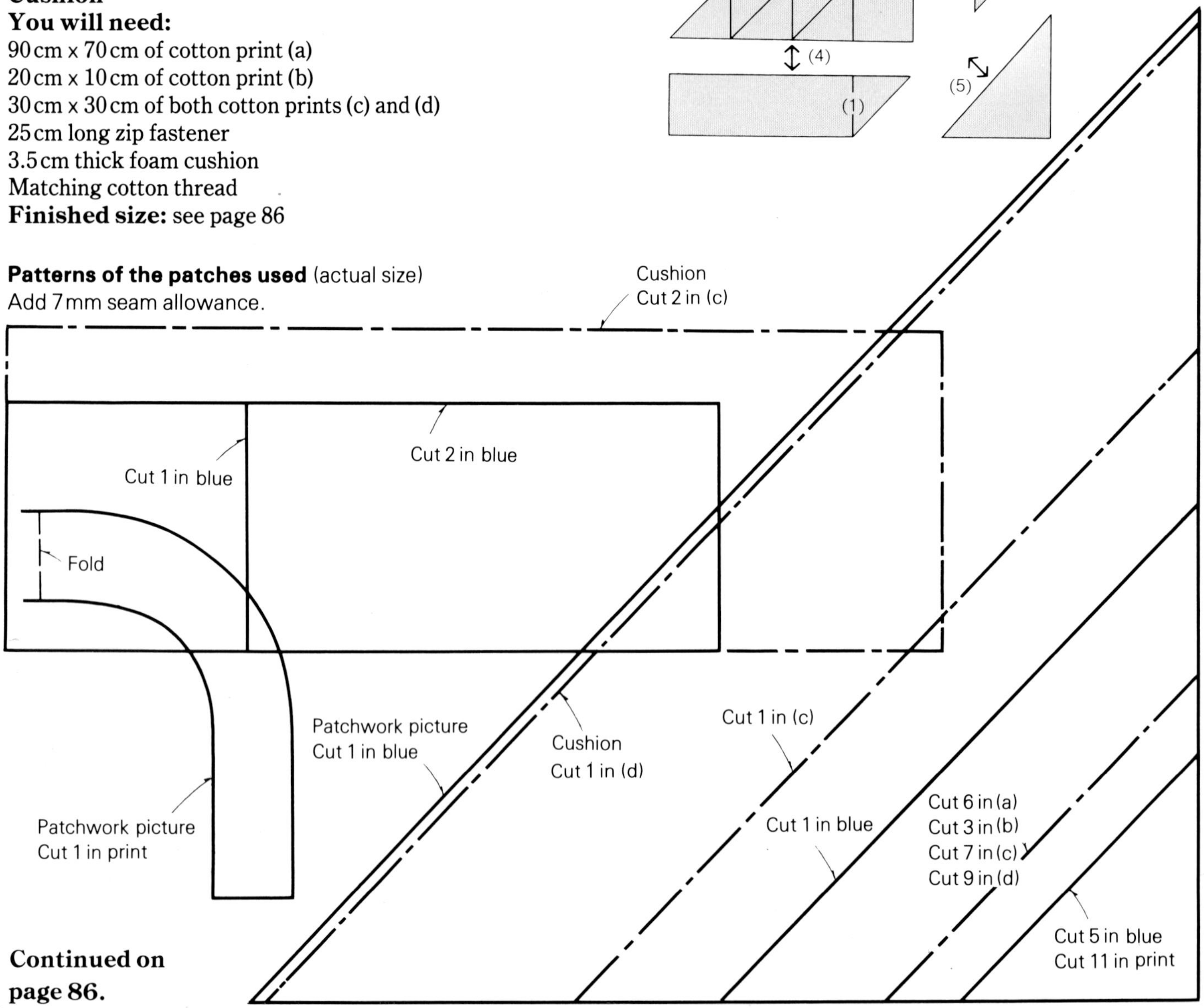

Cushion
Cut 2 in (c)
Cut 1 in blue
Cut 2 in blue
Fold
Patchwork picture
Cut 1 in blue
Cushion
Cut 1 in (d)
Cut 1 in (c)
Patchwork picture
Cut 1 in print
Cut 1 in blue
Cut 6 in (a)
Cut 3 in (b)
Cut 7 in (c)
Cut 9 in (d)
Cut 5 in blue
Cut 11 in print

Continued on page 86.

BABY BLOCKS
Quilt

This design is composed of print lozenges arranged to create a three-dimensional image of building blocks. This can only be made using the hand-stitched method (see page 101).

You will need:
3.4 m of 90 cm wide pale pink sheeting
1.90 m of 90 cm wide beige sheeting
50 cm of 90 cm wide yellow sheeting
1.30 m of 90 cm wide red-brown cotton
80 cm x 20 cm of lime green cotton
30 cm x 10 cm of tangerine yellow cotton
30 cm x 90 cm of cottons (a), (c) and (e).
70 cm x 20 cm of cotton (f)
70 cm x 10 cm of cottons (b), (d), (g) and (h)
2.40 m of 90 cm wide lightweight terylene wadding
White cotton thread
Finished size: 115.5 cm x 171 cm

To make up
Join in sequences (1)-(5)

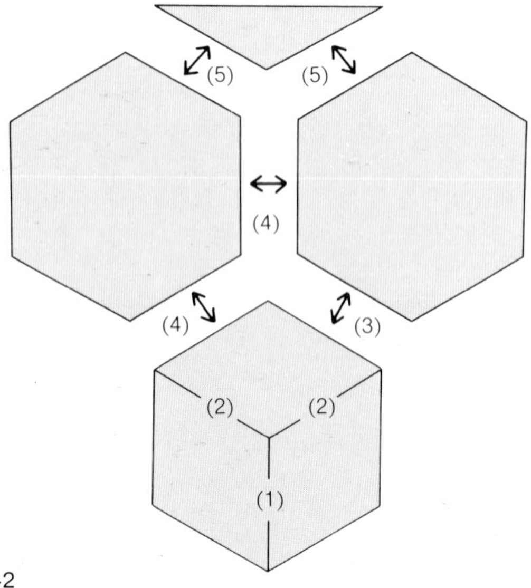

Patterns of the patches used (actual size)
Add 7 mm seam allowance.

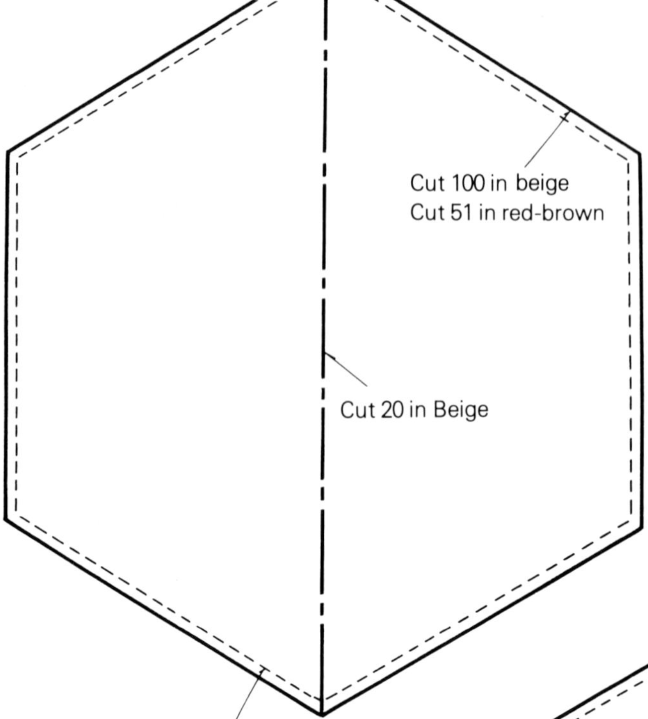

Cut 100 in beige
Cut 51 in red-brown
Cut 20 in Beige
Quilt with cotton thread.

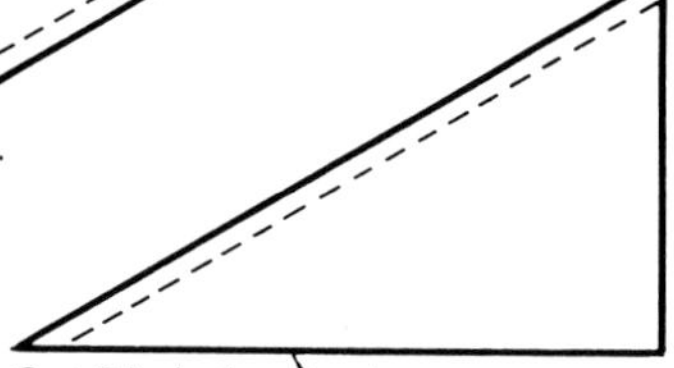

Cut 2 in beige as above
and 2 using the same pattern
reversed left to right

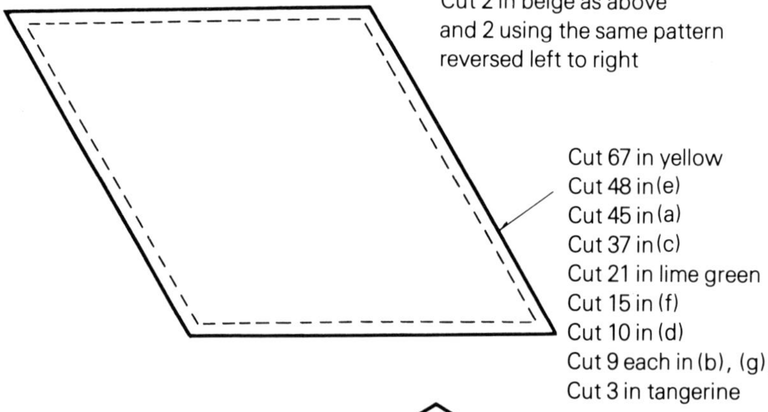

Cut 67 in yellow
Cut 48 in (e)
Cut 45 in (a)
Cut 37 in (c)
Cut 21 in lime green
Cut 15 in (f)
Cut 10 in (d)
Cut 9 each in (b), (g),
Cut 3 in tangerine

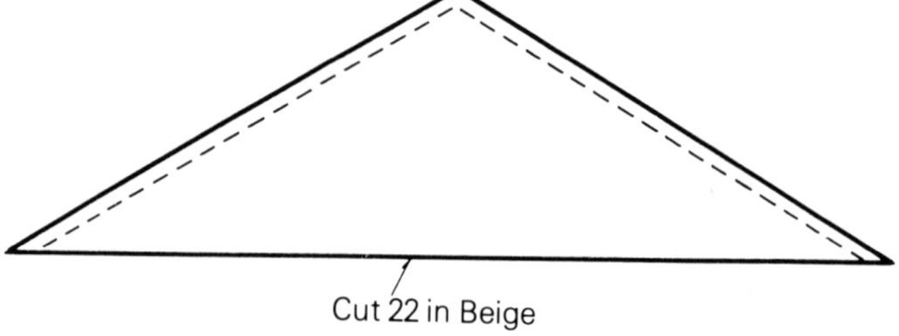

Cut 22 in Beige

Continued on page 93.

KALEIDOSCOPE
Bedspread

Isosceles triangles form the basis of this colourful design. By alternating bright and multi-coloured patches, a kaleidoscopic effect is achieved.

You will need:
1.80 cm of 90 cm wide white dressweight cotton
40 cm of 90 cm wide cream dressweight cotton
400 pieces, 11.5 cm x 10 cm of light-coloured dressweight cotton
400 pieces, 11.5 cm x 10 cm of dark-coloured dressweight cotton
5.50 m of 90 cm wide lining
5.50 m of 90 cm wide lightweight terylene wadding
White cotton thread
Finished size: 182.5 cm square

Patterns of the patches used (actual size)
Add 7 mm seam allowance.

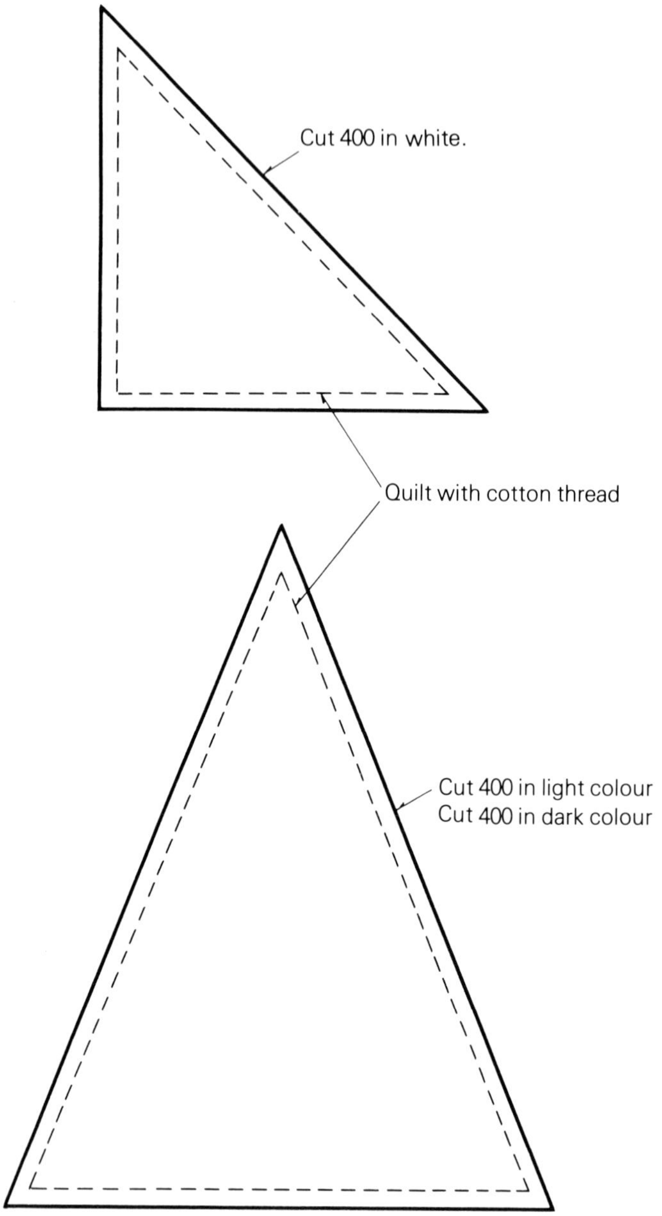

Cut 400 in white.
Quilt with cotton thread
Cut 400 in light colour
Cut 400 in dark colour

To make up
Join in sequences (1) and (2)

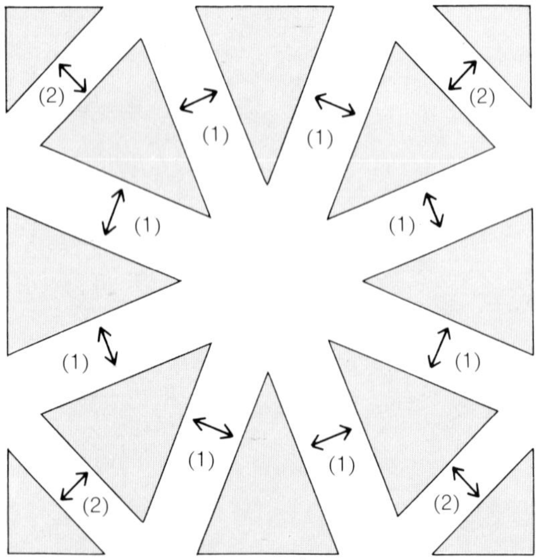

Continued on page 83.

WINDMILL
Table Mat & Tray Cloth

Squares of windmill patchwork are alternated with squares of sunflower quilting in plain fabric.

Tray Cloth
You will need:
70 cm x 30 cm of beige dressweight cotton
70 cm x 20 cm of red dressweight cotton
40 cm x 40 cm of moss green dressweight cotton
20 cm x 10 cm of red checked cotton
40 cm x 40 cm of lining
40 cm x 40 cm of lightweight terylene wadding
Red cotton thread
Finished size: 32 cm square

Table Mat
You will need:
80 cm x 50 cm of beige dressweight cotton
20 pieces, 15 cm x 5 cm, of coloured dressweight cottons
50 cm x 50 cm of olive green dressweight cotton
50 cm x 50 cm of lightweight terylene wadding
Beige cotton thread
Finished size: 47 cm square

To make up
Join in sequences (1)-(3).

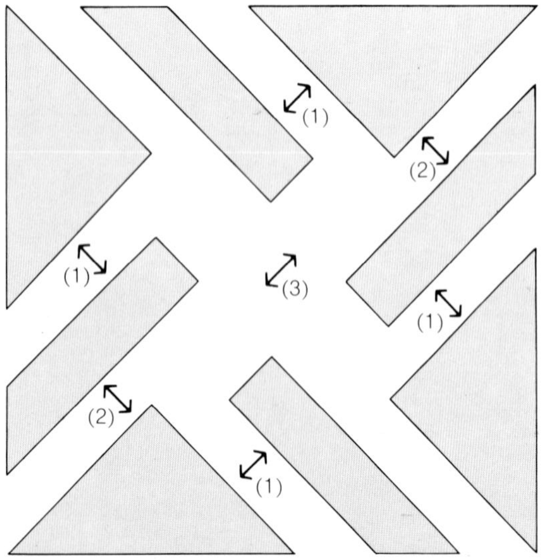

Patterns of the patches used (actual size)
Add 7 mm seam allowance.

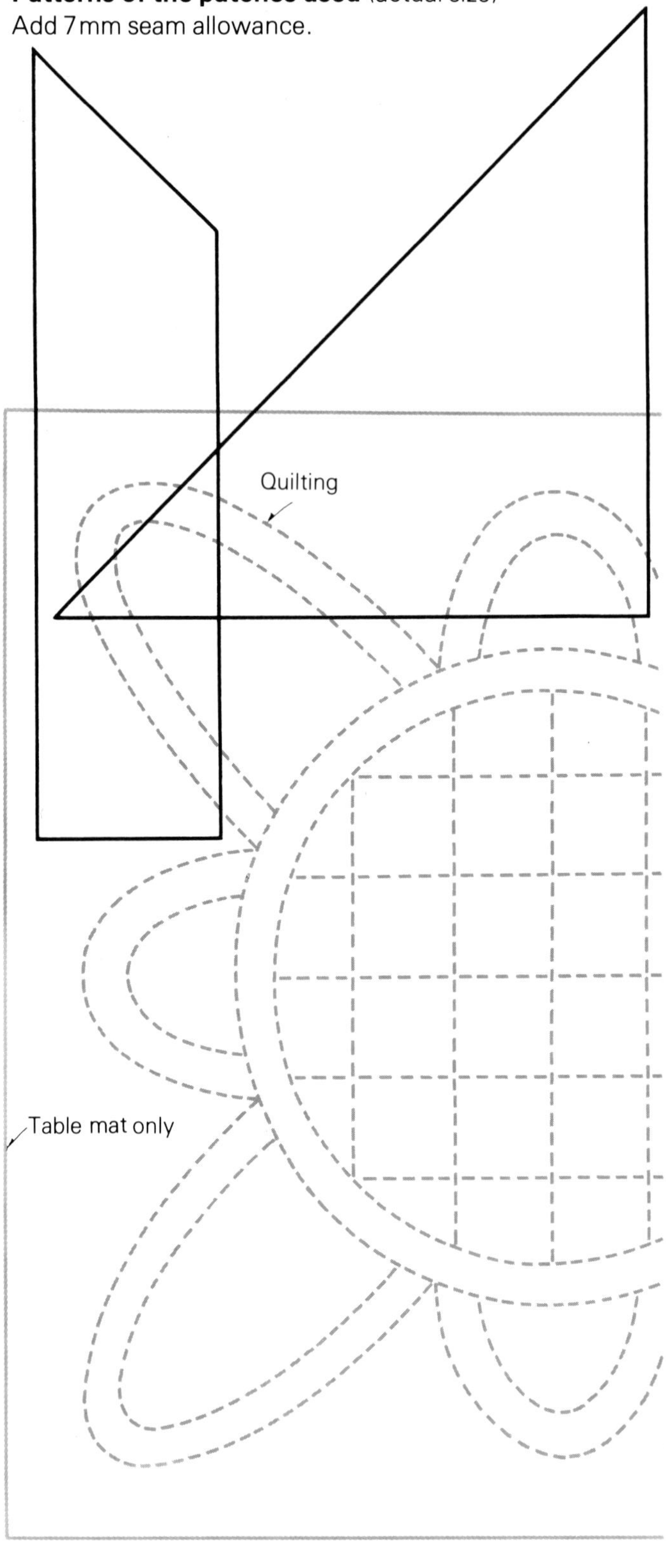

Continued on page 87.

OLD MAID'S PUZZLE
Spectacle Cases

Triangles and squares are combined in each block. This is an interesting puzzle to play with!

You will need:
Dressweight cotton (see pages 90-91)
20 cm x 20 cm of lightweight terylene wadding
Matching cotton thread
Finished size: see page 90

Continued on page 90.

To make up Join in sequences (1)-(8).

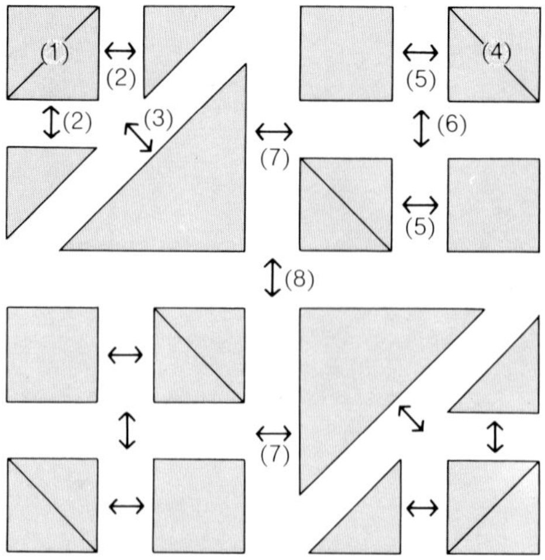

Patterns of the patches used (actual size)
Add 7 mm seam allowance.

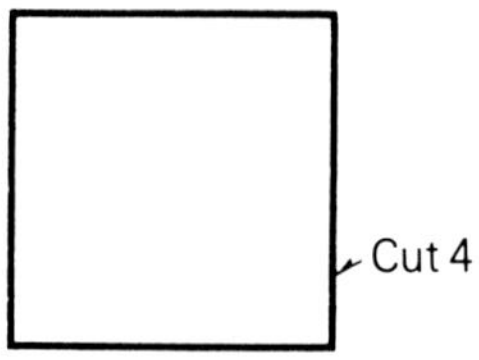

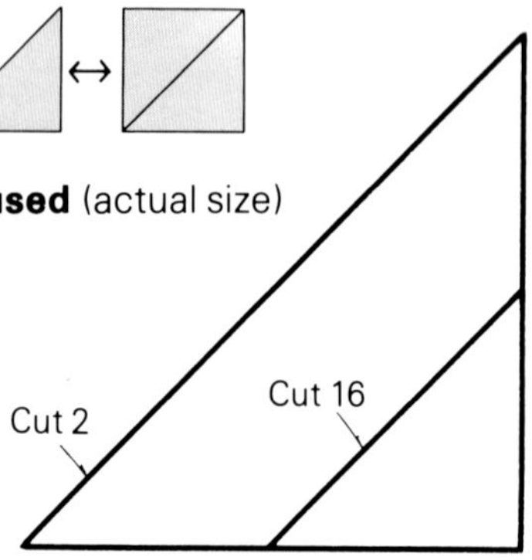

DUTCHMAN STYLE
Pincushions

In basic plain patchwork. Four octagons in a variety of prints attached to a square piece.

You will need:
30 cm x 20 cm of foundation fabric
6 cm squares of cottons (a), (b), (c) and (d)
15 cm square of wadding for each pincushion
Cotton wool
White cotton thread
Finished size: 11 cm square

Patterns of the patches used
(actual size)
Add 7 mm seam allowance.

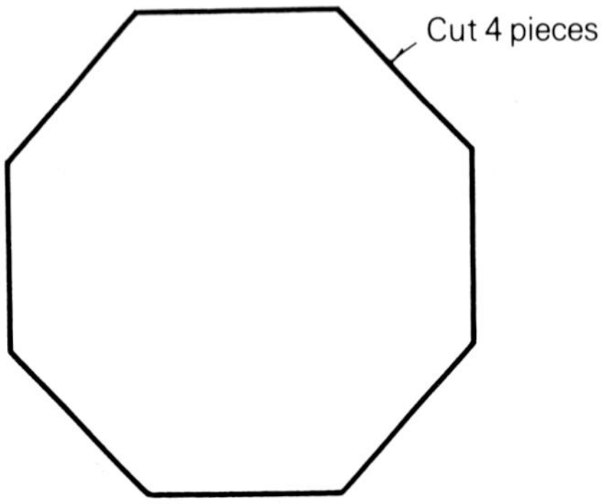

Join 4 pieces together first

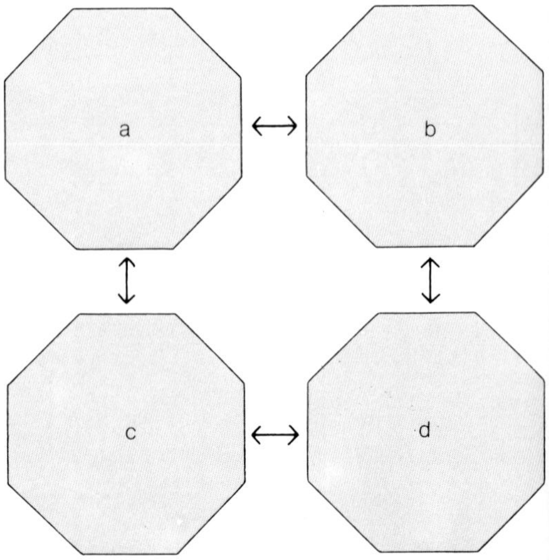

Continued on page 81.

Irish
Coffee

DAISY QUILT
Quilt & Pochette

Floral print petals are pieced together to make a daisy patch and arranged in a quilt and pochette.

Quilt
You will need:
420 cm x 70 cm of blue dressweight cotton
230 cm x 90 cm of red dressweight cotton
40 cm x 90 cm of dressweight cotton (a)
30 cm x 90 cm of dressweight cotton (b)
70 cm x 20 cm of cotton prints (c), (d), (e), (f), (g), (h), (i) and (j)
4.70 m of 90 cm wide cotton lining
4.70 m of 90 cm wide lightweight terylene wadding
Red and blue embroidery cotton
Finished size: 157 cm x 233 cm

Pochette
You will need:
40 cm x 90 cm of cotton print (a)
10 cm x 10 cm of cotton print (b)
20 cm x 10 cm of cotton prints (c), (d), (e) and (f)
40 cm x 20 cm of lightweight terylene wadding
1 matching embroidery cotton
White cotton thread
Finished size: see page 97

Patterns of the patches used
(actual size)
Add 7 mm seam allowance

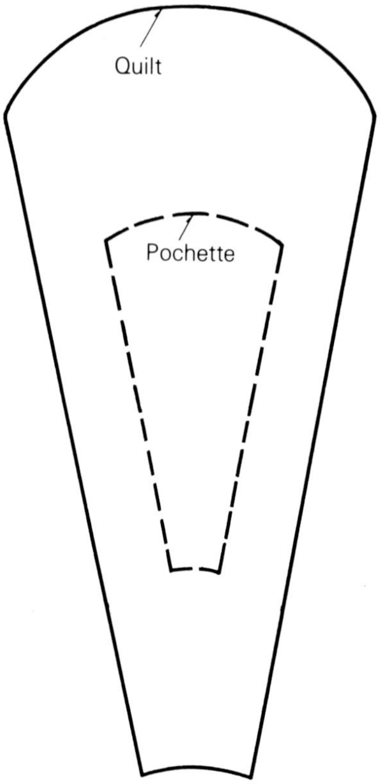

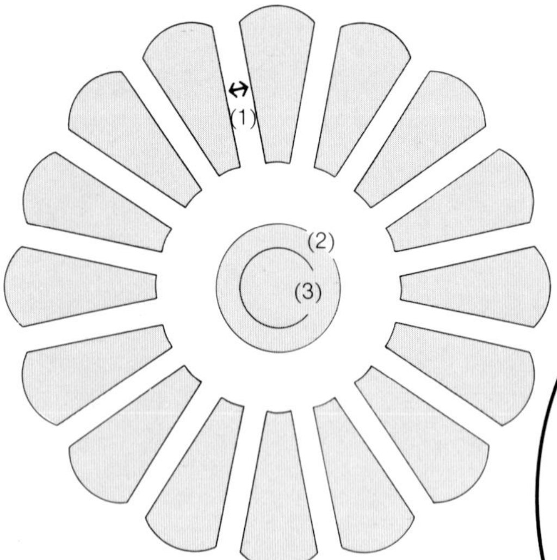

To make up
Join (1) with running stitch.
Slipstitch at stages (2) and (3)

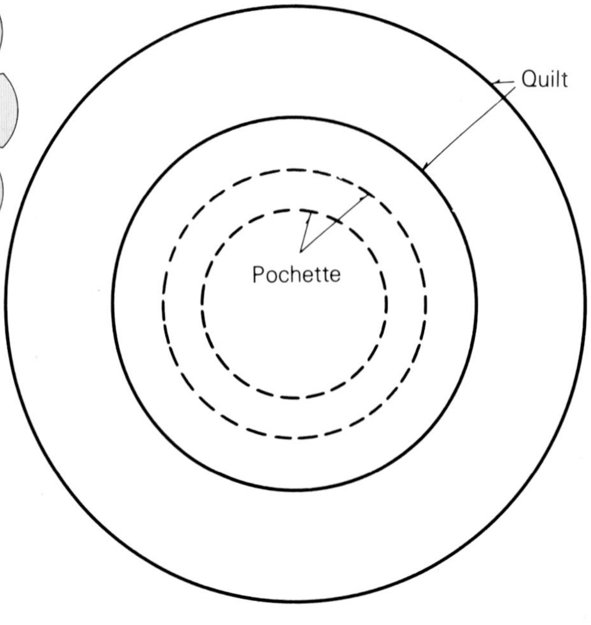

Continued on page 95.

Times

DUCK PADDLE
Mat & Pochette

"Duck paddle patchwork", named from its shape, is constructed in print and plain fabric.

Mat
You will need:
1.20 m of 90 cm wide dressweight cotton (a)
20 cm of 90 cm wide dressweight cotton (b)
40 cm of 90 cm wide dressweight cotton (c)
100 cm x 80 cm of lining
100 cm x 80 cm of lightweight terylene wadding
White cotton thread
Finished size: 97 cm x 70.5 cm

Pochette
You will need:
90 cm of 90 cm wide dressweight cotton (a)
60 cm x 10 cm of dressweight cotton (b)
40 cm x 10 cm of dressweight cotton (c)
50 cm x 30 cm of lining
30 cm of 90 cm wide lightweight terylene wadding
White cotton thread
Finished size: see page 89

To make up
Join in sequences (1)-(5).

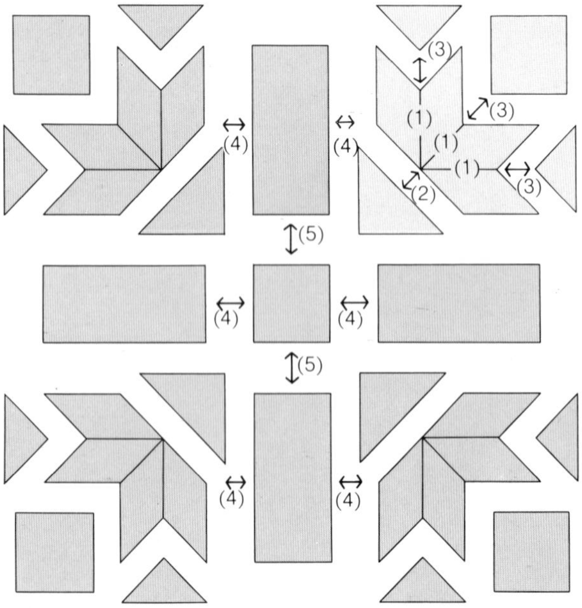

Patterns of the patches used (actual size)
Add 7 mm seam allowance.

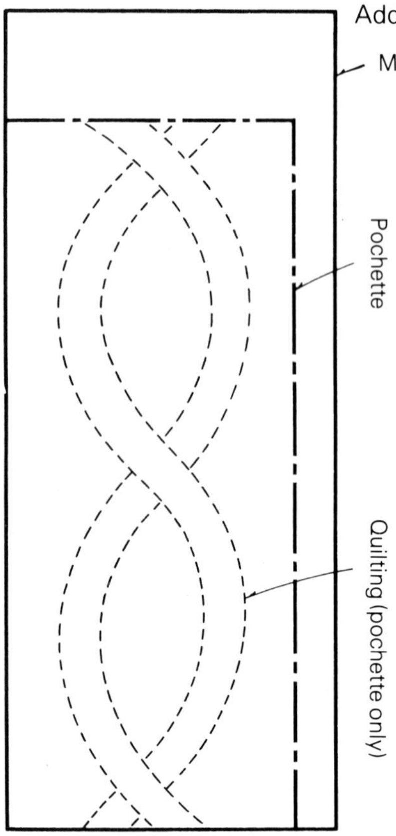

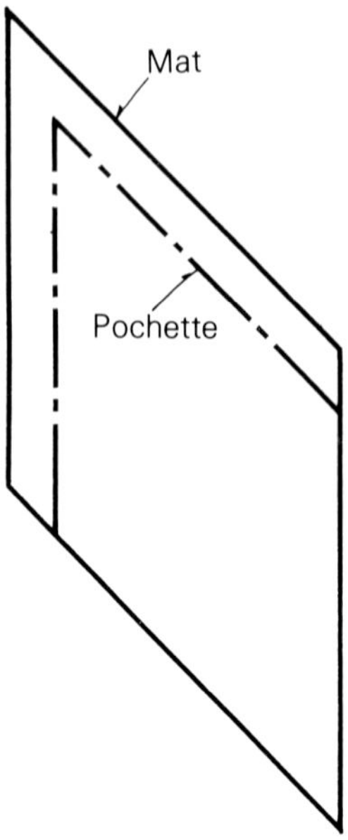

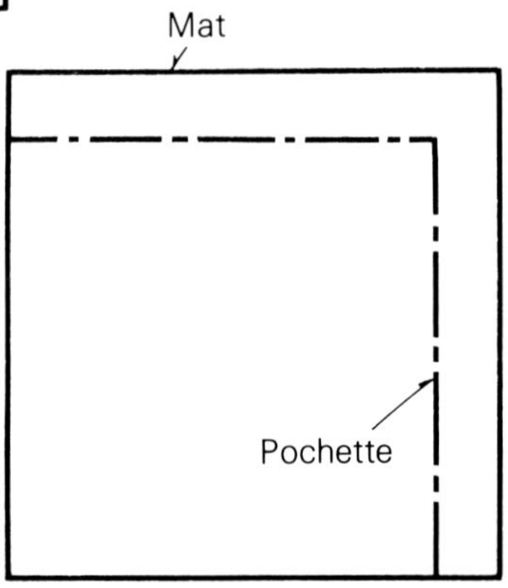

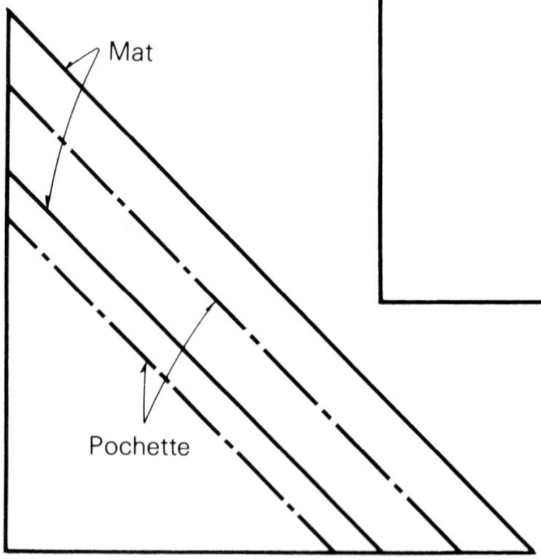

Continued on page 88.

SUPER STAR
Runner & Placemats

The eight-point star is the most traditional star pattern and is composed of squares and triangles.

Placemats
For each mat you will need:
70 cm x 30 cm of dressweight cotton (a)
70 cm x 20 cm of dressweight cotton (b)
40 cm x 30 cm of iron-on interlining
Matching cotton thread
Finished size: 37 cm x 21 cm

Runner
You will need:
40 cm of 90 cm wide black dressweight cotton
30 cm of 90 cm wide grey dressweight cotton
15 cm of 90 cm wide cotton print (a)
15 cm of 90 cm wide cotton print (b)
30 cm of 90 cm wide iron-on interlining
Matching cotton thread
Finished size: 85 cm x 21 cm

To make up
Join in sequences (1)-(4).

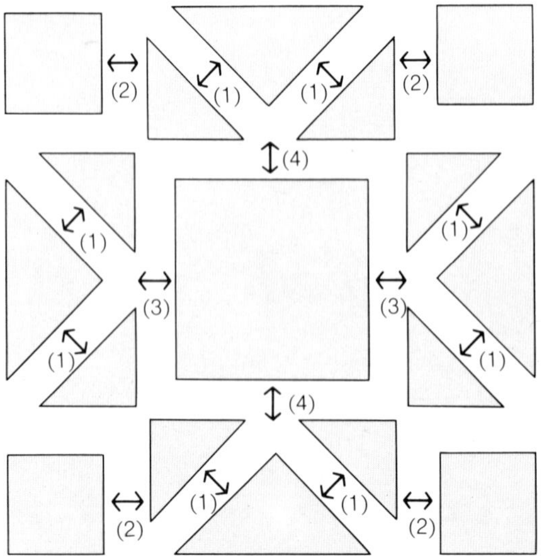

Patterns of the patches used (actual size)
Add 7 mm seam allowance.

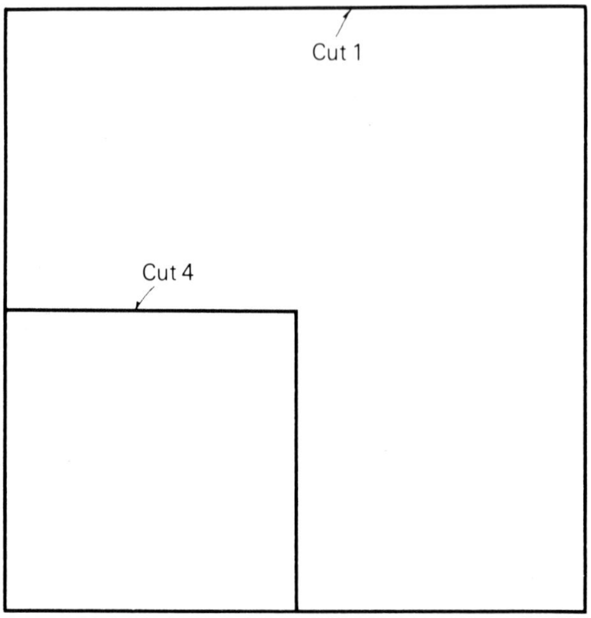

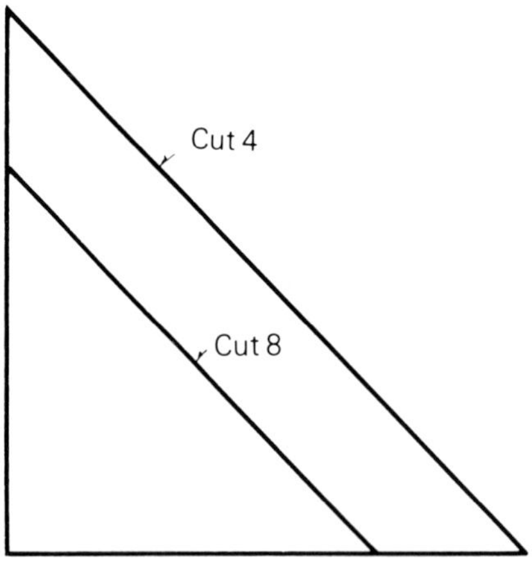

Continued on page 91.

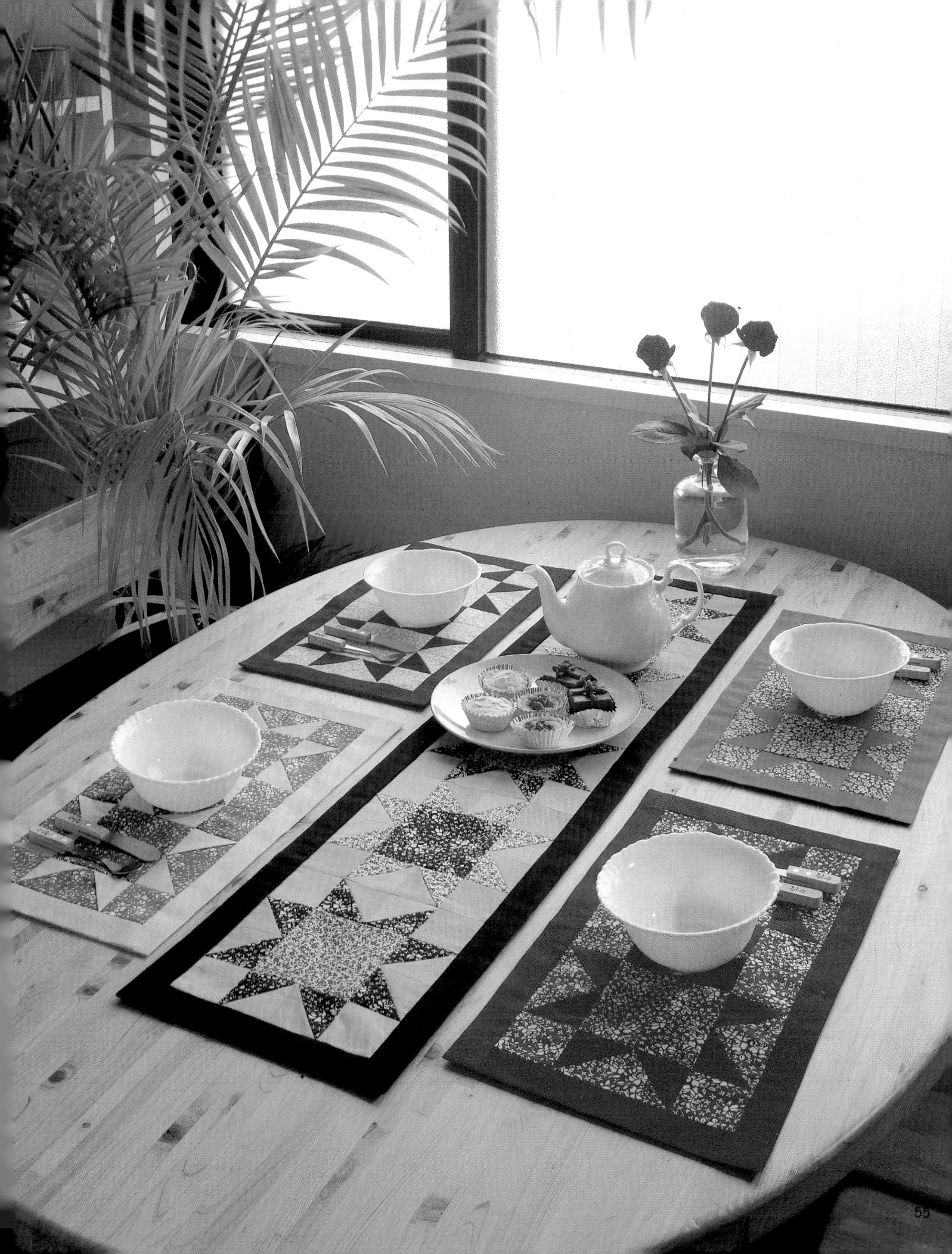

ROSE GARDEN
Pot Holder & Table Runner

One of the most popular rose patterns, composed with triangular patches attached to a centre square.

Table Runner
You will need:
50 cm x 90 cm of cotton (a)
70 cm x 10 cm of cotton (c)
20 cm x 90 cm of both cottons (b) and (d)
30 cm of 90 cm wide interlining
Matching cotton thread
Finished size: 81.5 cm x 21.5 cm

Pot Holder
For each pot holder, you will need:
40 cm x 30 cm of cotton (a)
50 cm x 20 cm of cotton (b)
20 cm x 20 cm of lightweight terylene wadding
20 cm x 20 cm of iron-on interlining
Matching cotton thread
Finished size: 19.5 cm square

To make up
Join in sequences (1)-(4).

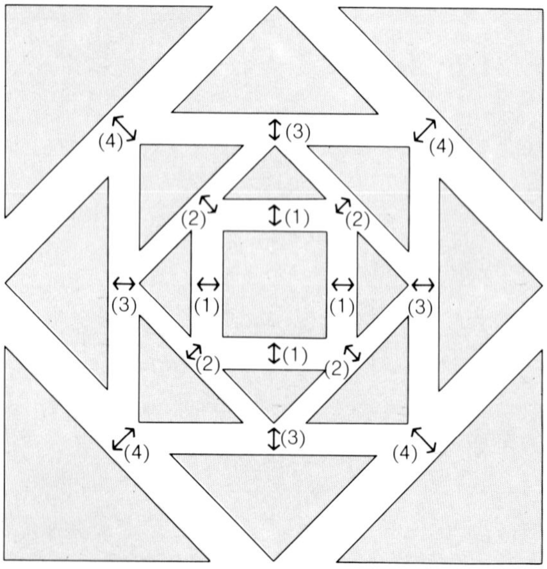

Patterns of the patches used (actual size)
Add 7 mm seam allowance.

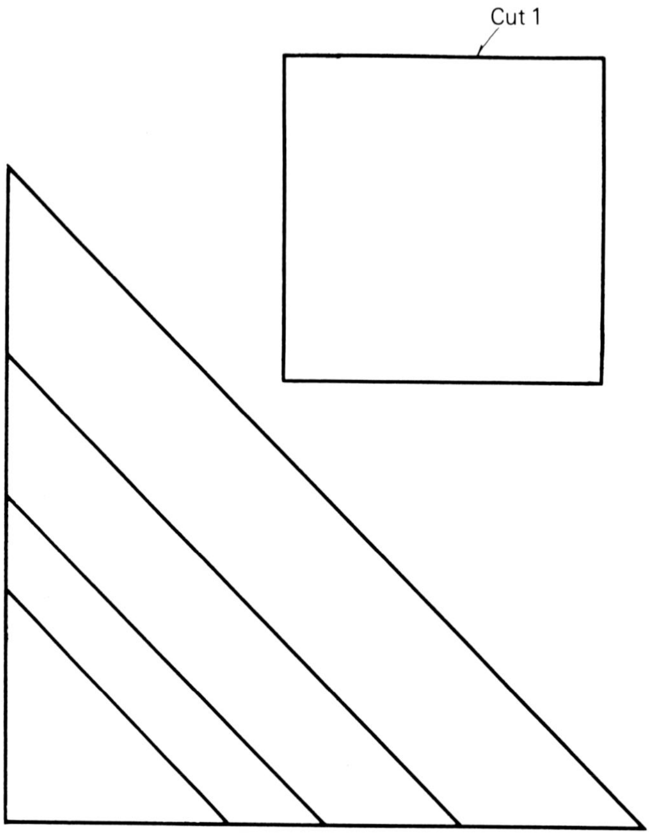

Cut 4 of each

Continued on page 92.

MONKEY WRENCH
Wall Hanging & Bags

The shape of the wrench is arranged in a square patch. Each square of the wall hanging can be used as a pot holder.

Wall Hanging
For each square you will need:
20 cm x 20 cm of dressweight cotton (a)
50 cm x 30 cm of dressweight cotton (b)
20 cm x 20 cm of lightweight terylene wadding
One button
White cotton thread
Finished size: see page 94

Bags
For each bag you will need:
80 cm x 80 cm of furnishing weight cotton hessian or denim (e)
30 cm x 20 cm of both cottons (a) and (b)
30 cm x 10 cm of both cottons (c) and (d)
80 cm x 60 cm of cotton to line bag
25 cm x 25 cm of lining
25 cm x 25 cm of lightweight terylene wadding
White cotton thread
Finished size: see page 94

To make up
Join in sequences (1)-(4)

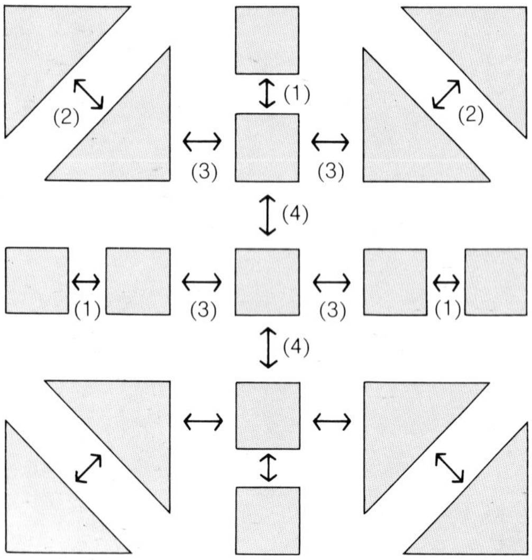

Patterns of the patches used (actual size)
Add 7 mm seam allowance.

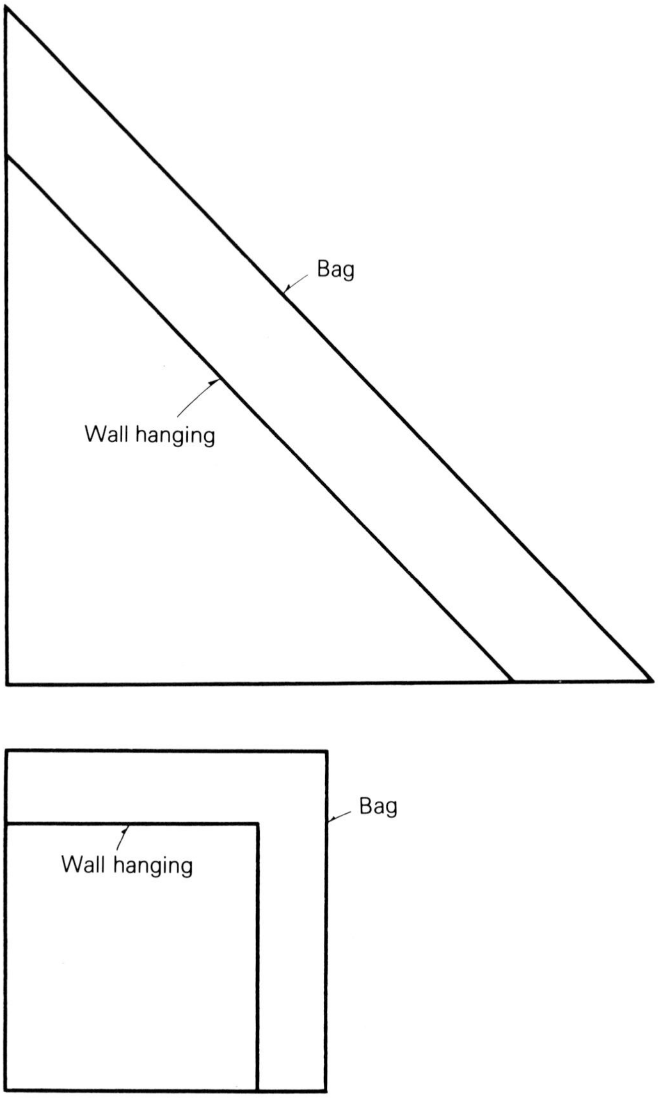

Continued on page 94.

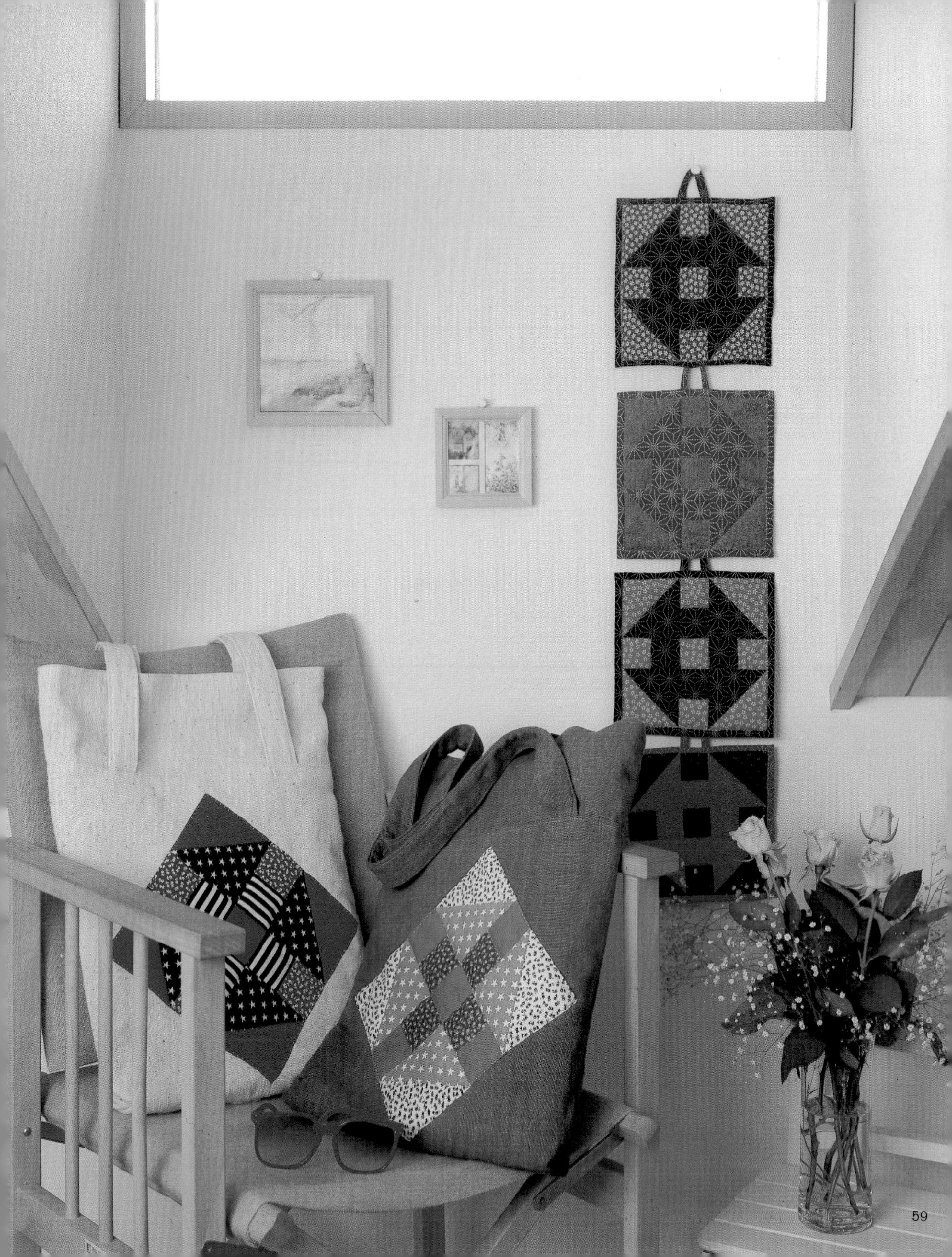

PINEAPPLE TREE VARIATION

Pen Cases & Phone Set

A series of plain and print trapeziums form a variation on the pineapple tree motif.

Phone Set
For the phone cover you will need:
50 cm x 40 cm of yellow dressweight cotton
70 cm x 10 cm of dressweight cottons (a), (b) and (c)
60 cm x 10 cm of dressweight cotton (d)
White cotton thread
Finished size: 33 cm x 37 cm

For the mat you will need:
30 cm x 30 cm of yellow dressweight cotton
50 cm x 10 cm of both dressweight cottons (a) and (b)
20 cm x 10 cm of both dressweight cottons (c) and (d)
30 cm x 30 cm of lining
30 cm x 30 cm of lightweight terylene wadding
White cotton thread
Finished size: 24 cm x 26 cm

Pen Case
For each pen case you will need:
60 cm x 30 cm of dressweight cotton (a)
40 cm x 40 cm of dressweight cotton (b)
30 cm x 30 cm of lightweight terylene wadding
1 cm of 2.5 cm wide Velcro
White cotton thread
Finished size: see page 98

Patterns of the patches used (actual size)
Add 7 mm seam allowance.

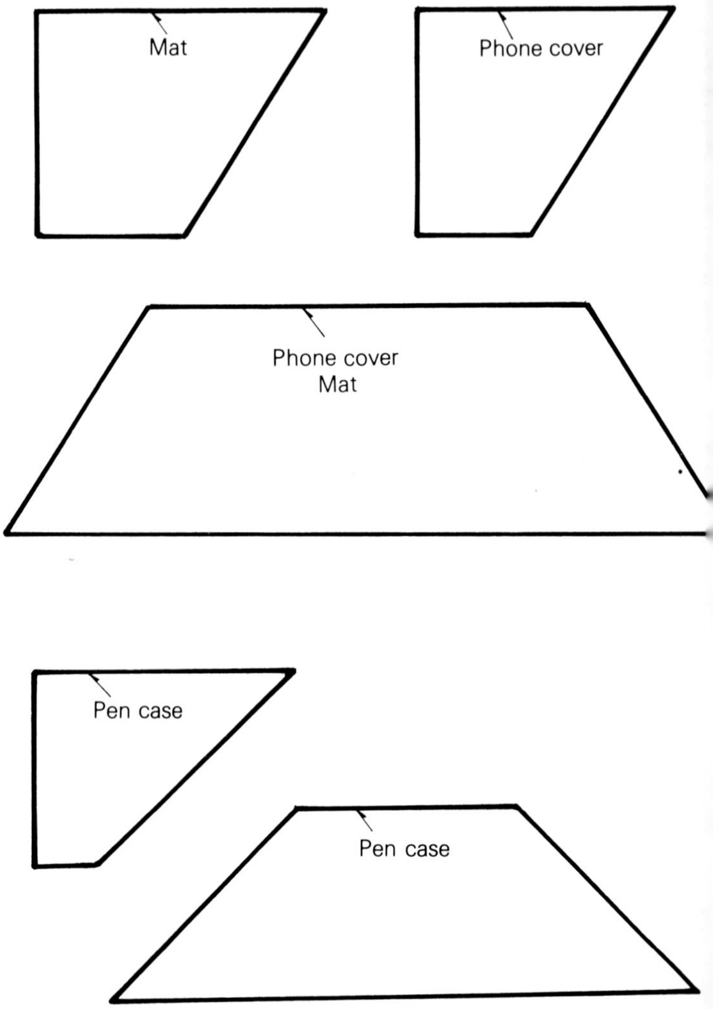

To make up
Press seam (1) open
Press seam (2) to one side for quilting

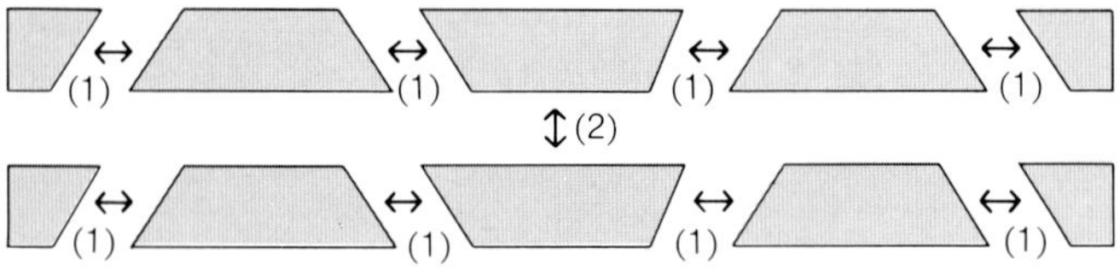

Continued on page 97.

WILD GOOSE CHASE

Cushion & Bags

A series of triangular patches point towards a central square.

Cushion
You will need:
70 cm x 90 cm of olive green cotton
80 cm x 30 cm of brown cotton
20 cm x 90 cm of floral print on red
70 cm x 70 cm of lightweight terylene wadding
34 cm long zip fastener
50 cm square inner cushion
Olive green and brown cotton thread
Finished size: 48 cm square

Bags
For the blue bag (bottom right) you will need:
60 cm of 90 cm wide navy blue heavyweight cotton
20 cm of 90 cm wide white cotton
20 cm x 70 cm of navy blue cotton
50 cm x 80 cm of lining
40 cm x 20 cm of backing fabric
Matching cotton thread

For the white bag (top right) you will need:
60 cm of 90 cm wide white heavyweight cotton
10 cm x 80 cm of plaid cotton
10 cm x 50 cm of pale blue cotton
10 cm x 40 cm of red cotton
70 cm x 80 cm of lining
20 cm x 20 cm of backing fabric
60 cm of 90 cm wide lightweight terylene wadding
Matching cotton thread
Finished size: see page 100

To make up Join in sequences (1)-(4)

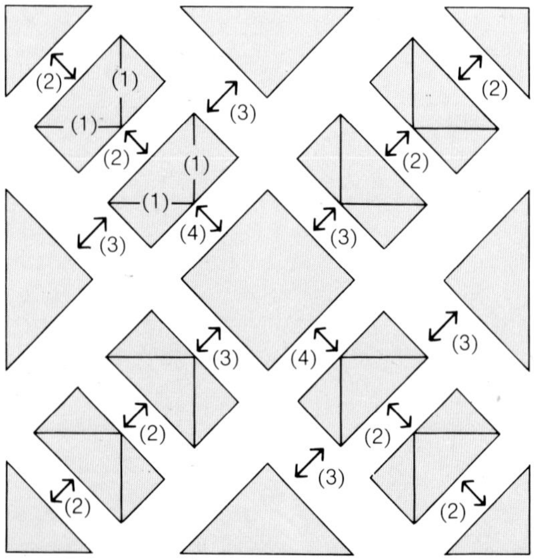

Patterns of the patches used (actual size)
Add 7 mm seam allowance.

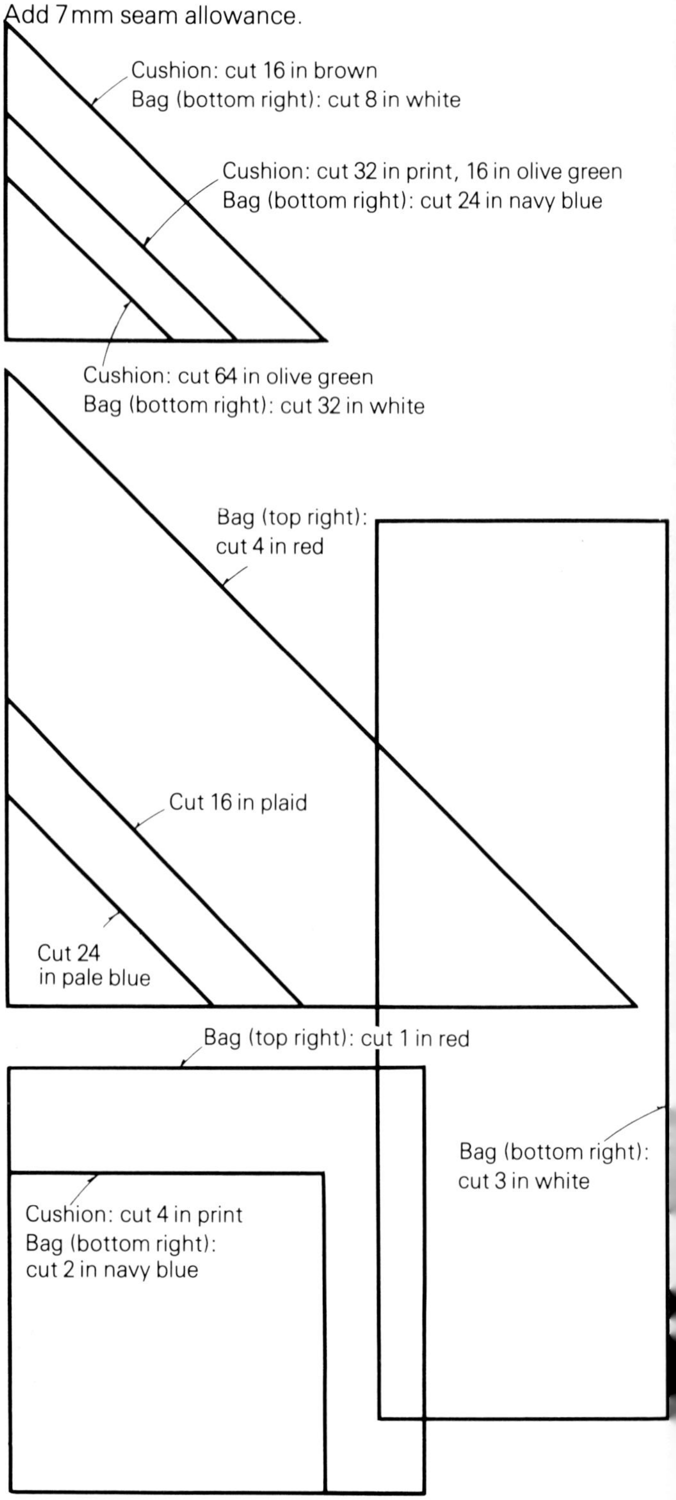
Cushion: cut 16 in brown
Bag (bottom right): cut 8 in white
Cushion: cut 32 in print, 16 in olive green
Bag (bottom right): cut 24 in navy blue
Cushion: cut 64 in olive green
Bag (bottom right): cut 32 in white
Bag (top right):
cut 4 in red
Cut 16 in plaid
Cut 24
in pale blue
Bag (top right): cut 1 in red
Bag (bottom right):
cut 3 in white
Cushion: cut 4 in print
Bag (bottom right):
cut 2 in navy blue

Continued on page 99.

COT QUILT

As shown on page 1

To make up:

(1) Cut out patch pieces, adding 7 mm seam allowance. Join as shown on the chart.

(2) Place the wadding between the patchwork and lining. Tack in place, starting at the centre and working outwards. Quilt and finish the edges with piping.

Chart of Measurements

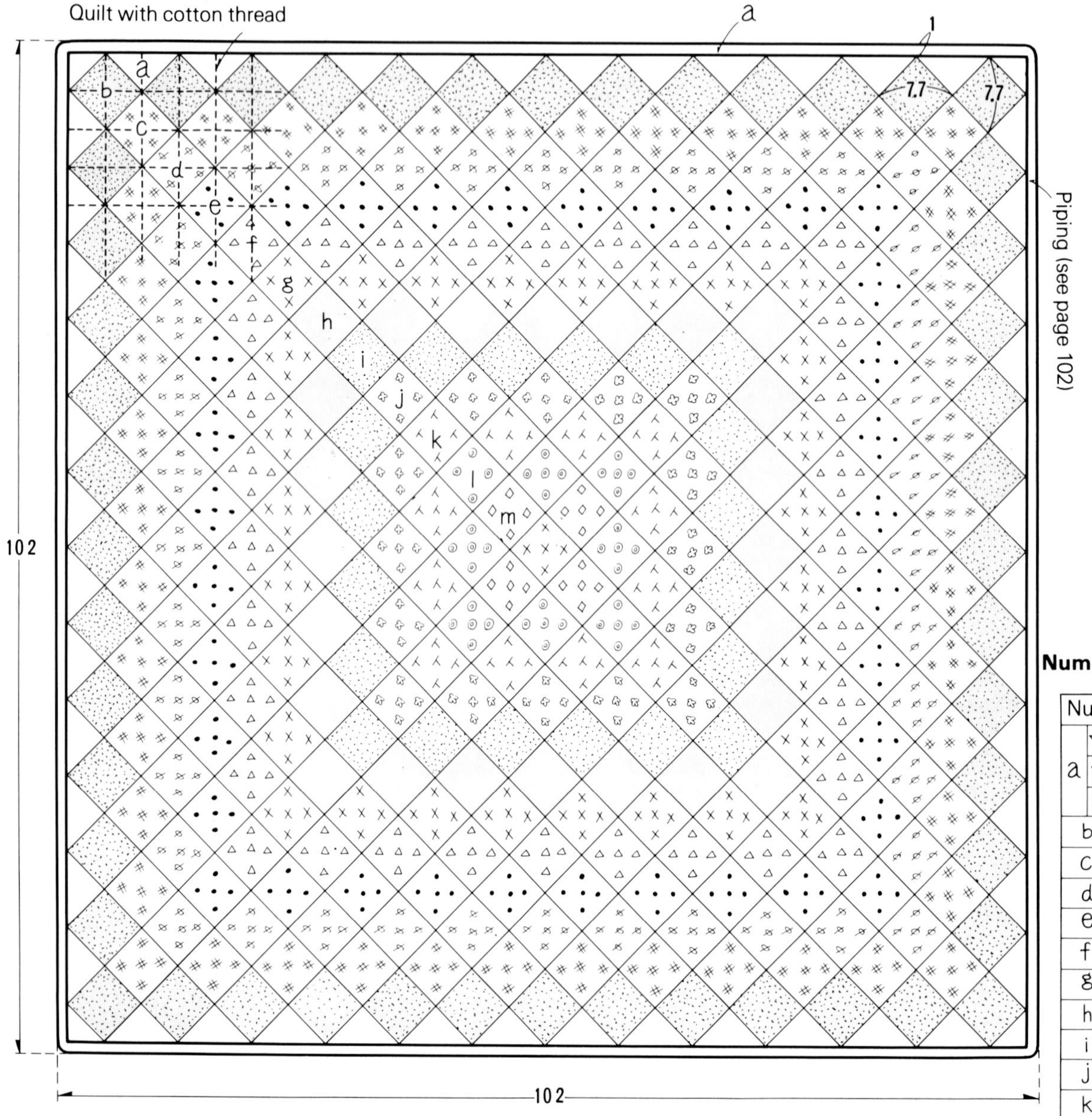

Quilt with cotton thread
a
1
7.7
7.7
Piping (see page 102)
102
102
a
b
c
d
e
f
g
h
i
j
k
l
m

Join lining to make a piece 102 cm square.

Number of patches & sizes

Numbers			Sizes (cm)
a	▽	48	65 × 65
	◁	4	
	Piping		
b		48	90 × 32
c		44	85 × 32
d		40	75 × 32
e		36	90 × 25
f		32	85 × 25
g		29	75 × 25
h		24	90 × 18
i		20	75 × 18
j		16	60 × 18
k		12	90 × 10
l		8	60 × 10
m		4	30 × 10

Bias strip for piping

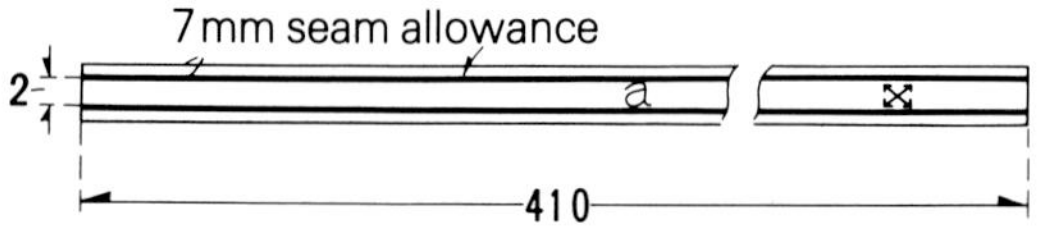

BEDSPREAD
As shown on page 5

To make up:

(1) Cut out patch pieces adding 7 mm seam allowance and join as shown on page 2. Alternate blocks A and B as shown below.

(2) Join border strips crosswise, and then lengthwise. Place wadding between top piece and lining, quilt and finish the edges with piping.

Chart of Measurements

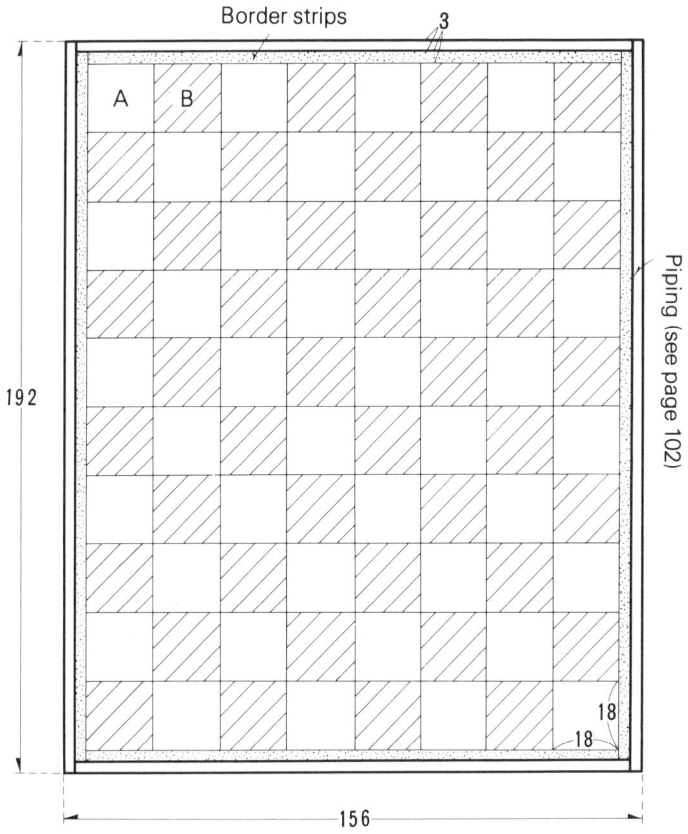

Cut lining and wadding to fit the finished size

Border strips

Cut 2 of each in navy blue

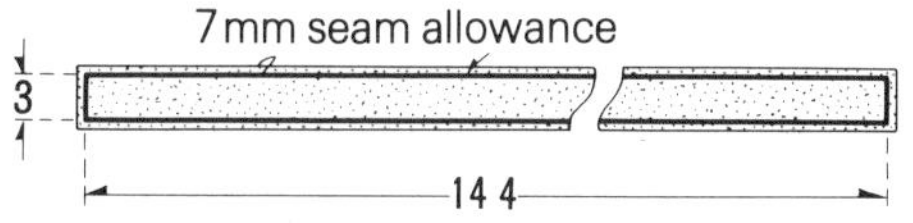

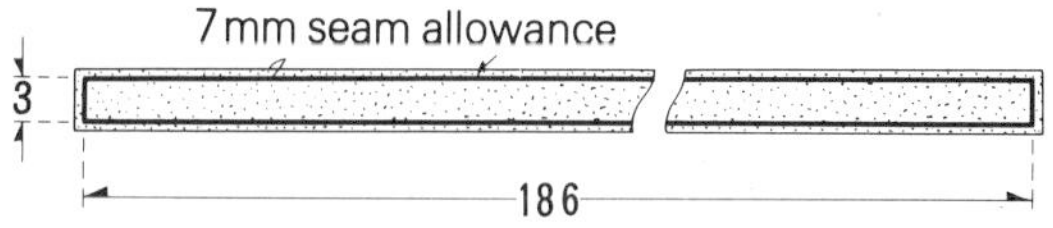

Piping strips

Cut 2 of each in unbleached calico

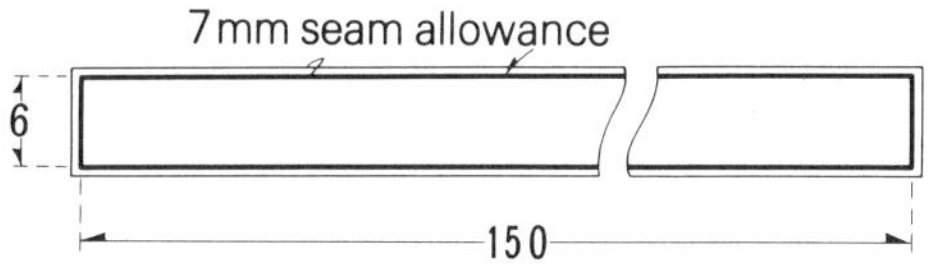

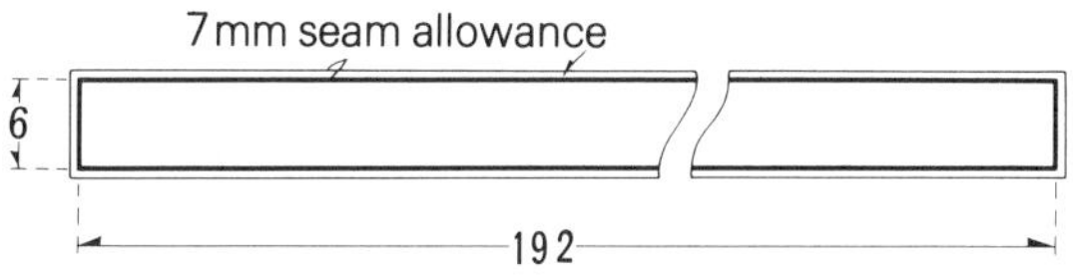

The quilt is composed of 40 patchwork blocks and 40 quilted blocks

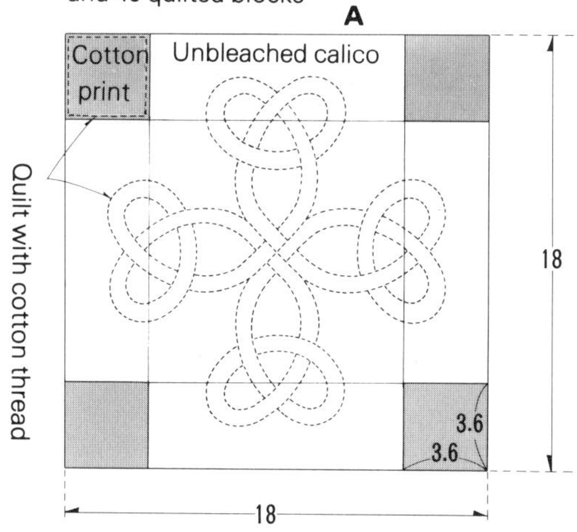

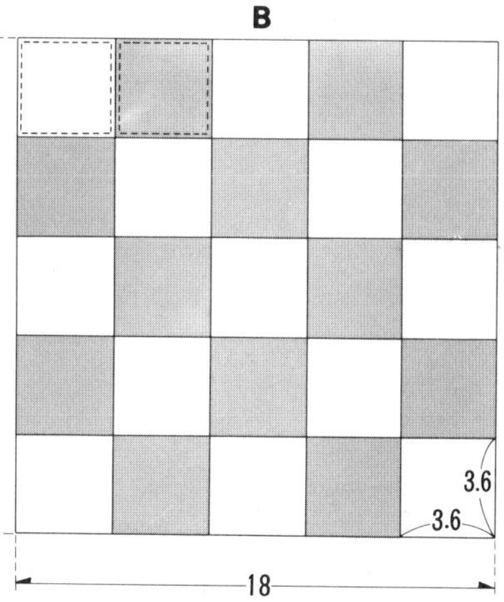

To finish corner of piping

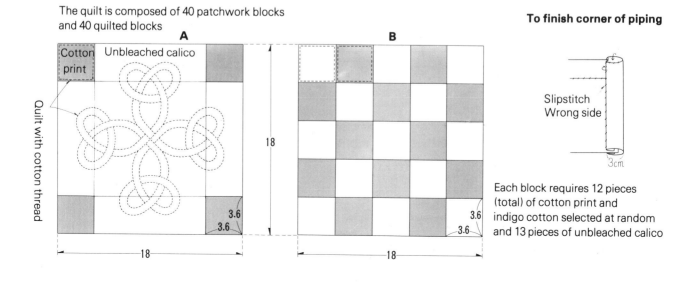

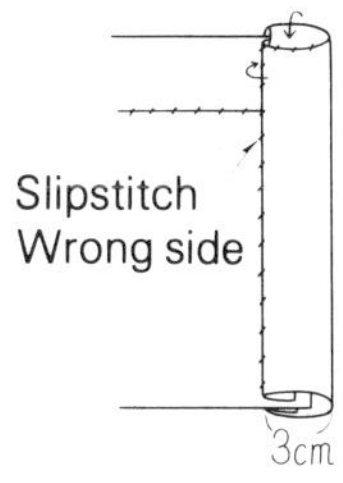

Each block requires 12 pieces (total) of cotton print and indigo cotton selected at random and 13 pieces of unbleached calico

COT QUILT
As shown on page 3

To make up:
(1) Cut out patch pieces, adding 7 mm seam allowance. Join as shown on the chart.
(2) Join border strips to patchwork crosswise then lengthwise. Place wadding between top piece and lining. Tack all three together, working from the centre outwards. Quilt and finish the edges with piping.

Chart of Measurements

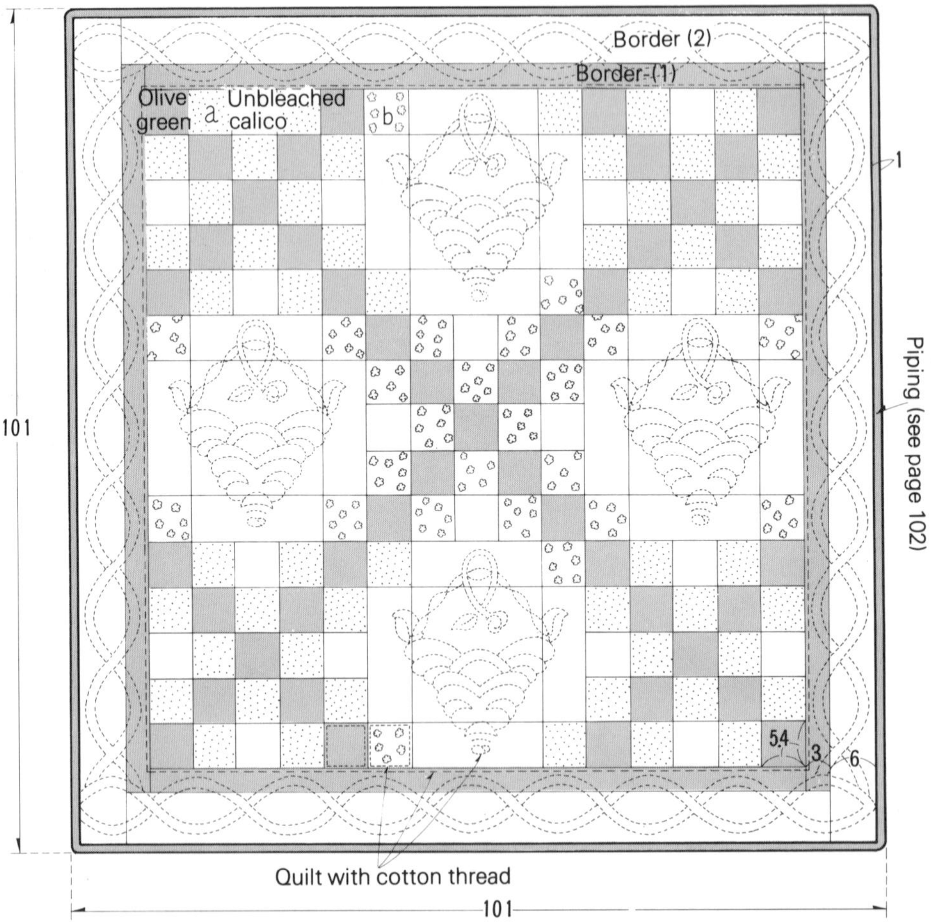
Border (2)
Border (1)
Olive green
a
Unbleached calico
b
1
Piping (see page 102)
101
5.4
3
6
Quilt with cotton thread
101

Cut lining in olive green and join to make a piece 101 cm square.

Border strips (1)
Cut 2 of each in olive green

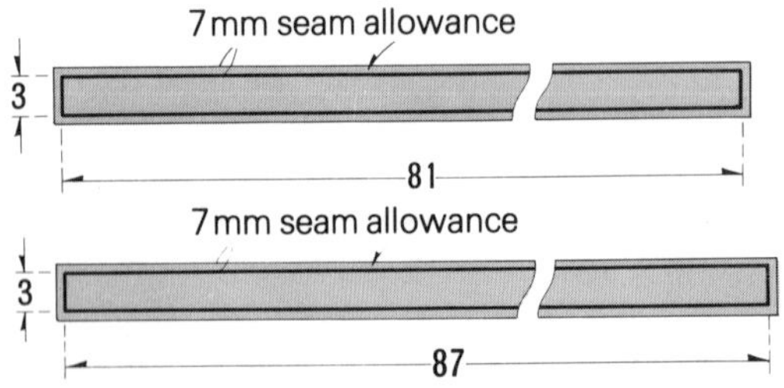
7 mm seam allowance
3
81
7 mm seam allowance
3
87

Border strips (2)
Cut 2 of each in unbleached calico

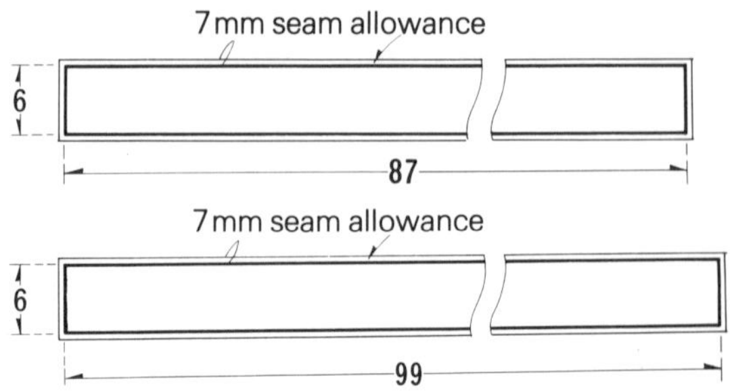
7 mm seam allowance
6
87
7 mm seam allowance
6
99

Bias strip for piping
(in olive green)

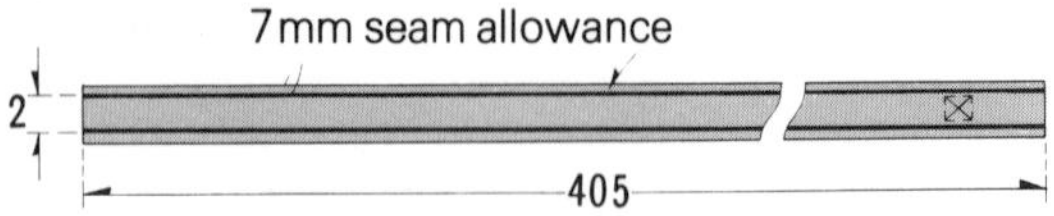
7 mm seam allowance
2
405

Quilting design (actual size)

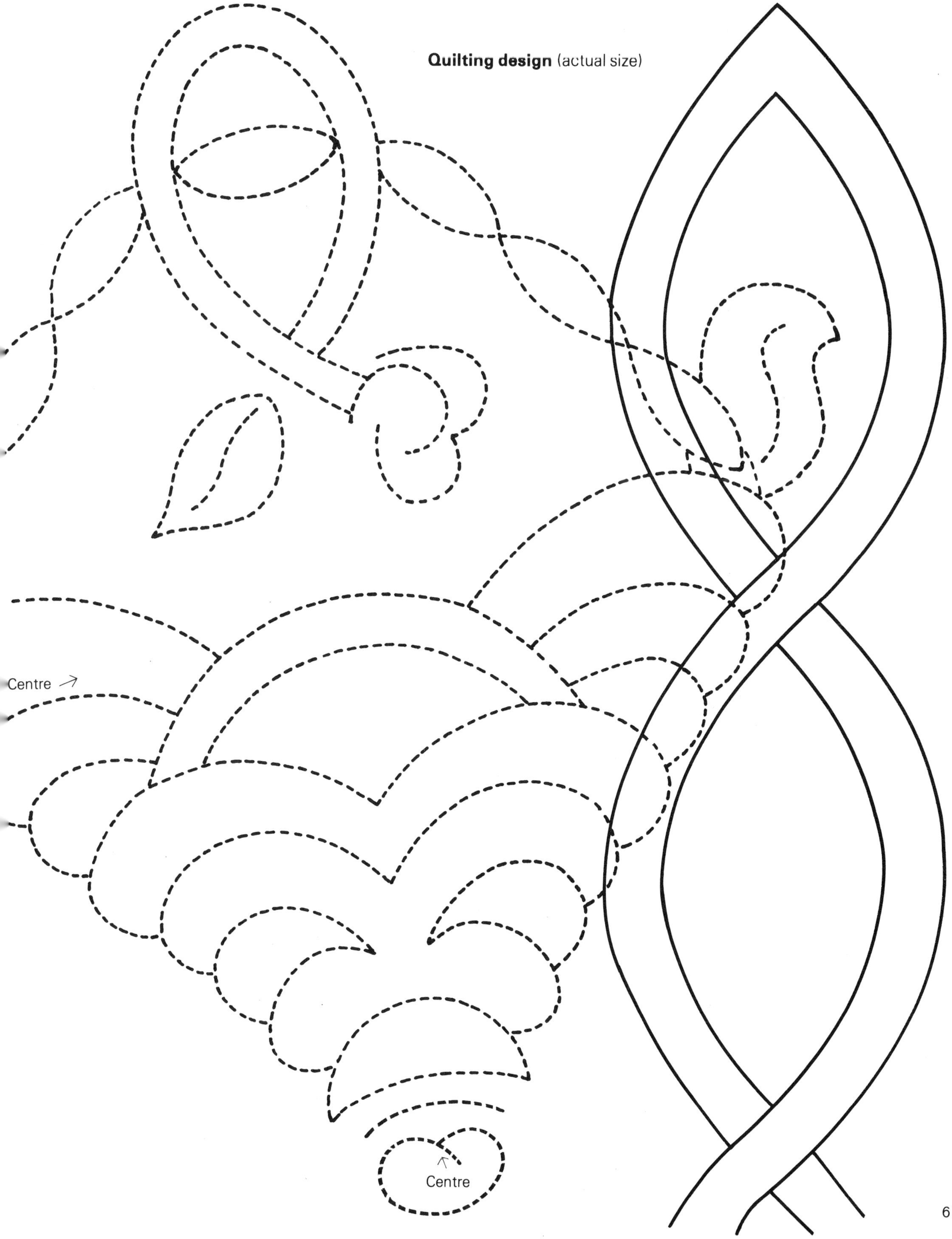

TOP QUILT FOR A SINGLE BED
As shown on page 7

To make up:

(1) Cut out patch pieces, adding 7 mm seam allowance. Cut squares in lining and wadding. With right sides together, join patch pieces to wadding and lining as shown.

(2) With right sides together, join top pieces of blocks. Overlap wadding and slipstitch lining in place.

(3) Finish the edges with piping.

Chart of Measurements

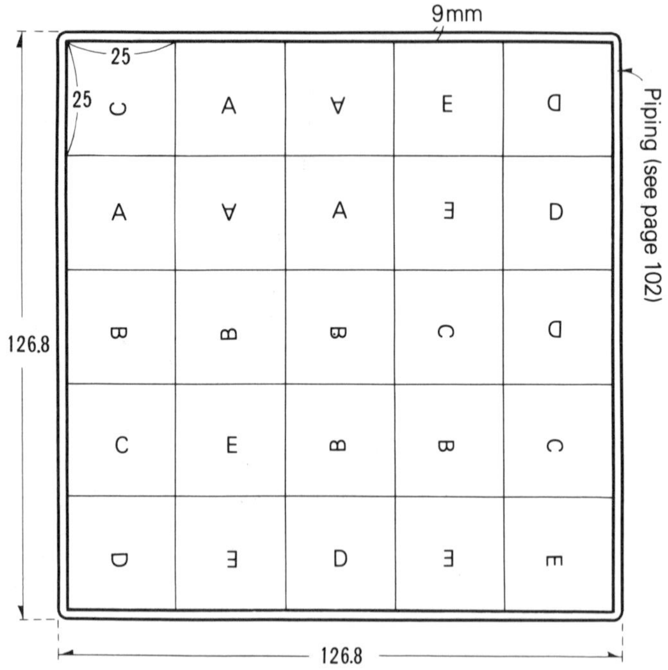

Cut 25 26.5cm squares in lining and wadding

Colours & sizes

Colours		Sizes (cm)
Lilac	a	72 × 10
	b	85 × 15
	c	90 × 15
	d	83 × 18
Brown	a	75 × 10
	b	75 × 15
	c	90 × 18
	d	83 × 22
Blue	a	60 × 10
	b	73 × 15
	c	80 × 18
	d	75 × 22
Pink	a	70 × 10
	b	75 × 15
	c	80 × 18
	d	90 × 22
Yellow	a	70 × 10
	b	75 × 15
	c	90 × 18
	d	82 × 20
Grey	a	80 × 5
	b	70 × 10
	c	75 × 15
	d	90 × 15
Green	a	75 × 10
	b	82 × 15
	c	80 × 18
	d	82 × 22
Orange	a	35 × 5
	b	60 × 5
	c	85 × 5
	d	67 × 10
Red		90 × 15

Colour scheme of each block

A
(5 pieces)

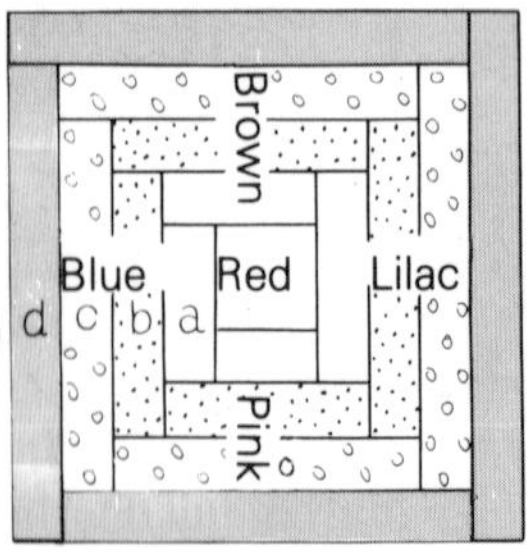

Brown
Blue
Red
Lilac
d c b a
Pink

B
(5 pieces)

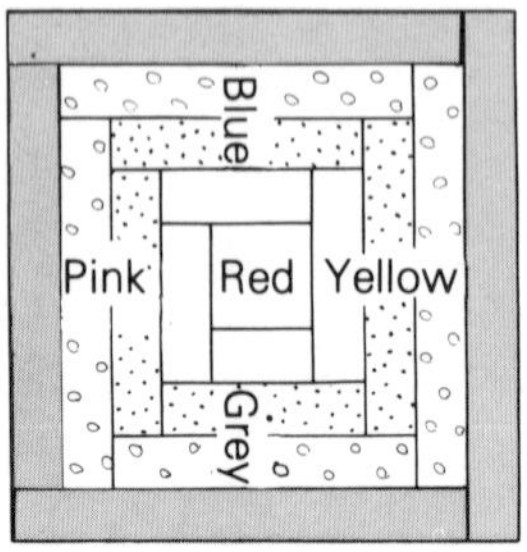

Blue
Pink
Red
Yellow
Grey

C
(4 pieces)

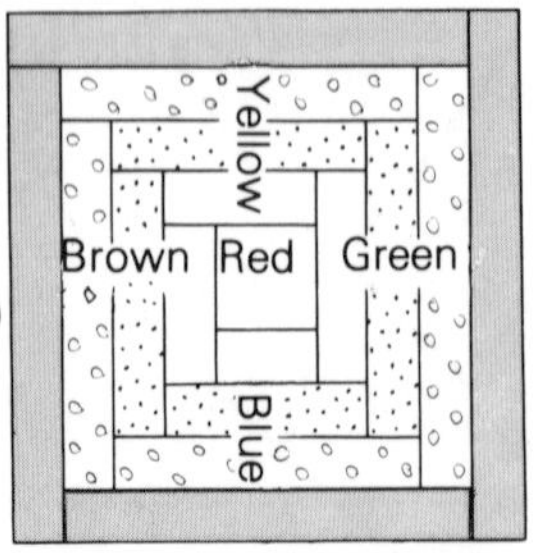

Yellow
Brown
Red
Green
Blue

D
(5 pieces)

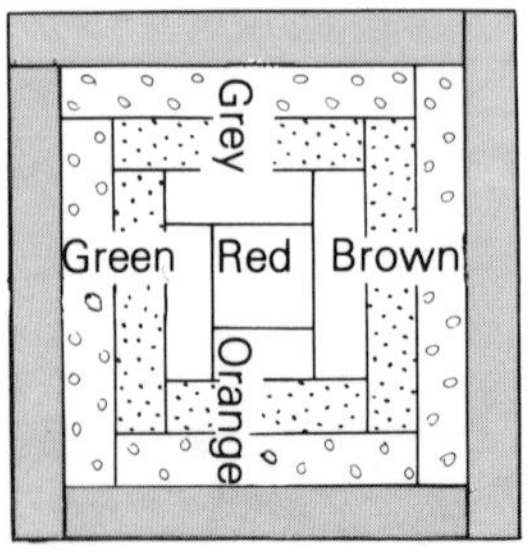

Grey
Green
Red
Brown
Orange

E
(6 pieces)

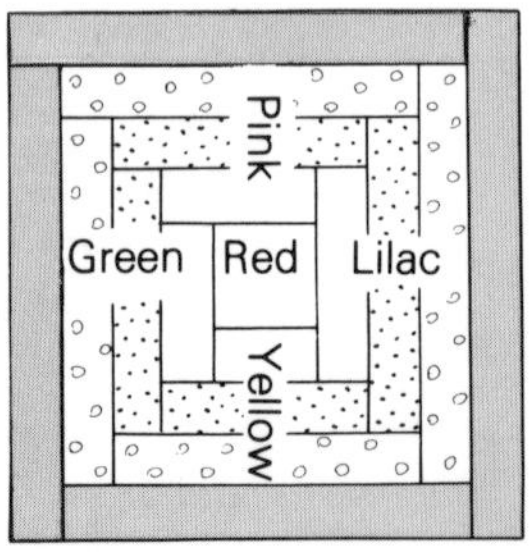

Pink
Green
Red
Lilac
Yellow

①

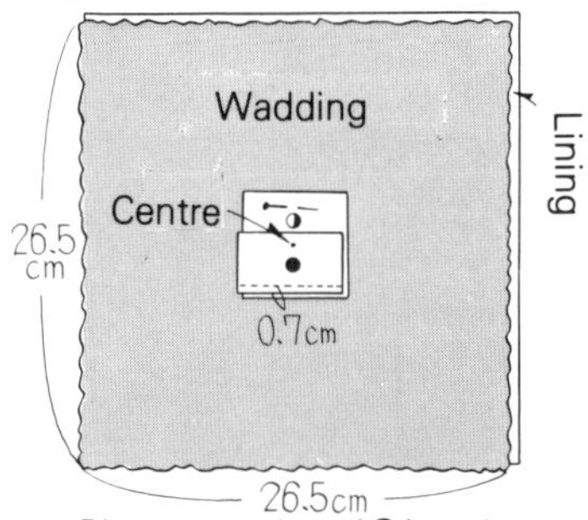

Pin centre piece (◑) to the centre of foundation block. Right sides together, join piece marked (●).

②

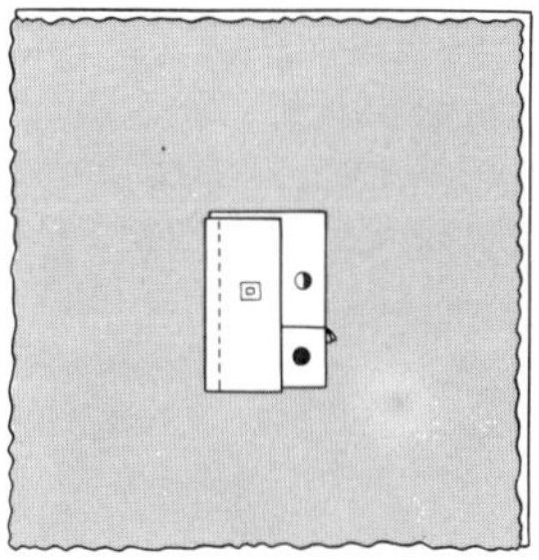

③

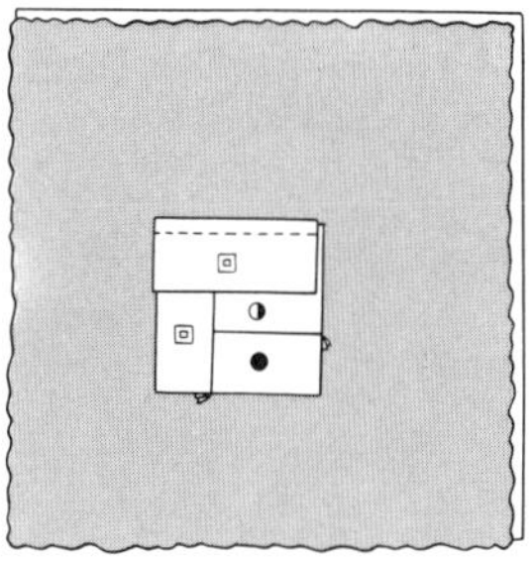

④

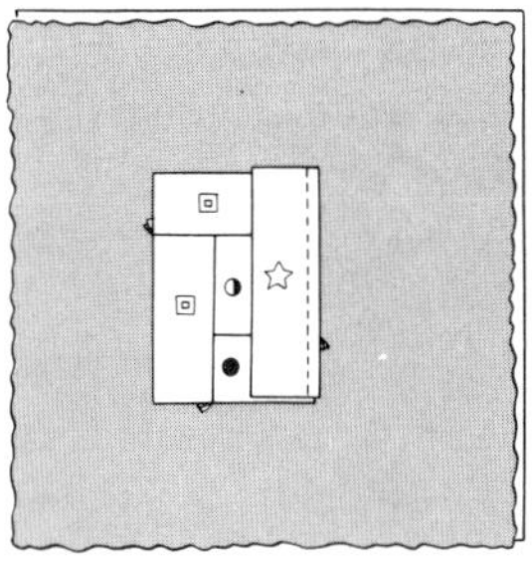

⑤

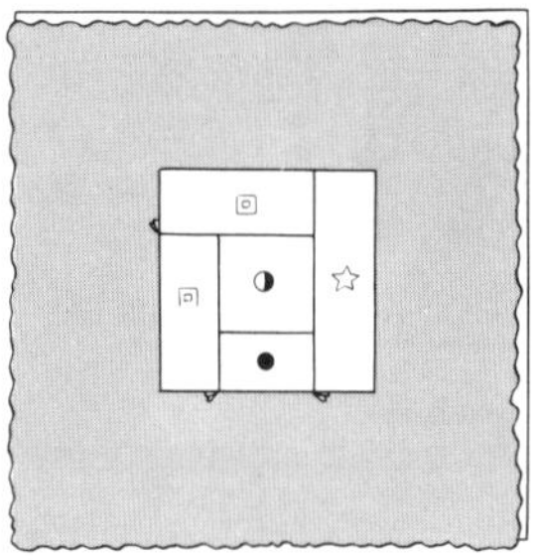

⑥

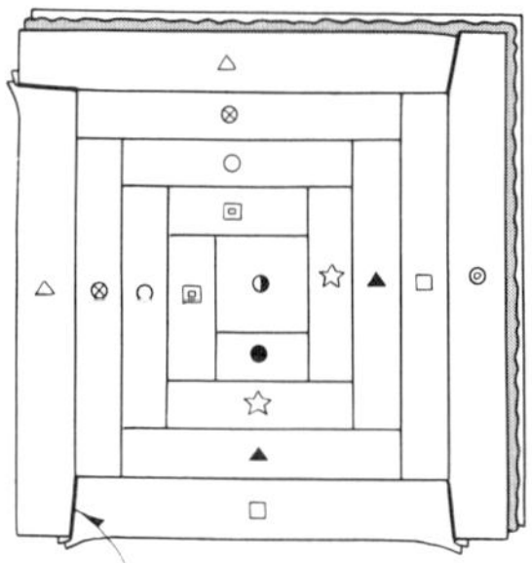

Right sides together, join the top layers of two blocks.

⑦ Sew top layer only at the four outer seams.

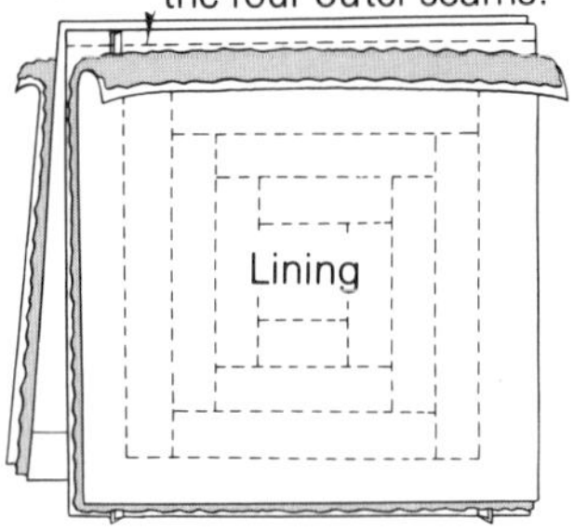

⑧

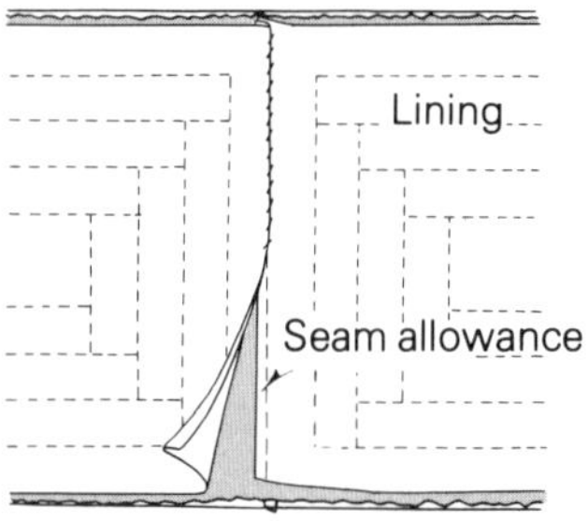

Overlap wadding. Fold in a small hem on one edge of the lining and slipstitch in place.

BED LINEN & MATCHING PICTURE

As shown on page 13

Patchwork Picture

To make up:

(1) Cut out patch pieces, adding 7 mm seam allowance. Join as shown on the chart.

(2) Place wadding between patchwork and lining. Quilt as indicated.

Chart of Measurements

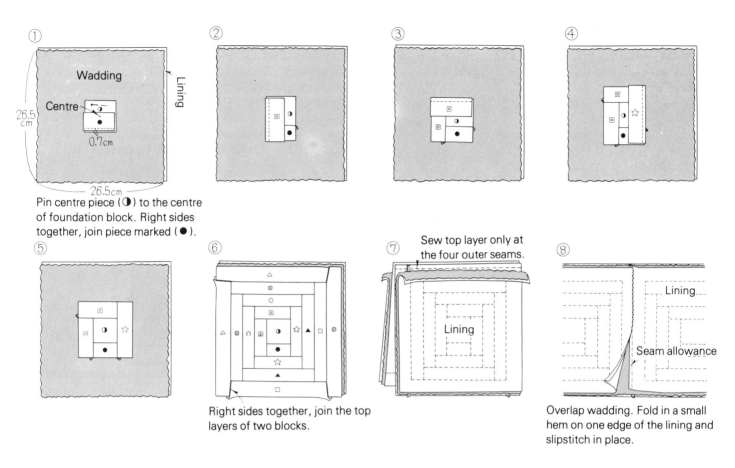

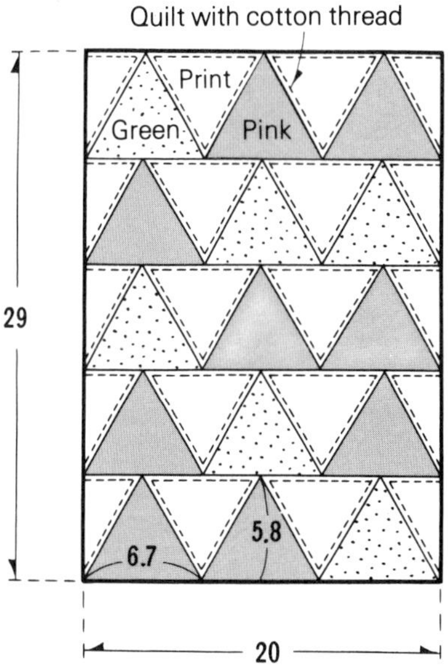
Quilt with cotton thread
Print
Green
Pink
29
6.7
5.8
20

Patchwork Border

To make up:

(1) Cut out and join patch pieces as for the patchwork picture.
(2) With right sides together, sew patchwork and lining together, leaving an opening for turning. Turn right side out and slipstitch the opening to close.
(3) Quilt as indicated.

Chart of Measurements

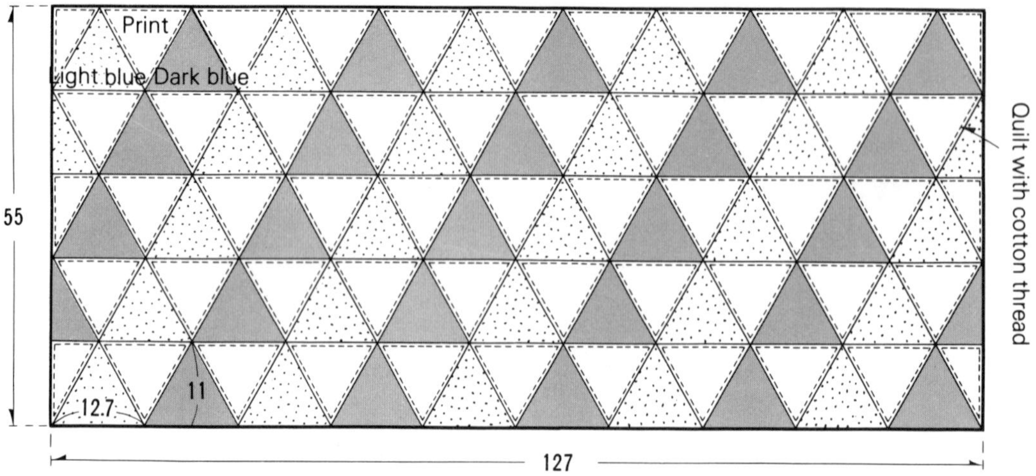

Join lining to make a piece 128cm x 56.5cm.

Pillow Case

To make up:

(1) Cut out and join patch pieces as for the patchwork picture.
(2) Wrong sides together, quilt patchwork to lining.
(3) Hem two edges for the back opening. Overlap pieces as shown and stitch to the front, right sides together.

Chart of Measurements

Front

Back
Add 1cm allowance unless specified

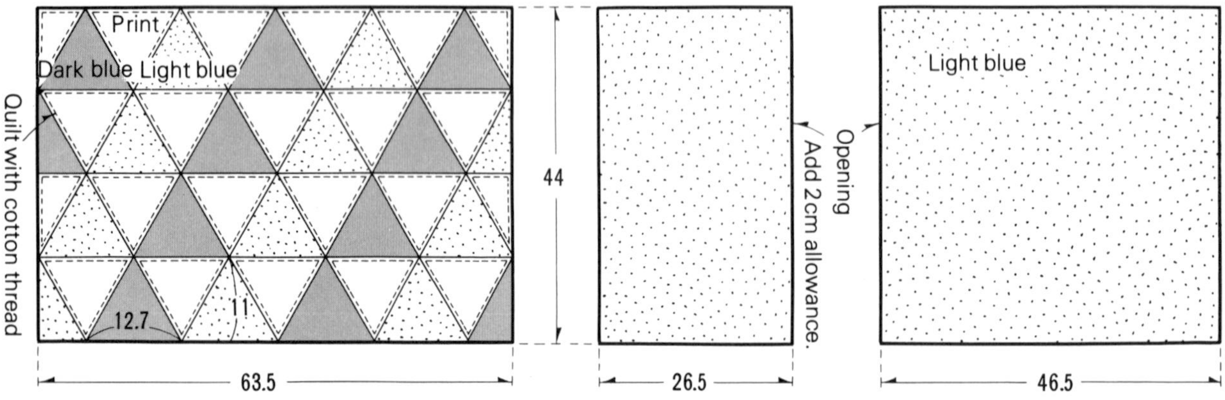

To overlap the two back pieces

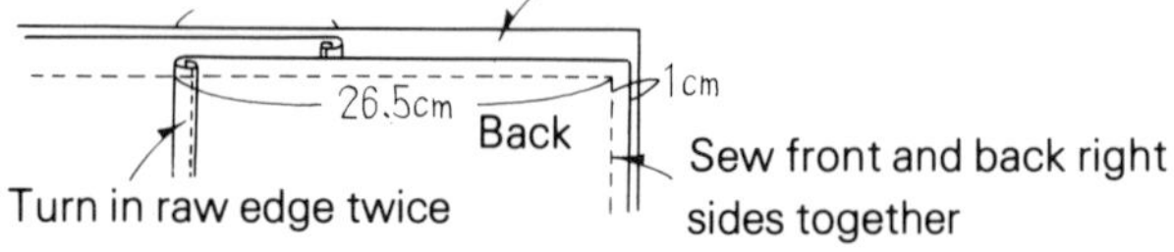

TOP QUILT FOR A SINGLE BED

As shown on page 9

To make up:

(1) Use the hand-stitched method (see page 101). Cut enough paper linings to make up a sizable section of the quilt before removing them.
(2) Cut out patch pieces, adding 7 mm seam allowance. Cut out a set of six patches from each print and join as shown on the chart.
(3) Place wadding between the patchwork and lining. Quilt along seamlines. Finish the edges with piping.

Chart of Measurements

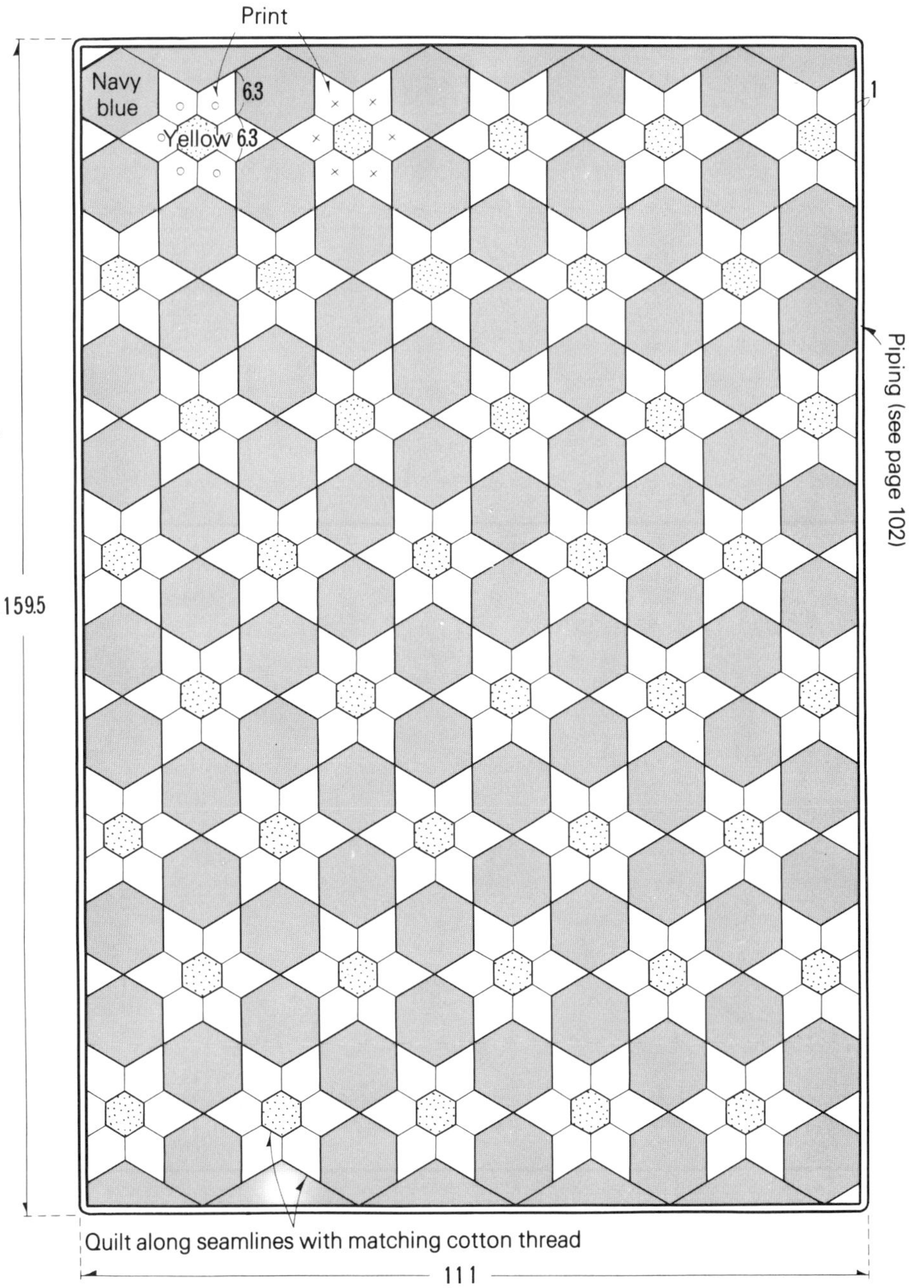
Print
Navy blue
6.3
Yellow 6.3
1
Piping (see page 102)
159.5
Quilt along seamlines with matching cotton thread
111

Join lining to make a piece 159.5cm x 111cm

Bias strip for piping
(polka dot print)

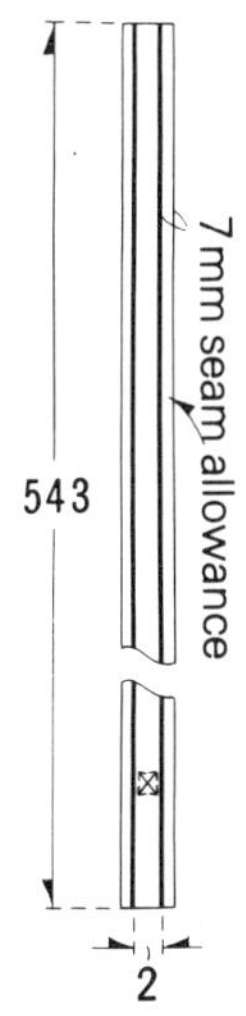

TABLECLOTH
As shown on page 11

To make up:

(1) Cut out patch pieces, adding 7 mm seam allowance. Cut ten pieces in aqua blue cotton for the background as shown on the chart and cutting guide.

(2) Join and sew patches, referring to the chart.

(3) Place top piece and lining right sides together. Sew, leaving opening for turning. Turn right side out. Slipstitch the opening to finish.

Chart of Measurements

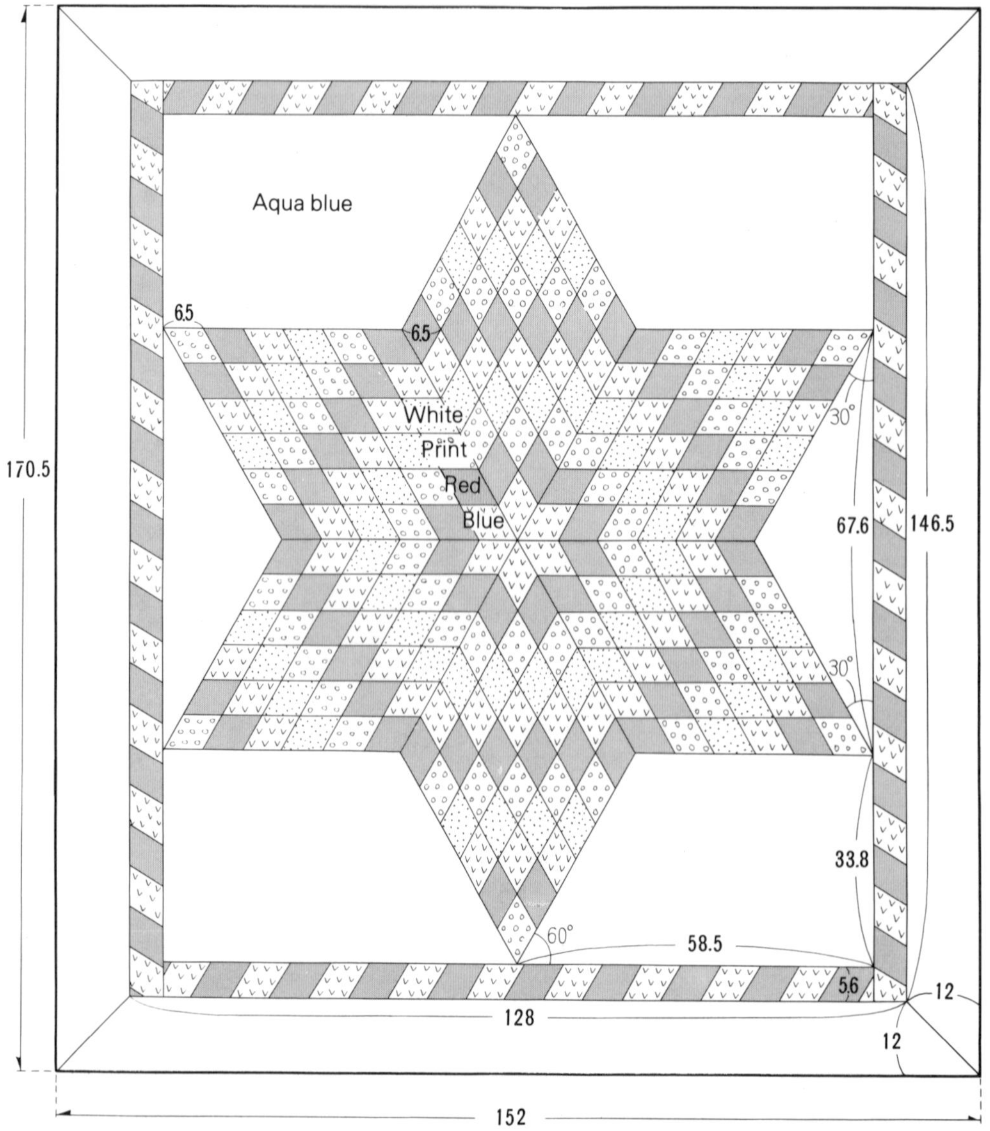

Aqua blue
6.5
6.5
White
Print
Red
Blue
30°
30°
60°
170.5
67.6
146.5
33.8
58.5
5.6
12
12
128
152

Join lining to make a piece 154cm x 172.5cm

Add 1 cm seam allowance unless specified

Cutting guide

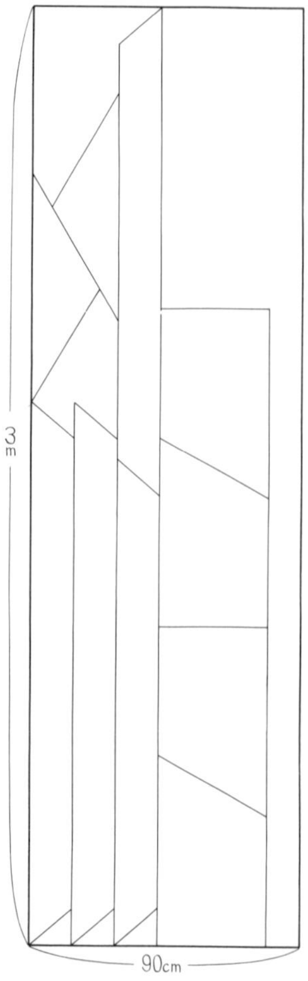

PLACEMATS & PINCUSHIONS

As shown on page 15

Placemat

To make up:

(1) Cut out patch pieces, adding 7 mm seam allowance. Join as shown on the chart.

(2) Place wadding on the wrong side of patchwork. Quilt together.

(3) Wrong sides together, attach lining. Finish edges with piping.

Chart of Measurements

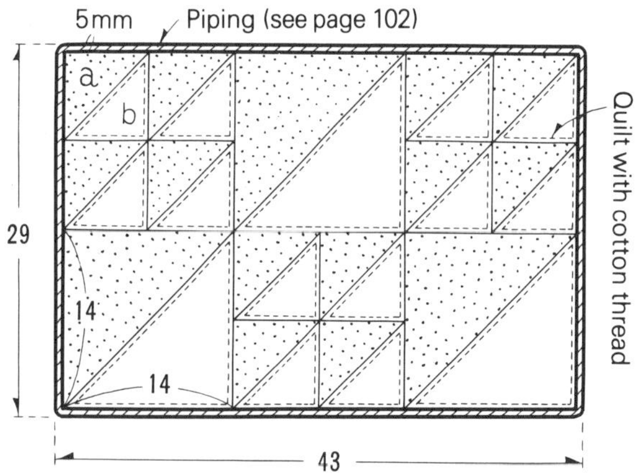

Pincushions

To make up:

(1) Cut out and join patch pieces as for the placemat.

(2) Right sides together, sew front to back, leaving an opening for turning. Turn right side out and stuff with cotton wool. Slipstitch opening to finish.

Chart of Measurements

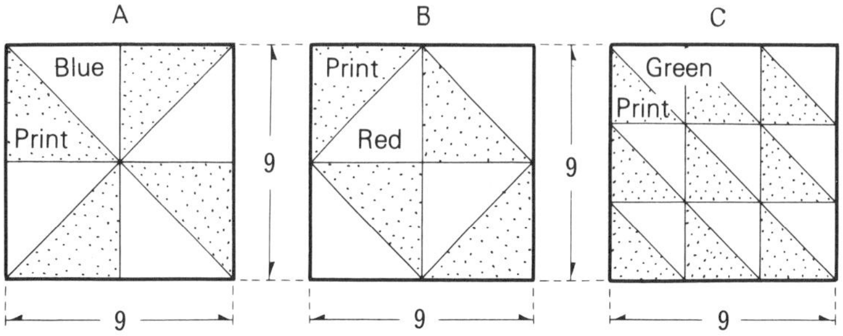

Cut three 10.5 cm squares in blue, red and green for the back of pincushions A, B and C respectively.

BED LINEN & TRAY CLOTH

As shown on page 19

Tray Cloth

To make up:

(1) Cut out patch pieces, adding 7 mm seam allowance. Join as shown on the chart.

(2) Place wadding between patchwork and lining. Quilt as indicated.

Chart of Measurements

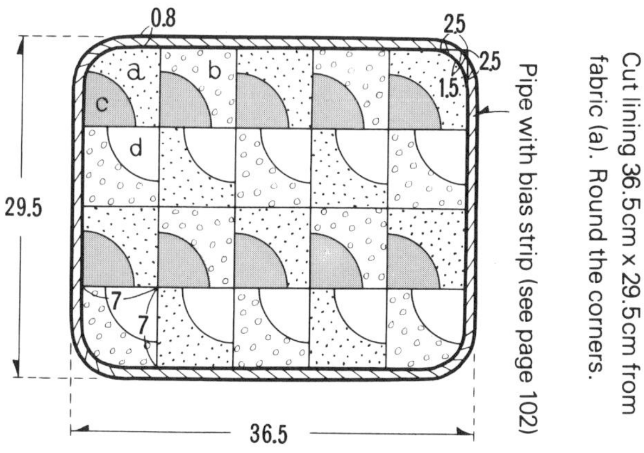

Patchwork Border

To make up:

(1) Assemble patches as for the tray cloth.
(2) Topstitch as indicated.
(3) With right sides of lace and lining to right side of patchwork, stitch the edges, leaving an opening for turning. Turn right side out. Slipstitch the opening to close.

Chart of Measurements

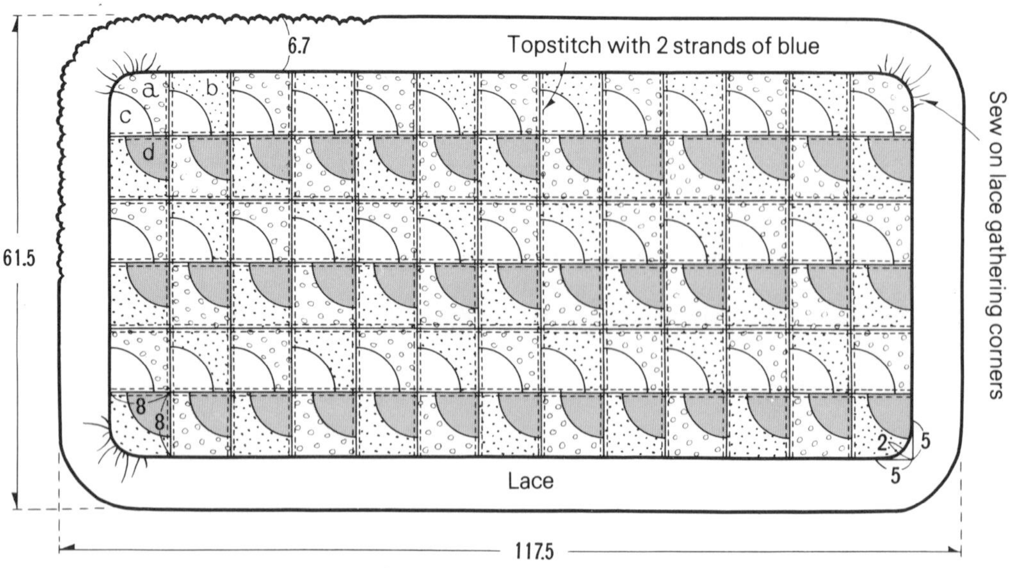

6.7
Topstitch with 2 strands of blue
Sew on lace gathering corners
61.5
a
b
c
d
8
8
2
5
5
Lace
117.5

Cut lining 50 cm x 106 cm

Pillow Case

To make up:

(1) Assemble patches as for the tray cloth.
(2) Topstitch as indicated.
(3) Hem two edges for back opening and overlap as shown. With right sides of lace and back to the patchwork stitch edges.

Chart of Measurements

Front

Topstitch with 2 strands blue thread

Back

Add 1 cm seam allowance unless specified

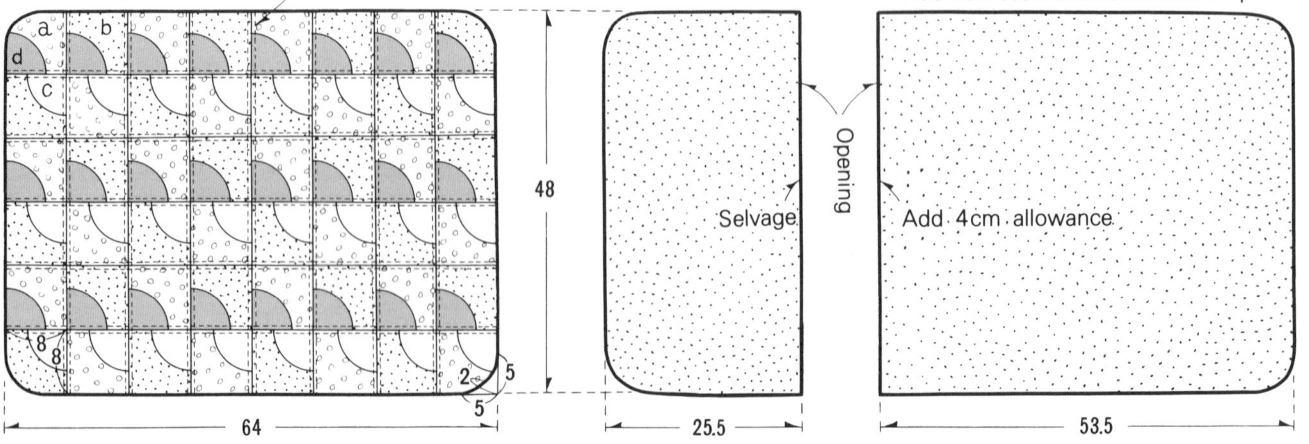

a
b
c
d
8
8
2
5
5
48
64
Selvage
Opening
Add 4 cm allowance
25.5
53.5

To finish

To overlap

Overlap by 15 cm

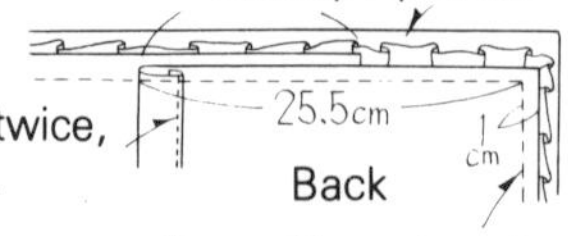

Turn in raw edge twice, slipstitch in place.

Sew with gathered lace between front and back.

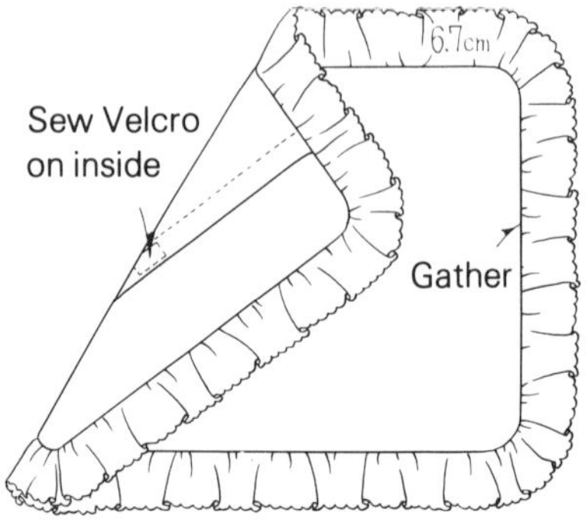

6.7cm
Sew Velcro on inside
Gather

TABLECLOTH
As shown on page 17

To make up:
(1) Cut out patch pieces adding 7 mm seam allowance. Join as shown on page 16.
(2) Assemble patches as shown on the chart, positioning the twelve brown patches at the edge.
(3) Make up lining to size. Right sides together, tack to patchwork top. Stitch edge leaving an opening for turning. Turn right side out.
(4) Quilt top to lining, stitching round the edges of print patches as shown on page 16, so that lining forms the central patch.

Chart of Measurements

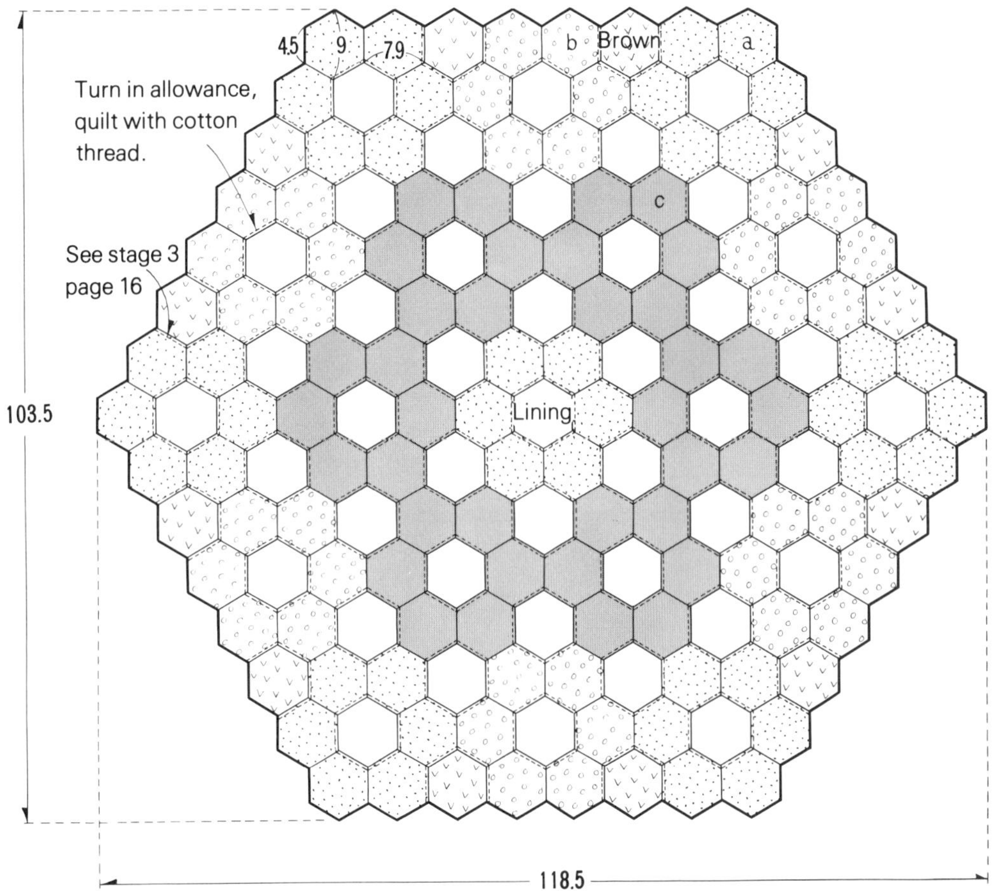

Make up lining to fit the patchwork adding 7mm seam allowance at each edge

CUSHIONS
As shown on page 35

To make up:
(1) Cut out patch pieces adding 7 mm seam allowance. Join patches to make flower as shown.
(2) Slipstitch flower, stem and leaves to pillow front.
(3) Join front and back right sides together leaving opening for turning.
(4) Make up inner case to same measurments as cushion. Insert into cover and close opening.

Chart of Measurements

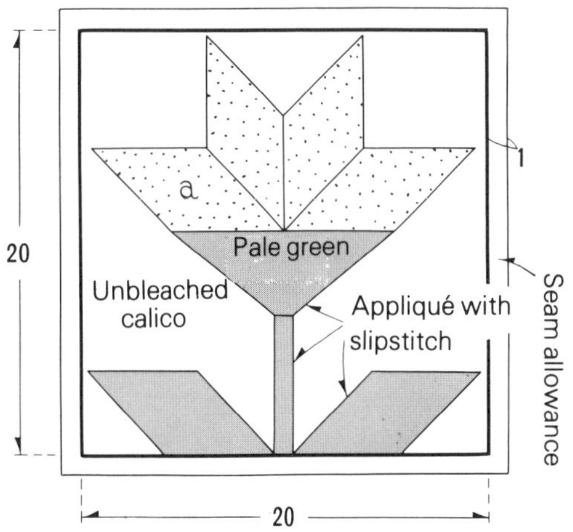

Cut a 22 cm square from pale green cotton for lining.

PANEL

As shown on page 21

To make up:

(1) Cut out patch pieces, adding 7 mm seam allowance. Join as shown on the chart.

(2) Place patchwork and lining wrong sides together, and finish the edges with bias strip.

Chart of Measurements

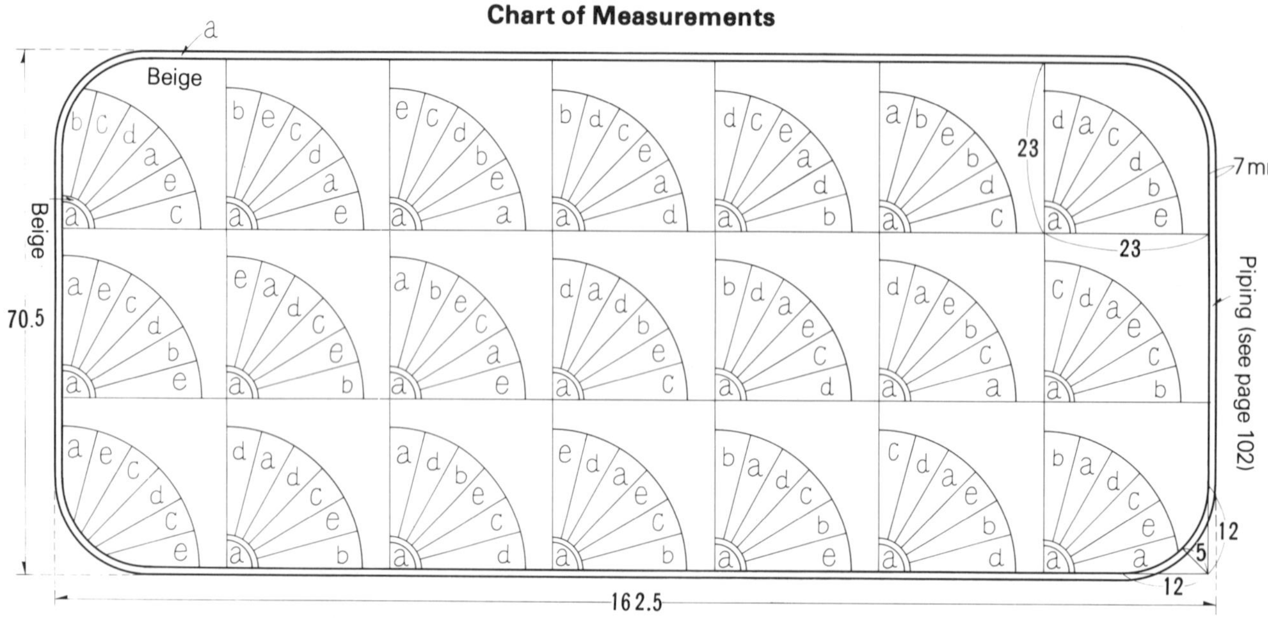

Round corners of lining to fit top

Piping strip

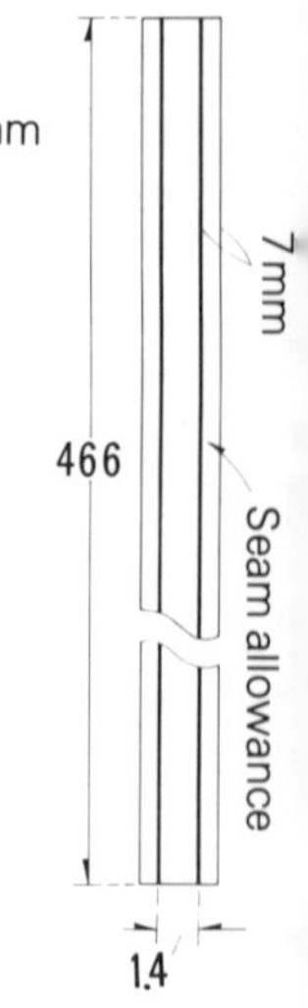

WALL HANGING & PHONE SET

As shown on page 21

Phone Cover

To make up:

(1) Cut out patch pieces, adding 7 mm seam allowance. Join as shown on the chart.

(2) Join centre strips to blocks. Place top and lining wrong sides together, and finish the edges with piping. Quilt as shown.

Chart of Measurements

Phone Cover

Quilt with cotton thread

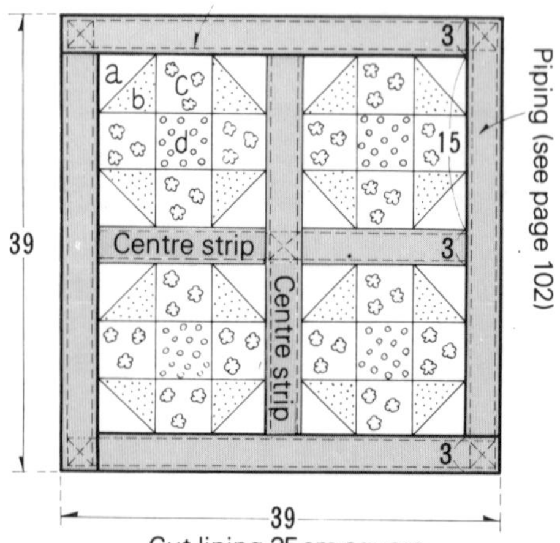

Cut lining 35 cm square

Centre strip

Cut 2 in brown

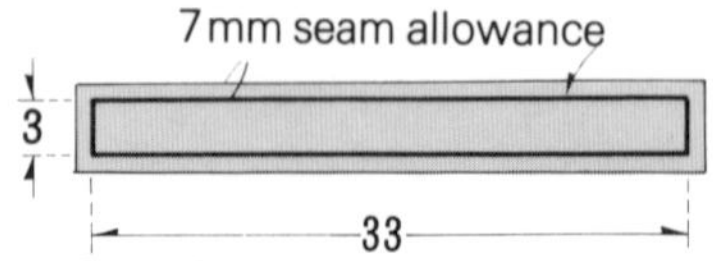

Cross 2 strips in the middle

Piping strip

Cut 4 in brown

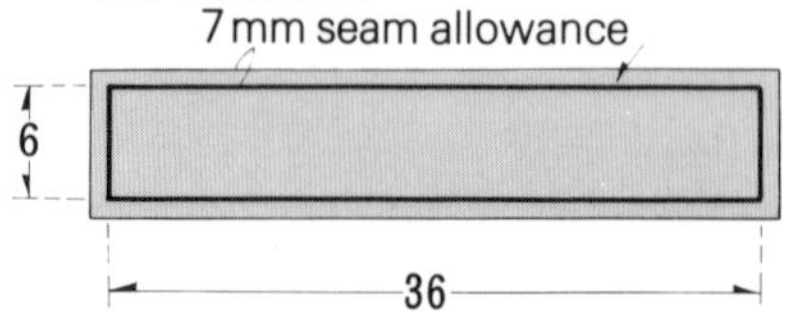

Mat

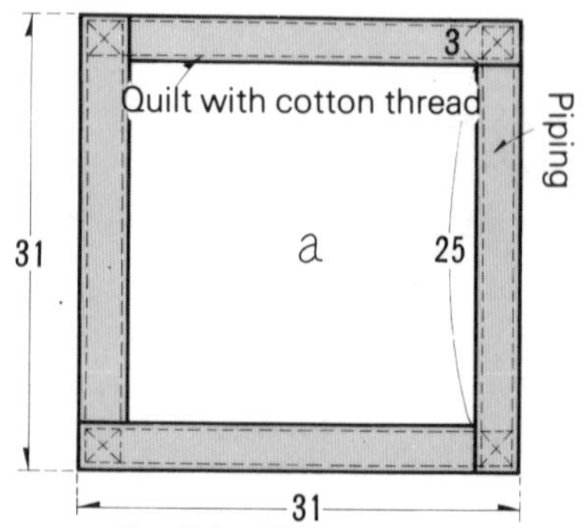

Cut lining 27 cm square

Piping Strip

Cut 4 in brown

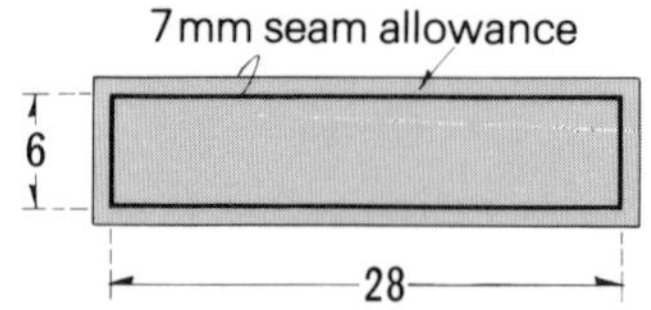

Mat:

Lay wadding between fabric and lining, edge with piping, and quilt together.

Wall Hanging
To make up:
(1) Make up pocket square as shown for phone cover.
(2) Place wadding between patchwork and lining. Quilt together. Finish edges with piping.
(3) Place wadding between foundation fabric and lining. Sew pockets in position and quilt. Finish edges with piping. Sew loops to top.

Chart of Measurements

Pocket (make 2)

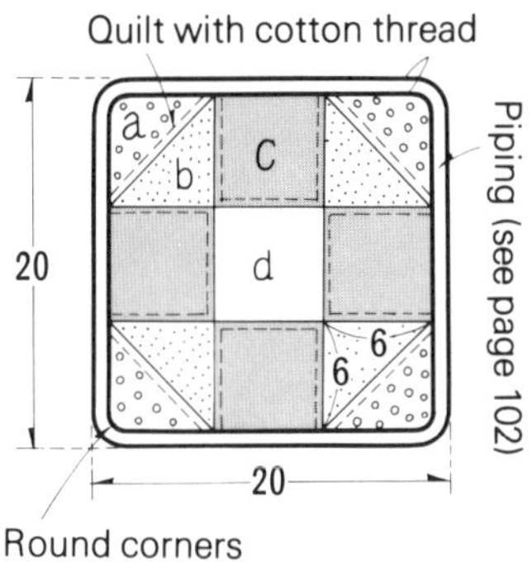
Quilt with cotton thread
a
b
c
d
6
6
6
20
20
Piping (see page 102)
Round corners

Piping strip (cut 2 in (d))

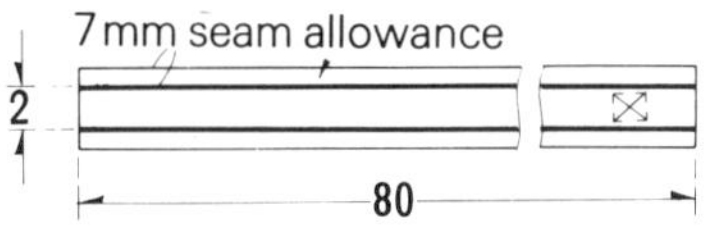

Cut 20cm square of lining and wadding for each pocket.

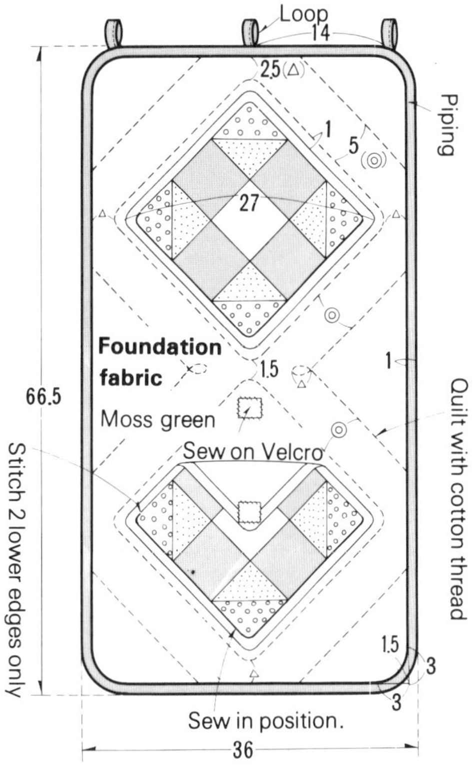
Loop
14
2.5(△)
1
5
27
Piping
Foundation fabric
Moss green
1.5
1
Sew on Velcro
66.5
Stitch 2 lower edges only
Quilt with cotton thread
1.5
3
3
Sew in position.
36

Cut a piece 66.5cm x 36cm in moss green foundation fabric, lining and wadding. Round corners.

Piping strip

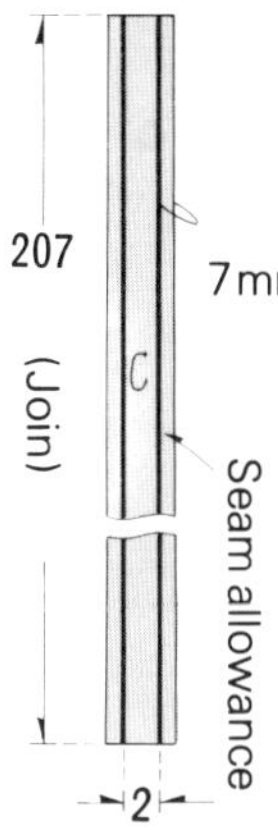
207
(Join)
7mm
c
Seam allowance
2

Loop (cut 3 in (c))

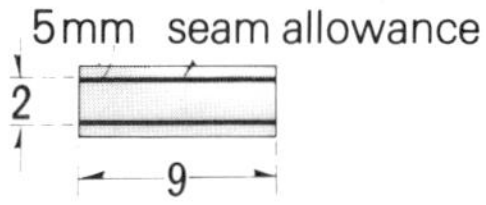

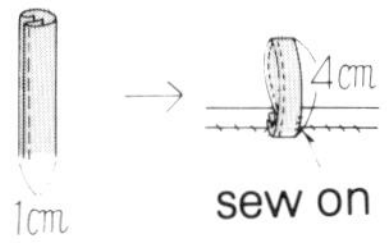

TABLE MAT & POT HOLDER
As shown on page 23

Table Mat
To make up:
(1) Cut out patch pieces, adding 7mm seam allowance. Join as shown on the chart.
(2) Place wadding between patchwork and lining. Quilt together.
(3) Finish edges with piping. Quilt as shown.

Chart of Measurements

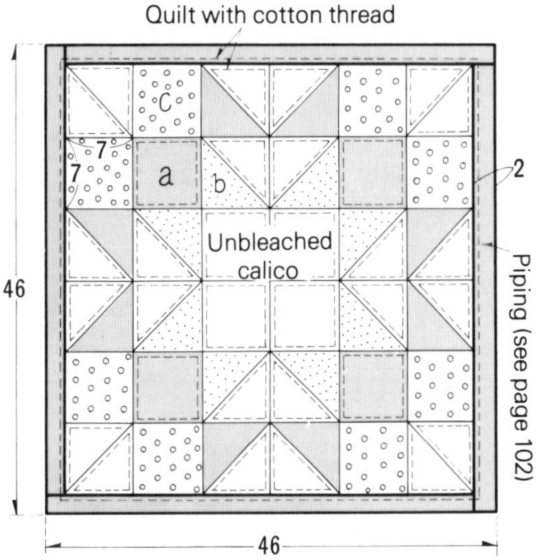
Quilt with cotton thread
c
7
7
a
b
2
Unbleached calico
46
Piping (see page 102)
46

Cut lining 46cm square in unbleached calico

Piping strip
Cut 4 in (a)

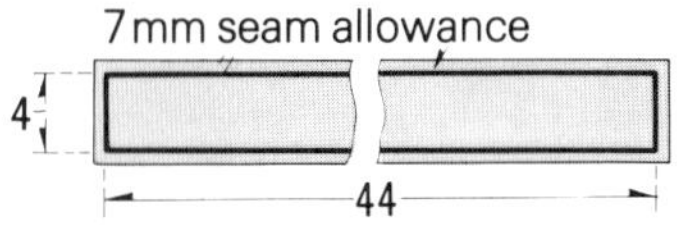

To finish piping

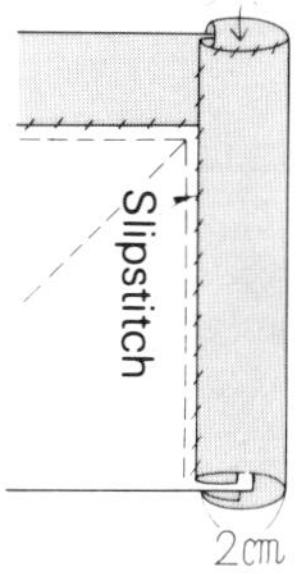

Pot Holder
To make up:
(1) Cut out patch pieces, adding 7mm seam allowance. Join as shown on the chart.
(2) Place wadding between patchwork and lining. Quilt together.
(3) Finish edges with piping. Sew on loop.

Chart of Measurements

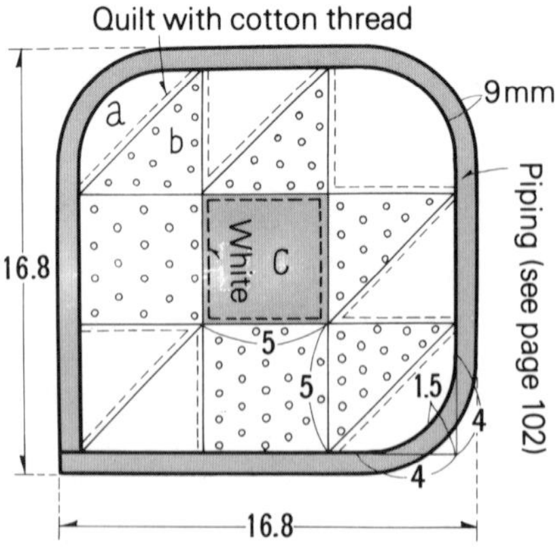
Quilt with cotton thread
9mm
Piping (see page 102)
a
b
White
c
16.8
5
5
1.5
4
4
16.8

Cut lining 16.8cm square from fabric (c).
Round corners to fit top piece.

Sewing on a Loop

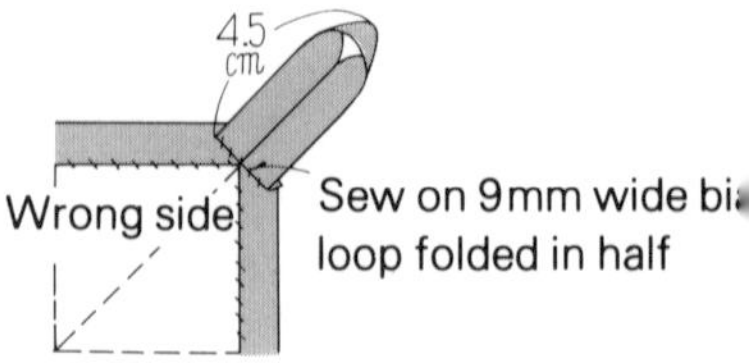
4.5 cm
Wrong side
Sew on 9mm wide bi
loop folded in half

BAG & PEN CASE

As shown on page 25

Bag
To make up:
(1) Cut out patch pieces, adding 7mm seam allowance. Join as shown on the chart.
(2) Place wadding on wrong side of patchwork. Quilt together. Finish edges with piping.
(3) Cut out each piece as shown. Pipe front piece and strap. Sew motif to front flap.
(4) Put front and back wrong sides together. Pipe the edges. Sew on strap and ties.

Chart of Measurements

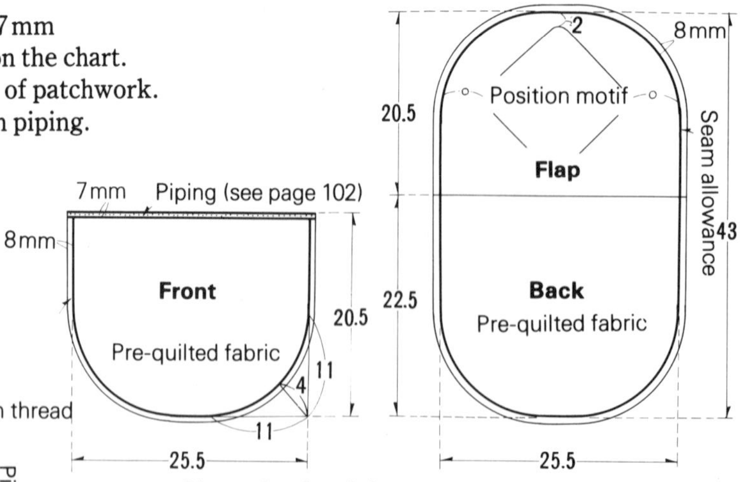
7mm
Piping (see page 102)
8mm
Front
Pre-quilted fabric
20.5
11
4
11
25.5
2
8mm
Position motif
Flap
Seam allowance
20.5
43
22.5
Back
Pre-quilted fabric
25.5

Strap

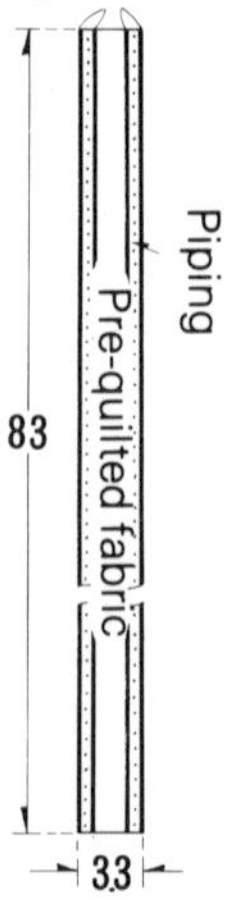
8mm
Piping
Pre-quilted fabric
83
3.3

Tie (cut 2 in

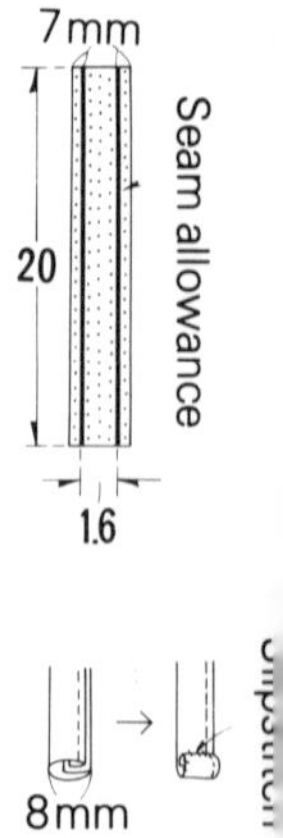
7mm
Seam allowance
20
1.6
8mm

Motif

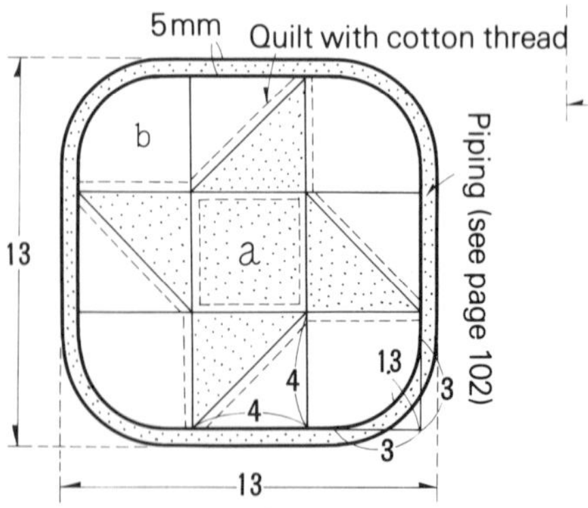
5mm
Quilt with cotton thread
Piping (see page 102)
b
a
13
1.3
3
4
4
3
13

Cut wadding 13cm square.
Round corners.

Bias strips for piping

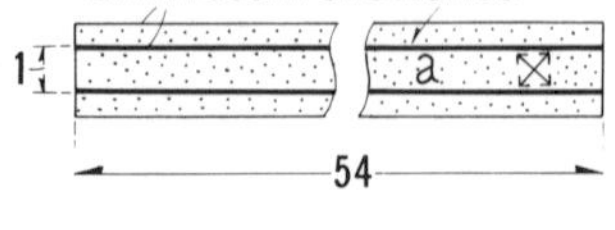
5mm seam allowance
1
a
54

Bias strips for piping
(Cut from fabric (a))

Front (cut 1)

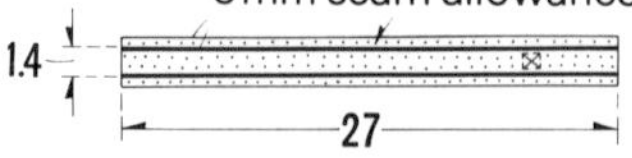
5mm seam allowance
1.4
27

Flap, Back (cut 1)

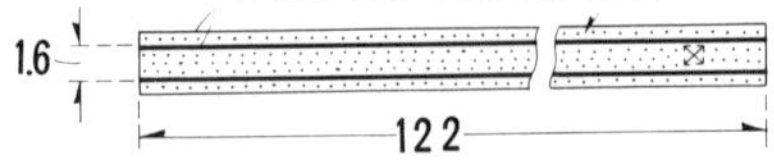

Strap (cut 2)

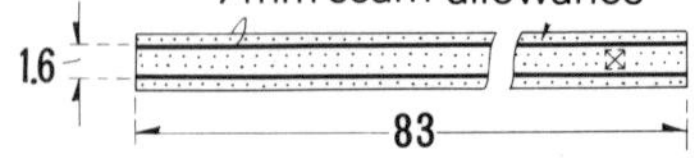

To finish

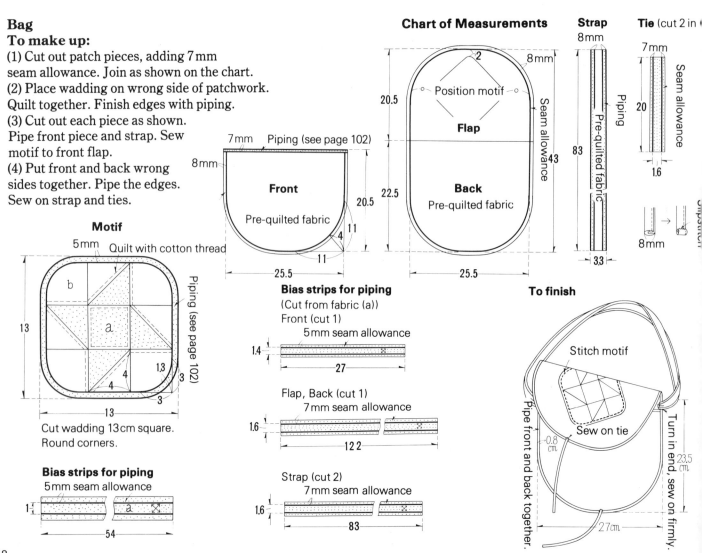

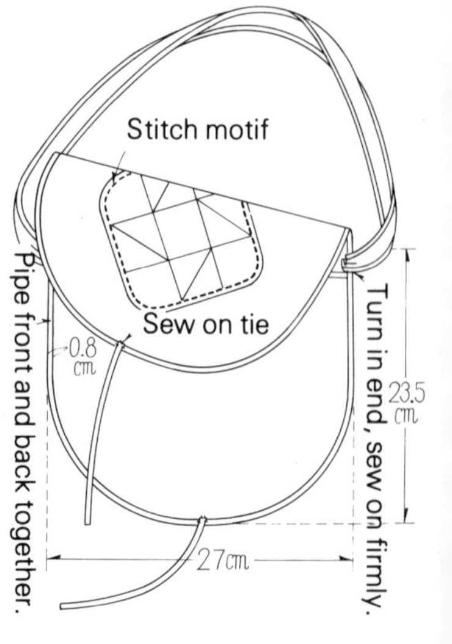
Stitch motif
Sew on tie
Pipe front and back together.
0.8 cm
Turn in end, sew on firmly.
23.5 cm
27cm

Pen Case
To make up:
(1) Compose motif as for the bag. Sew to front.
(2) Place wadding between front piece and lining. Quilt together.
Pipe top edge with bias tape as shown.
(3) Place wadding between back piece and lining. Sew front to back, wrong sides facing. Pipe edges.
(4) Sew on press studs.

Chart of Measurements

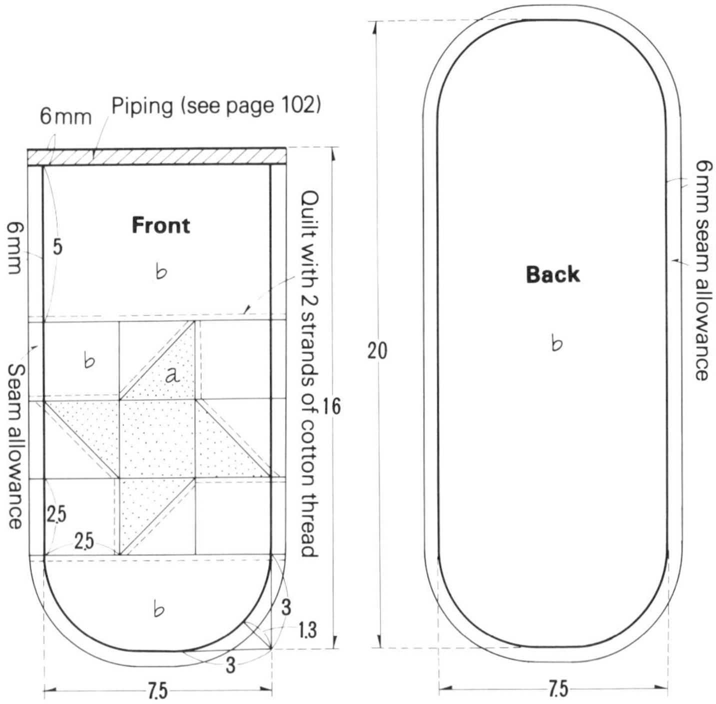

Cut wadding and lining to the size of back and front pieces

To finish

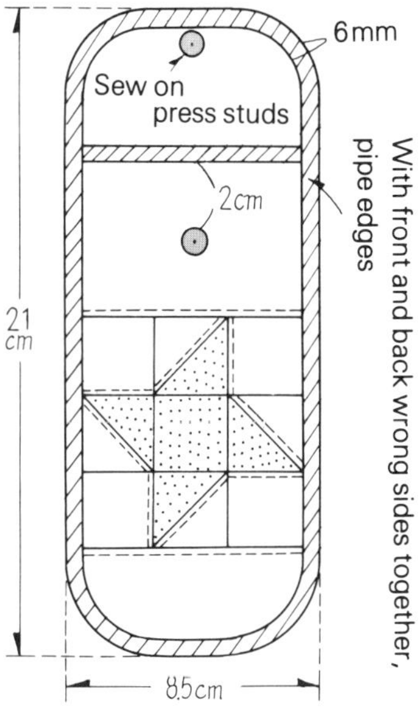

VANITY CASE & SPECTACLE CASE
As shown on page 25

Vanity Case
To make up:
(1) Cut out patch pieces, adding 7 mm seam allowance. Join as shown on the chart, sewing strips of fabric (b) to each side of patchwork centre.
(2) Place wadding between patchwork and lining. Quilt together. Pipe top edges with bias tape.
(3) Stitch zip as shown. Pipe sides to finish.

Chart of Measurements

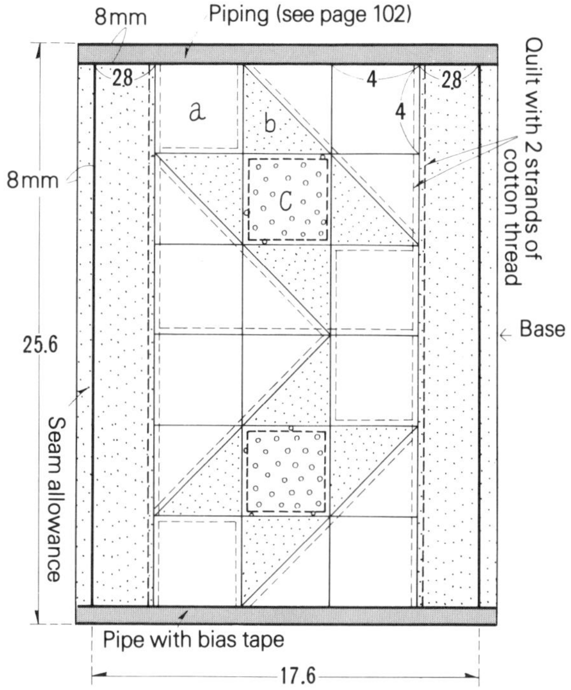

To finish
Stitch zip tape to piping

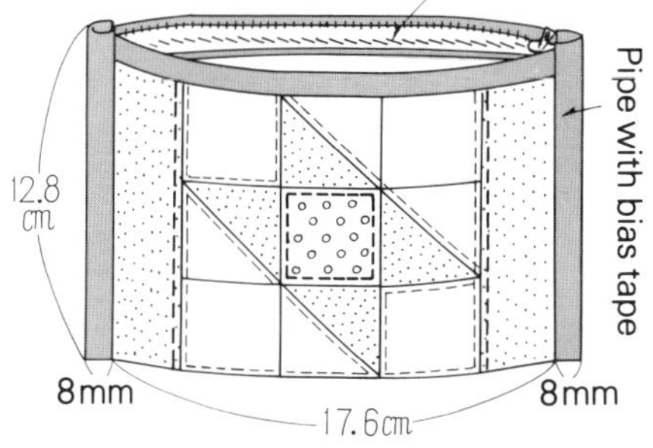

Spectacle Case

To make up:

(1)-(2) Assemble in the same way as the pen case.

(3) Place front and back wrong sides together. Pipe edges to end of opening. Sew on press studs.

Chart of Measurements

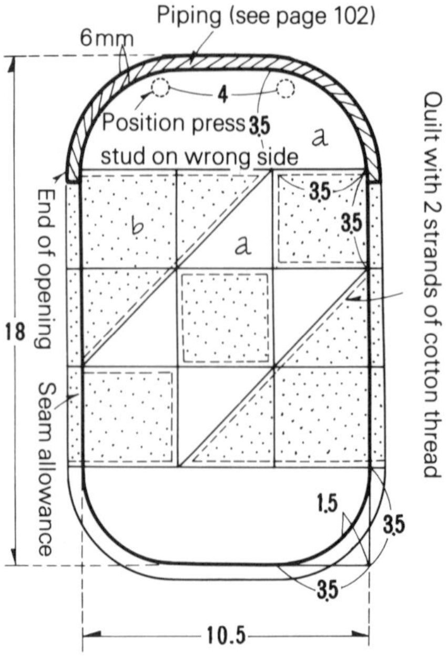

Cut 1 piece in (b) for back and 2 pieces of lining and wadding

To finish

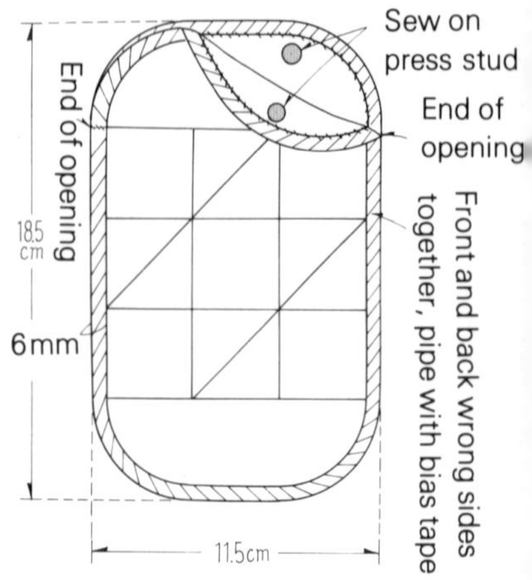

COT QUILT

As shown on page 27

To make up:

(1) Cut out patch pieces for the front and lining. Sew as shown on page 26. Join, refering to chart. Stuff.

(2) Tack back piece to the front, wrong sides together. Pipe edges crosswide them lengthwise, stuffing gently before hemming to the back.

Chart of Measurements

Front

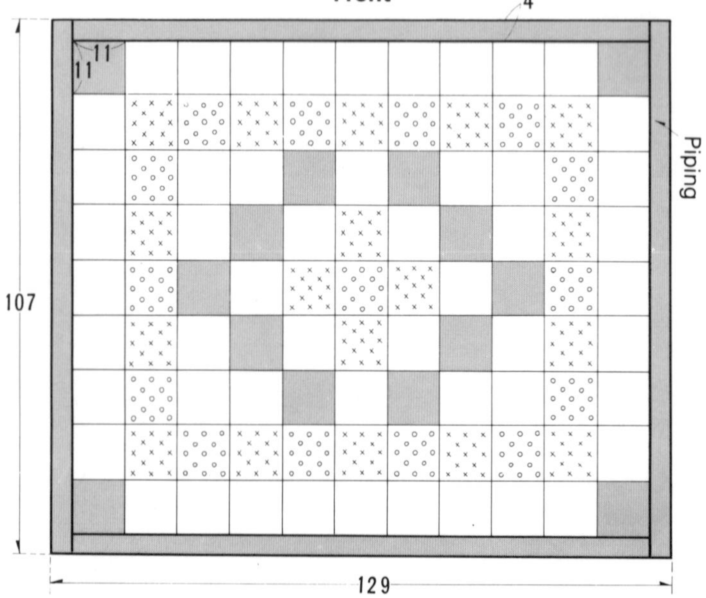

Cut the back piece in grey-green cotton 129cm x 107cm

Piping strips
(cut 2 of each)

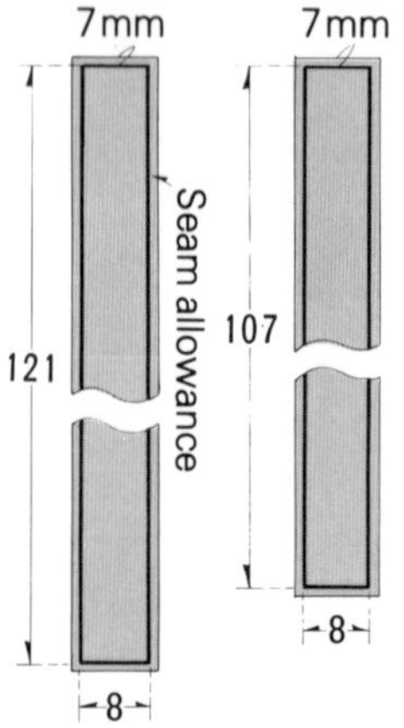

Colour scheme & number of patches

	Colour	Number
☐	Pink	52
☒	Print on pink	18
☒	Print on white	15
■	Grey-green	4

To finish piping

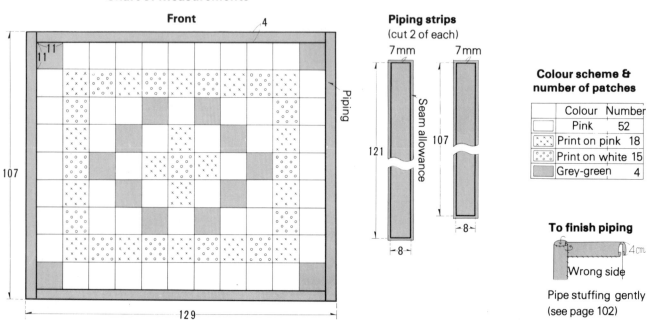

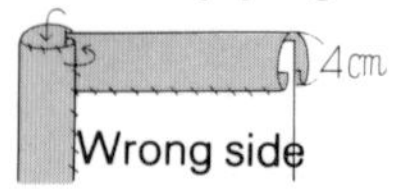

Pipe stuffing gently (see page 102)

CUSHION & PINCUSHIONS
As shown on page 31

Cushion
To make up:
(1) Cut out patch pieces in appropriate cottons. Join as shown on page 30.
(2) Cut out pieces for the back. Sew in zip. Right sides together, join back to front. Insert inner cushion.

Chart of Measurements

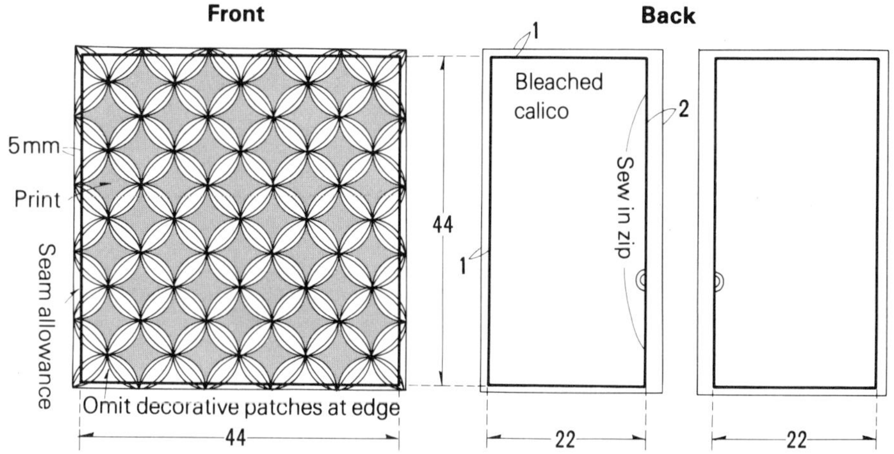

Front
Back
5mm
Print
Seam allowance
Omit decorative patches at edge
44
44
1
1
Bleached calico
2
Sew in zip
22
22

Pincushions
To make up:
(1) Cut out patches. Join as for cushion.
(2) Sew front and back, right sides together, leaving opening for turning. Turn right side out, stuff with cotton wool. Close opening.
For the pink pincushion, join front and back wrong sides together. Finish the edges with piping. Stuff.

Chart of Measurements

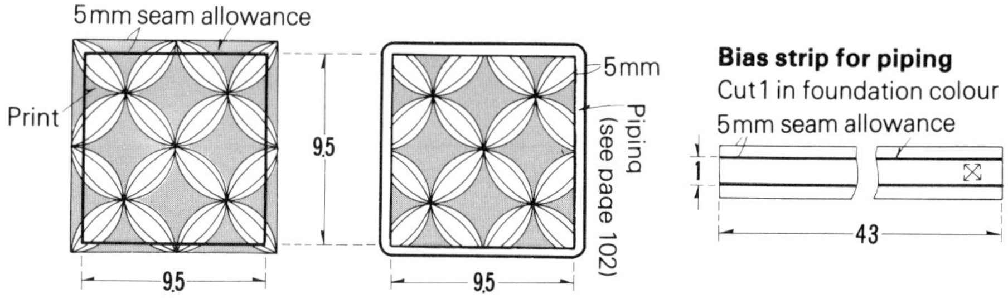

5mm seam allowance
Print
9.5
9.5
5mm
Piping (see page 102)
9.5
Bias strip for piping
Cut 1 in foundation colour
5mm seam allowance
1
43

Cut out a 10.5cm square in foundation fabric for the back

PINCUSHION
As shown on page 49

To make up:
(1) Cut out patch pieces, adding 7mm seam allowance. Join four pieces together.
(2) Appliqué patchwork centre to foundation fabric. Place wadding on wrong side and quilt together.
(3) Sew front and back right sides together, leaving opening for turning. Turn right side out, and stuff with cotton wool. Close opening.

Chart of Measurements

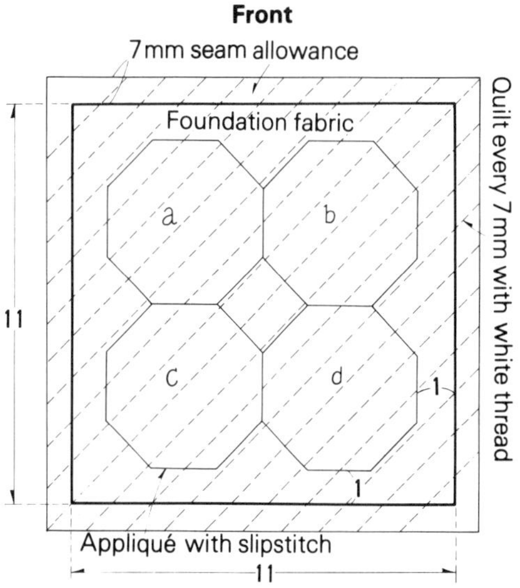

Front
7mm seam allowance
Foundation fabric
a
b
c
d
11
1
1
Quilt every 7mm with white thread
Appliqué with slipstitch
11

Cut out back foundation fabric same size as front

QUILT
As shown on page 29

To make up:
(1) Cut out patch pieces, adding 7 mm seam allowance. Join patches to make up pieces A and B, then arrange and sew as shown on the chart.
(2) Sew front and back right sides together, leaving opening for turning. Cut wadding to size and tack in place on the wrong side of patchwork before turning right side out.
(3) Close opening. Topstitch along the edge and quilt as indicated.

Chart of measurements

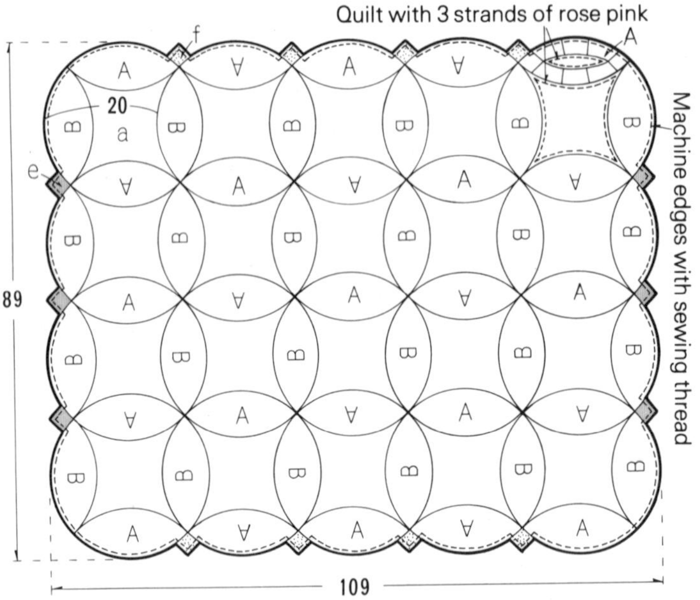

Cut the back piece in fabric (a) to fit the front

Make 25 pieces of A

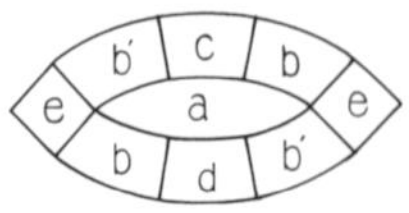

Make 24 pieces of B

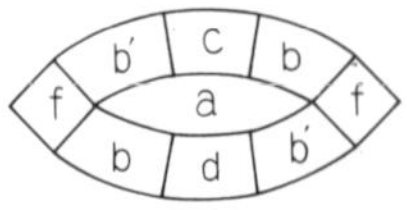

BAG
As shown on page 33

To make up:
(1) Cut out patch pieces, adding 7 mm seam allowance. Join as shown on the chart.
(2) Position motif and topstitch to main piece.
(3) Finish edges of pocket with piping. Stitch pocket in place.
(4) Hem top edge and attach handles. Stitch sides. Make a base by sewing corners as shown.

Chart of measurements

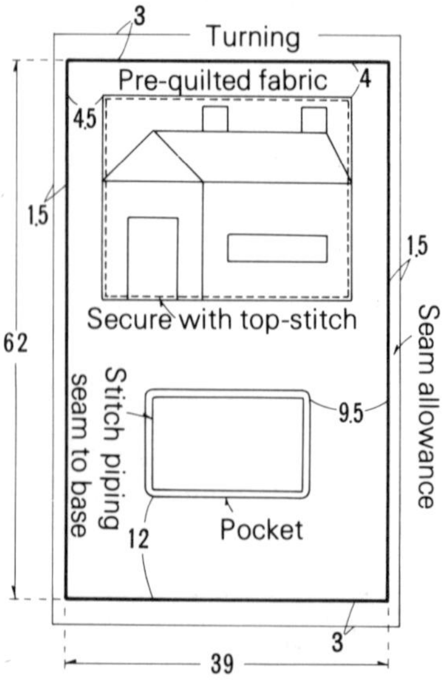

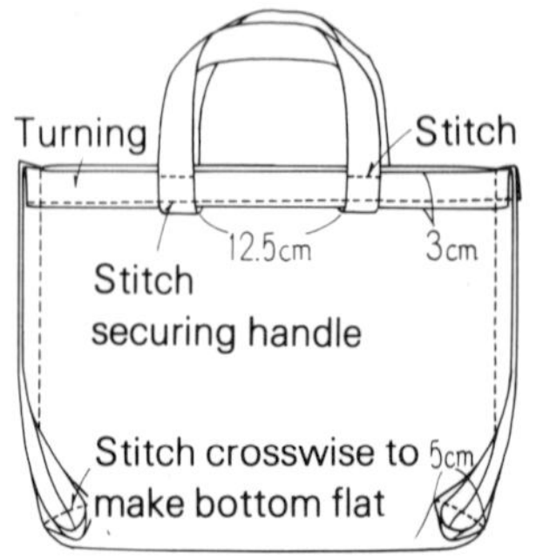

Pocket (make 1)

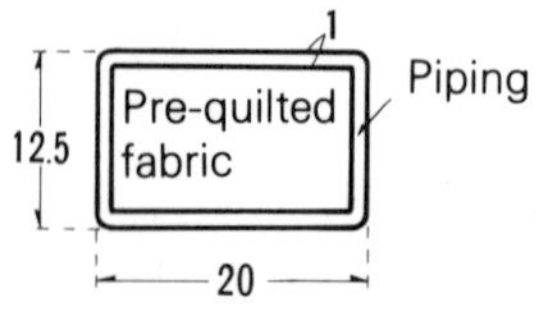

To finish

BEDSPREAD
As shown on page 45

To make up:
(1) Cut out patch pieces, adding 7mm seam allowance. Assemble, alternating light and dark cottons as shown.

(2) Lay wadding between patchwork and lining. Quilt together and pipe edges.

Chart of Measurements

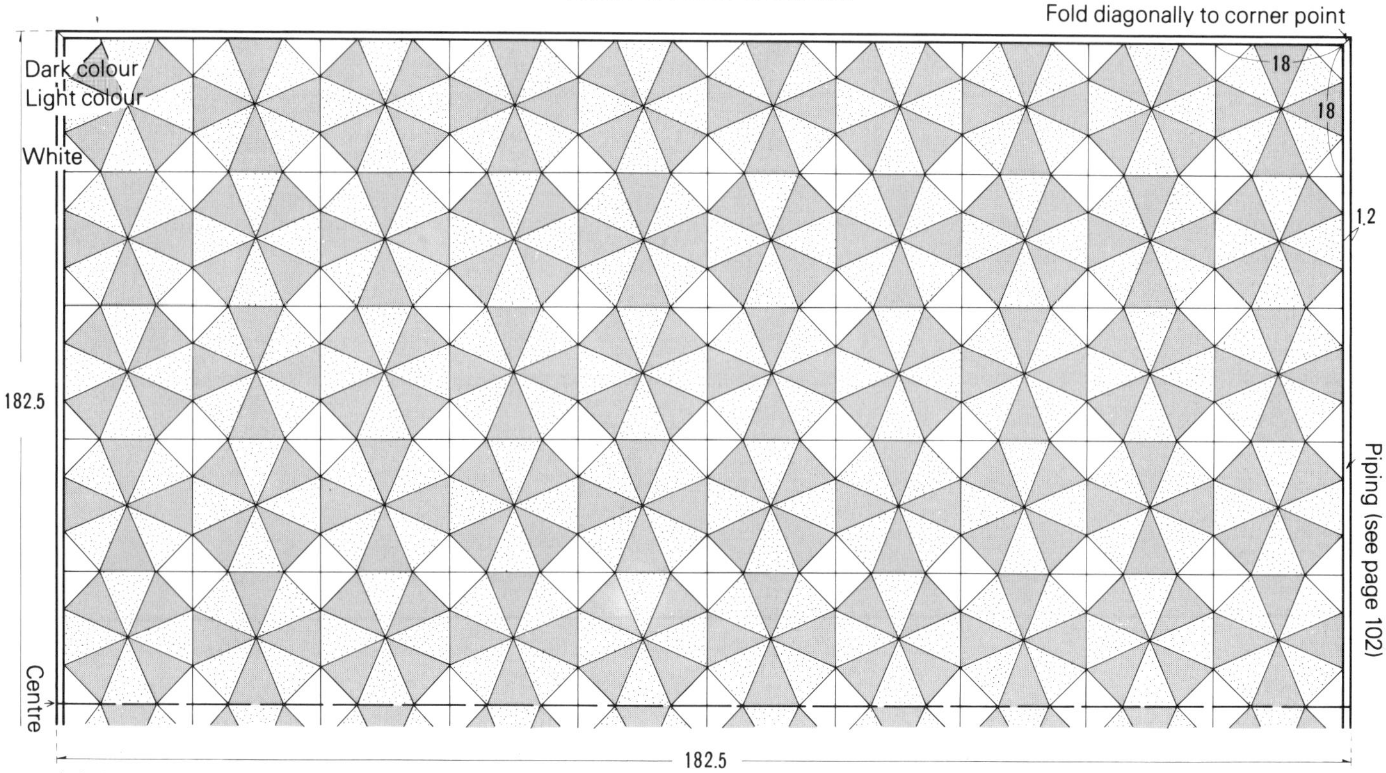

Fold diagonally to corner point
Dark colour
Light colour
White
18
18
1.2
182.5
Piping (see page 102)
Centre
182.5

Join lining to make a piece 182.5cm square

Piping Strip
(Cream)

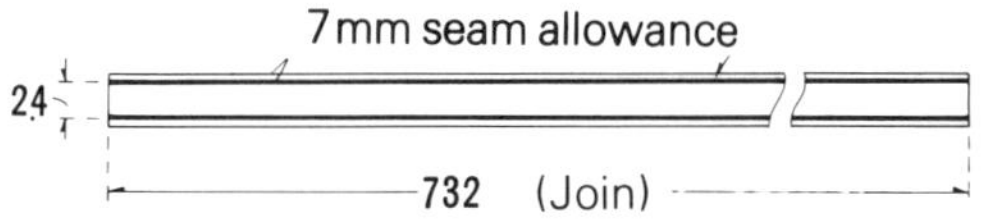

7mm seam allowance
2.4
732 (Join)

TOASTER COVER, TEA COSY & CUSHIONS
As shown on page 37

Toaster Cover
To make up:
(1) Scale up design to 1 square = 2.7cm. Cut out pieces, adding 7mm seam allowance.
(2) Cut out pieces for front, back and centre panel as shown. Appliqué figures to front, inserting plait between hat and foundation fabric on girl. Finish with embroidery.

(3) Press iron-on interlining to lining. Fold tape over piping cord to encase. Stitch edge. Right sides together, sew front and back pieces to centre panel, with piping between. Turn right sides out. Right sides facing, stitch piping and bias tape along bottom edge. Turn tape to lining and hem.

Chart of Measurements
Add 1 cm seam allowance.

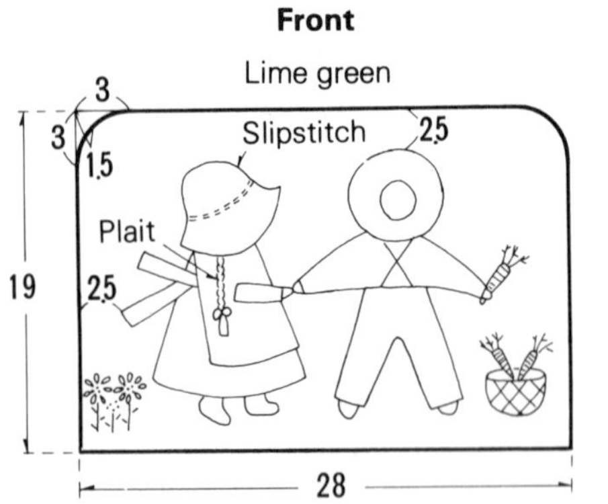
Front
Lime green
3
3
1.5
Slipstitch
2.5
Plait
19
2.5
28

Cut 1 piece in lime green for back, 2 in wadding and lining same size as front

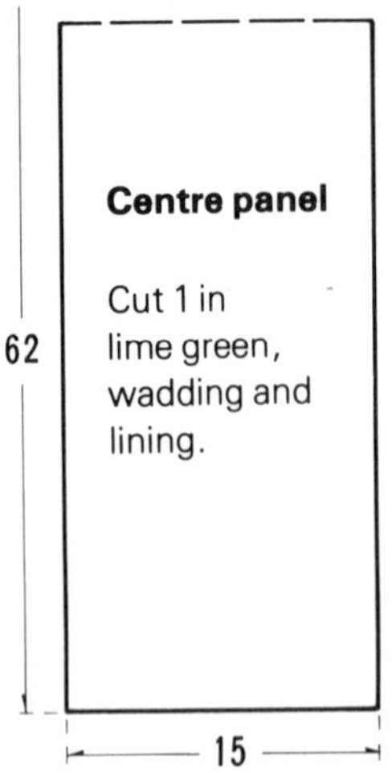
Centre panel
Cut 1 in lime green, wadding and lining.
62
15

To finish

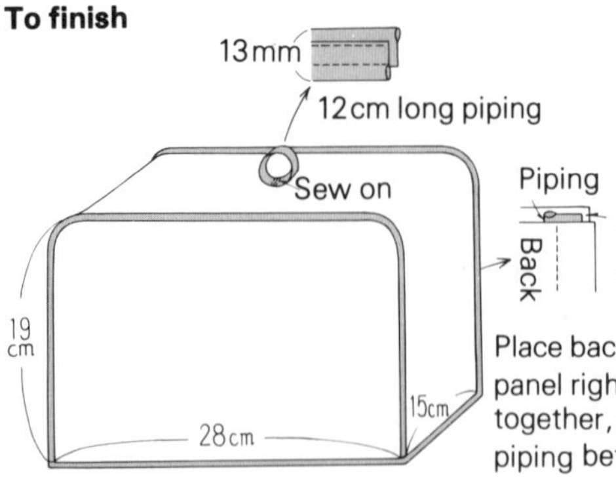
13mm
12cm long piping
Sew on
Piping
Back
Centre panel
19 cm
15cm
28cm

Place back and centre panel right sides together, sew with piping between.

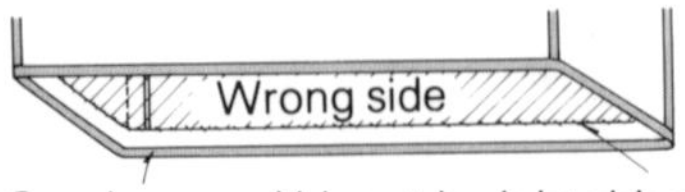
Wrong side

(1) Sew base and bias strip right sides together with piping between.
(2) Slipstitch to wrong side of base.

Embroidery (actual size)
Use 3 strands of embroidery cotton

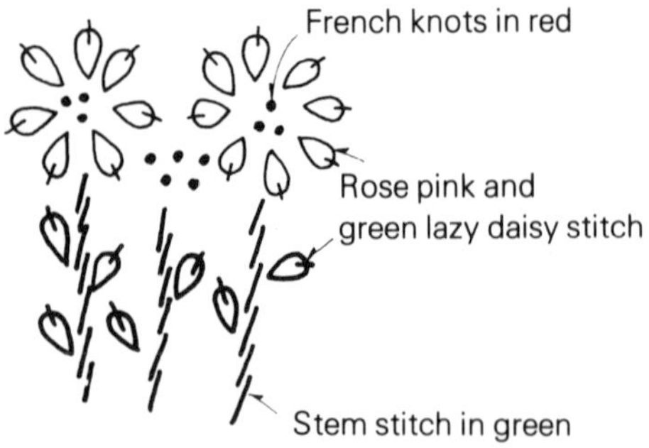
French knots in red
Rose pink and green lazy daisy stitch
Stem stitch in green

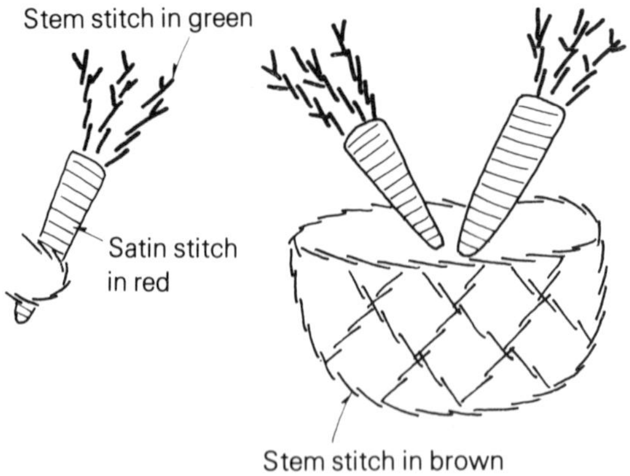
Stem stitch in green
Satin stitch in red
Stem stitch in brown

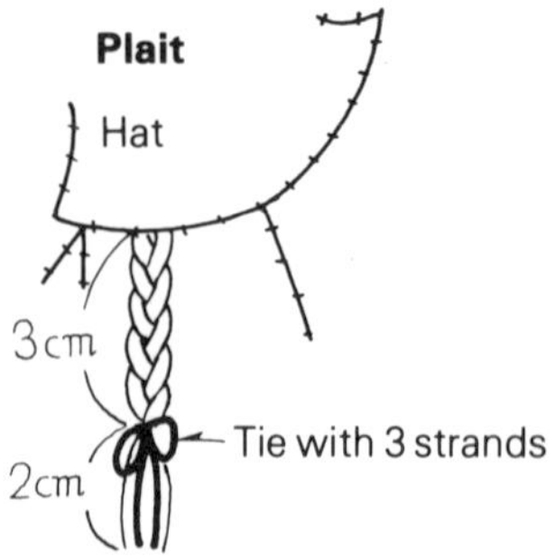
Plait
Hat
3cm
Tie with 3 strands
2cm

Sew on hat after the hair is plaited with 12 strands in brown

Tea Cosy
To make up:
(1) Scale up design to 1 square = 3 cm. Cut out pieces, adding 7 mm seam allowance.
(2) Cut out front and back as shown. Appliqué figure to front, stuffing gently. Embroider.
(3) Leaving straight edge open, stitch front to back, right sides together, positioning red balloon as indicated. Sew lining together. Spread stuffing over wrong side of top piece and attach lining right side out. Turn in hem on lining and top piece. Slipstitch together.

Patterns (actual size)
Add 7 mm seam allowance

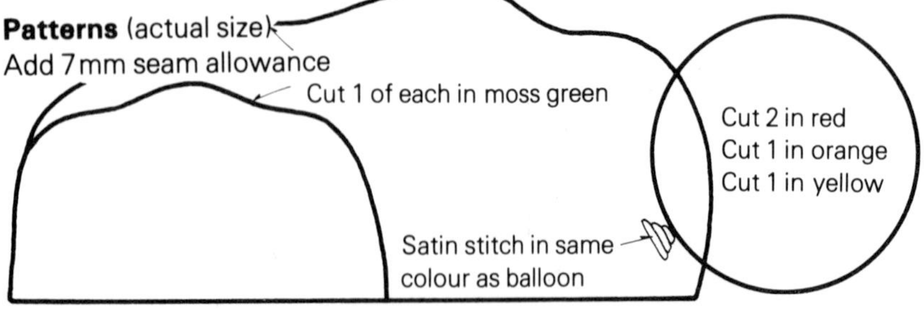
Cut 1 of each in moss green
Cut 2 in red
Cut 1 in orange
Cut 1 in yellow
Satin stitch in same colour as balloon

Chart of Measurements

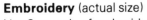

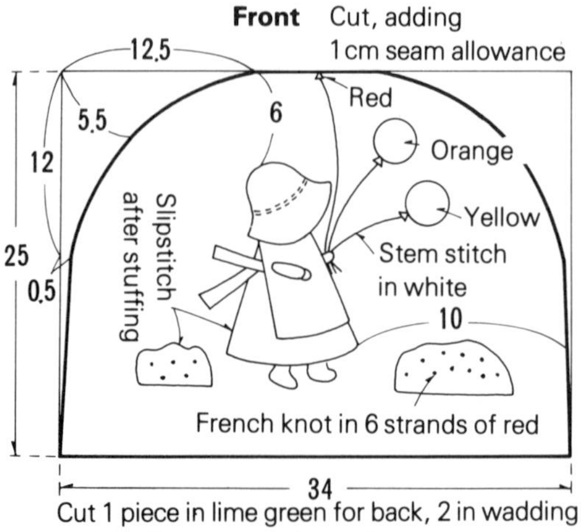
Front
Cut, adding 1 cm seam allowance
12.5
5.5
6
Red
Orange
Yellow
12
25
0.5
Slipstitch after stuffing
Stem stitch in white
10
French knot in 6 strands of red
34

Cut 1 piece in lime green for back, 2 in wadding and 2 in lining same size as front.

To finish

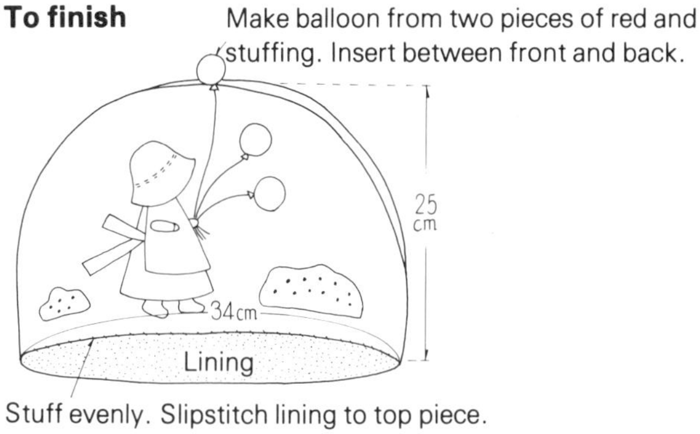
Make balloon from two pieces of red and stuffing. Insert between front and back.
25 cm
34cm
Lining
Stuff evenly. Slipstitch lining to top piece.

Cushion

To make up:

(1) Cut out patch pieces as for tea cosy.

(2) Appliqué boy and girl respectively on white fabric. Finish with embroidery.

(3) Cut out foundation fabric, place white patched piece in the centre. Trim with ribbon.

(4) Sew front and back right sides together, with ties between. Sew zip in place.

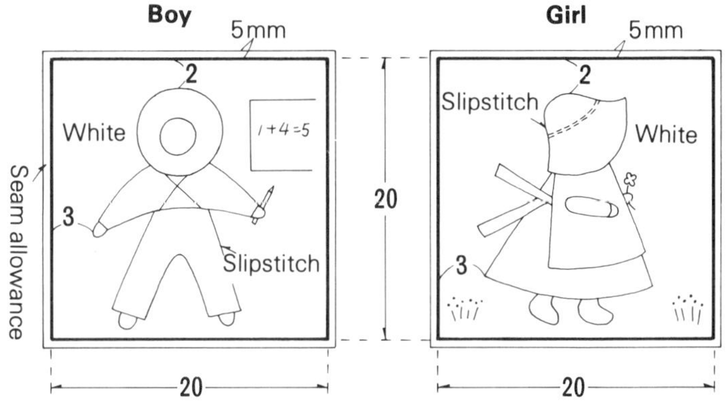

Chart of Measurements

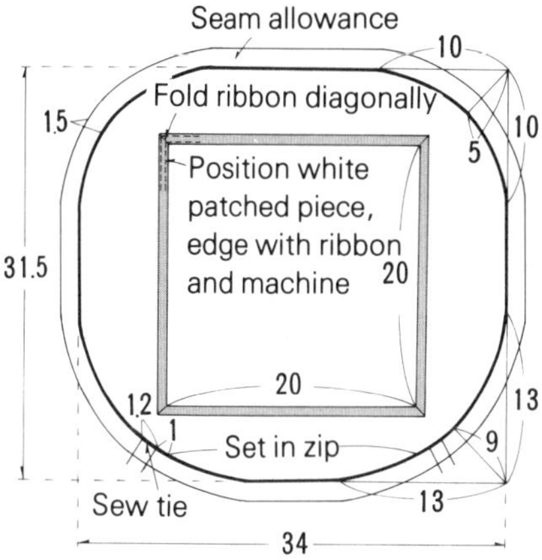

Cut foundation fabric in (c) for boy, in (a) for girl.
Cut the pieces for back in same way

Embroidery (actual size)

Boy

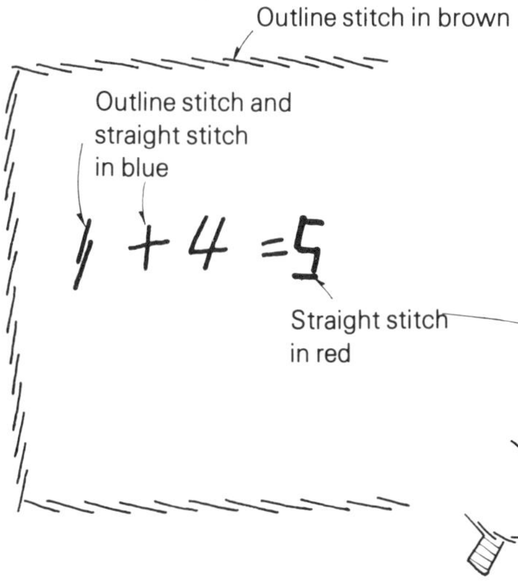

Girl

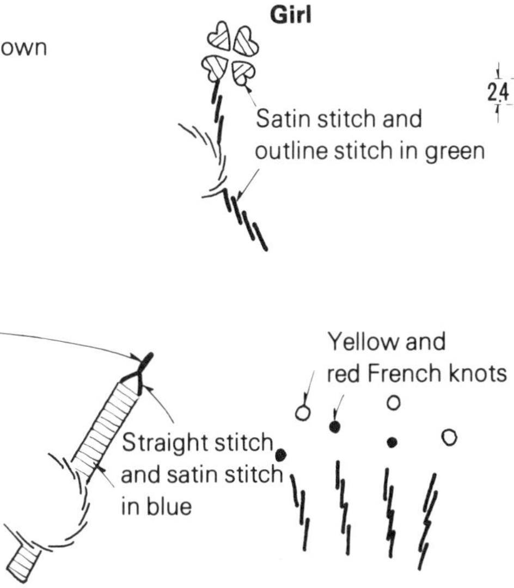

Ties (cut 2 in (c) for boy, (a) for girl)

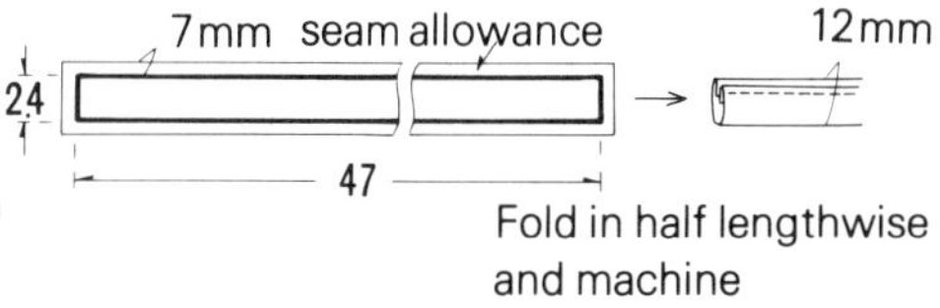

To finish

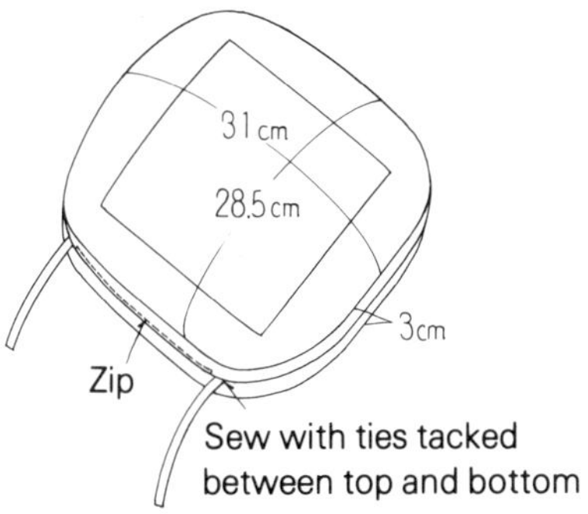

Running Stitch

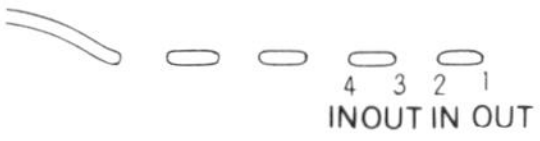

Chain Stitch

French Knot

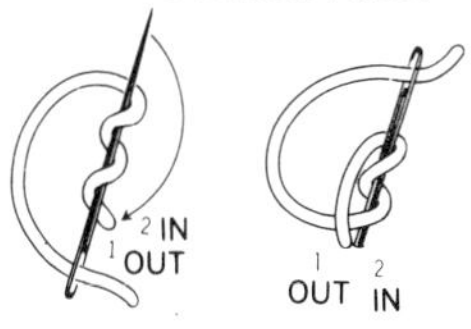

Lazy Daisy Stitch

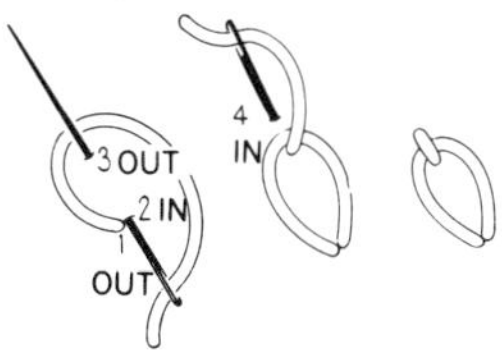

Straight Stitch

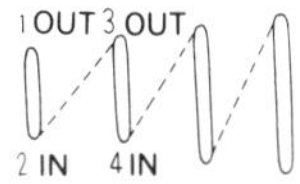

Outline Stitch

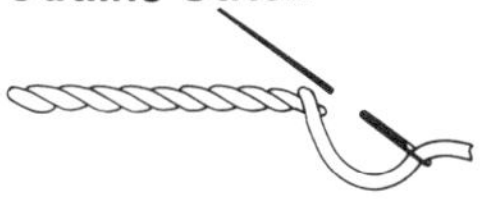

Satin Stitch

CUSHION
As shown on page 39

To make up:
(1) Cut out patch pieces, adding 7 mm seam allowance. Join as shown on the chart.
(2) Place wadding between front and lining. Quilt together.
(3) Cut out back pieces. Set in zip. Join front and back right sides together. Insert inner cushion.

Chart of measurements

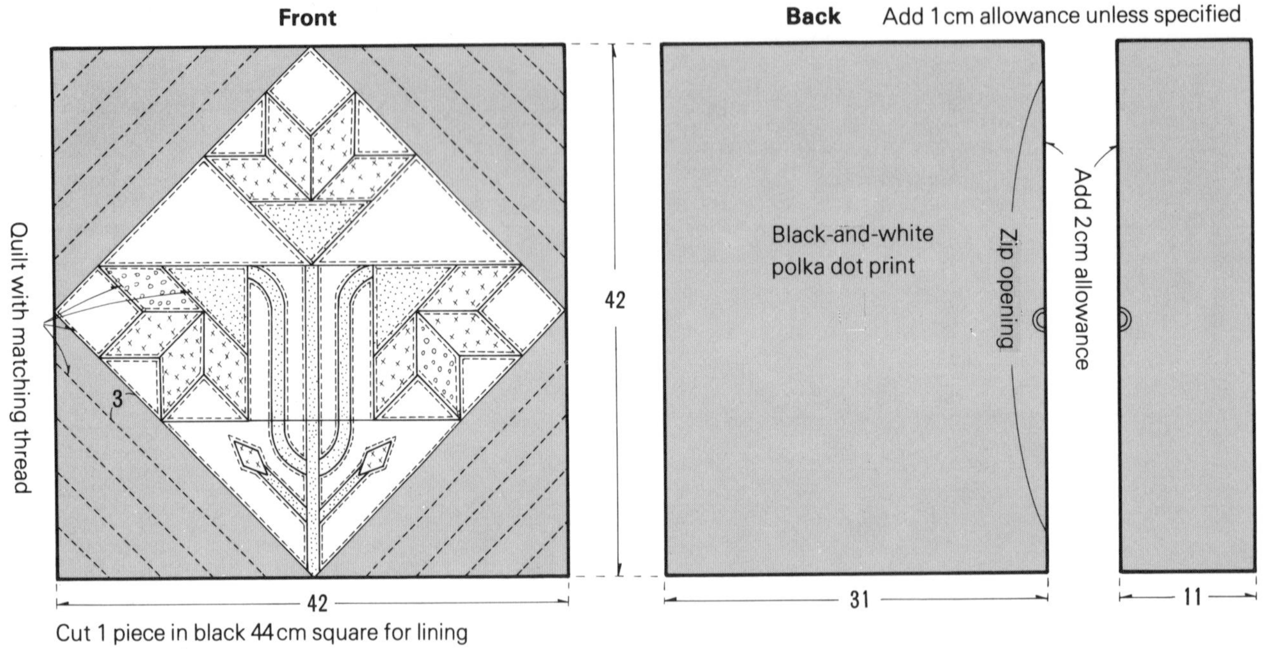

Front
Back
Add 1 cm allowance unless specified
Quilt with matching thread
3
42
42
Black-and-white
polka dot print
Zip opening
Add 2cm allowance
31
11
Cut 1 piece in black 44cm square for lining

PATCHWORK PICTURE & CUSHION
As shown on page 41

Patchwork Picture
To make up:
(1) Cut out patch pieces, adding 7 mm seam allowance. Join as shown on the chart.
(2) Lay wadding between top piece and lining. Quilt together.

Chart of measurements

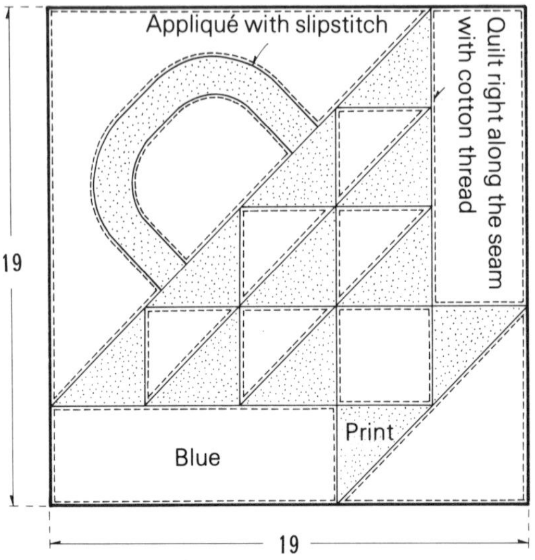

Appliqué with slipstitch
Quilt right along the seam with coton thread
19
Print
Blue
19

Cushion
To make up:

(1) Assemble patches as for the patchwork picture.
(2) Cut out pieces in (a) as shown on the chart. Join to patchwork centre. Cut out back and ties in (a). Sew ties wrong sides together, turning in cut edges.
(3) Sew front and back right sides together, placing ties between. Sew in zip and insert foam cushion.

Chart of Measurements

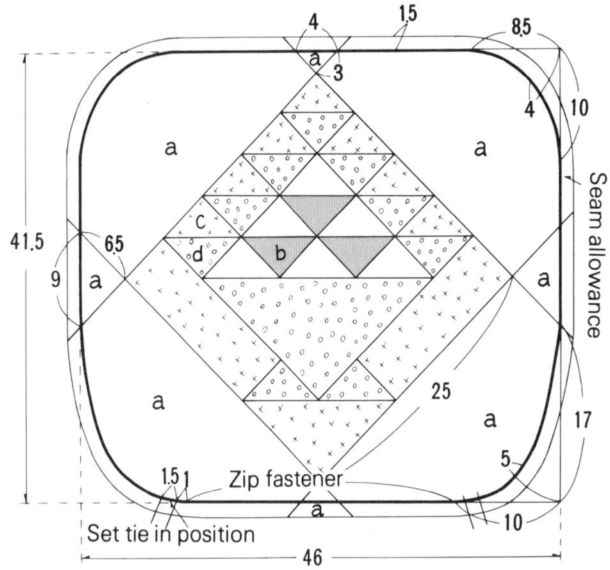

Cut pieces in (a), adding 7mm seam allowance.
Cut back in (a), 49cm x 44.5cm, and round corners.

To finish:

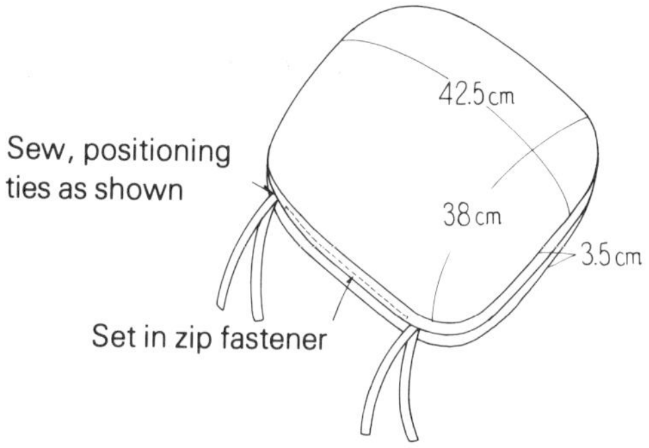
42.5cm
Sew, positioning ties as shown
38cm
3.5cm
Set in zip fastener

Tie (cut 4)

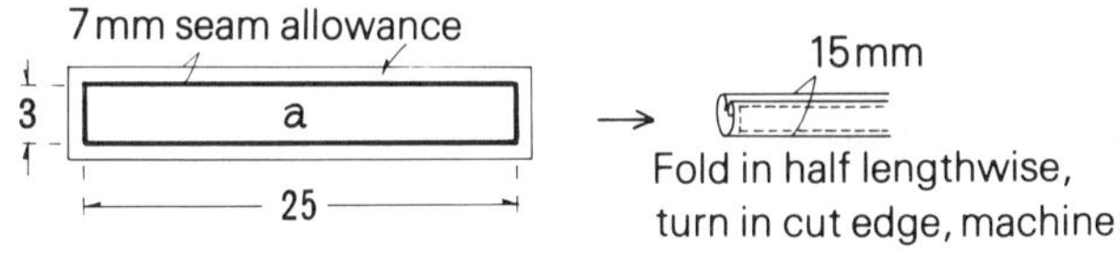
7mm seam allowance
3
a
25
15mm
Fold in half lengthwise, turn in cut edge, machine

TABLE MAT & TRAY CLOTH

As shown on page 47

Chart of Measurements

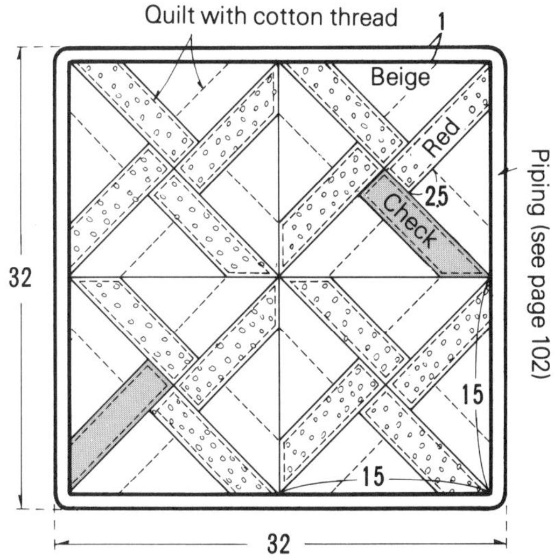
Quilt with cotton thread
1
Beige
Red
2.5
Check
Piping (see page 102)
32
15
15
32

Tray Cloth
To make up:

(1) Cut out patch pieces, adding 7mm seam allowance.
(2) Lay wadding between patchwork and lining. Quilt together. Finish edges with piping.

Bias strip for piping
Moss green

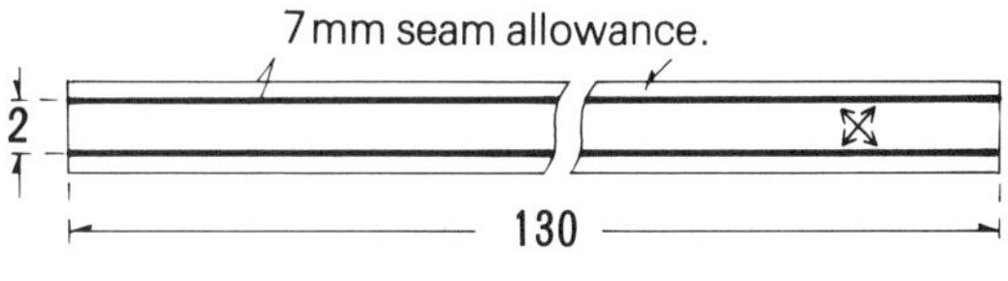

Table Mat
To make up:
Work in the same way as for the tray cloth.

Chart of Measurements

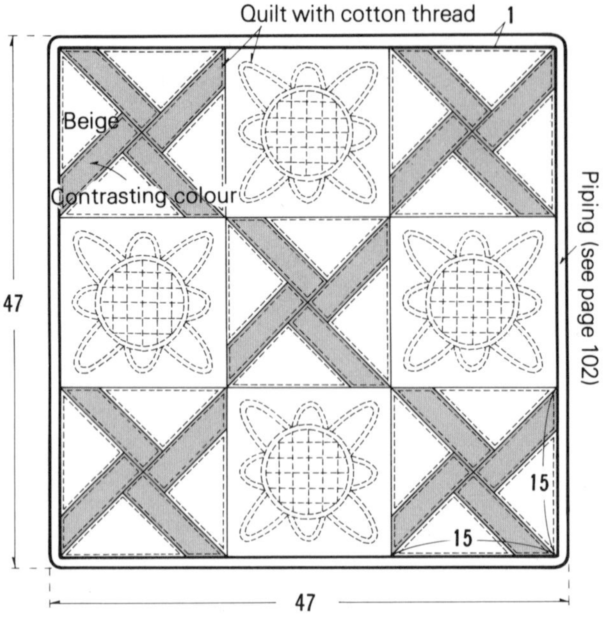

Bias strip for piping

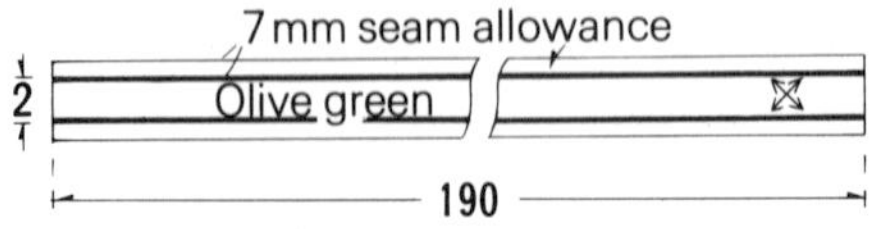

MAT & POCHETTE

As shown on page 53

Mat
To make up:
(1) Cut out patch pieces, adding 7 mm seam allowance. Join as shown on the chart.
(2) Assemble blocks as shown. Join borders to patchwork centre, lengthwise then crosswise.
(3) Lay wadding between patchwork top and lining. Quilt together and finish edges with piping.

Chart of Measurements

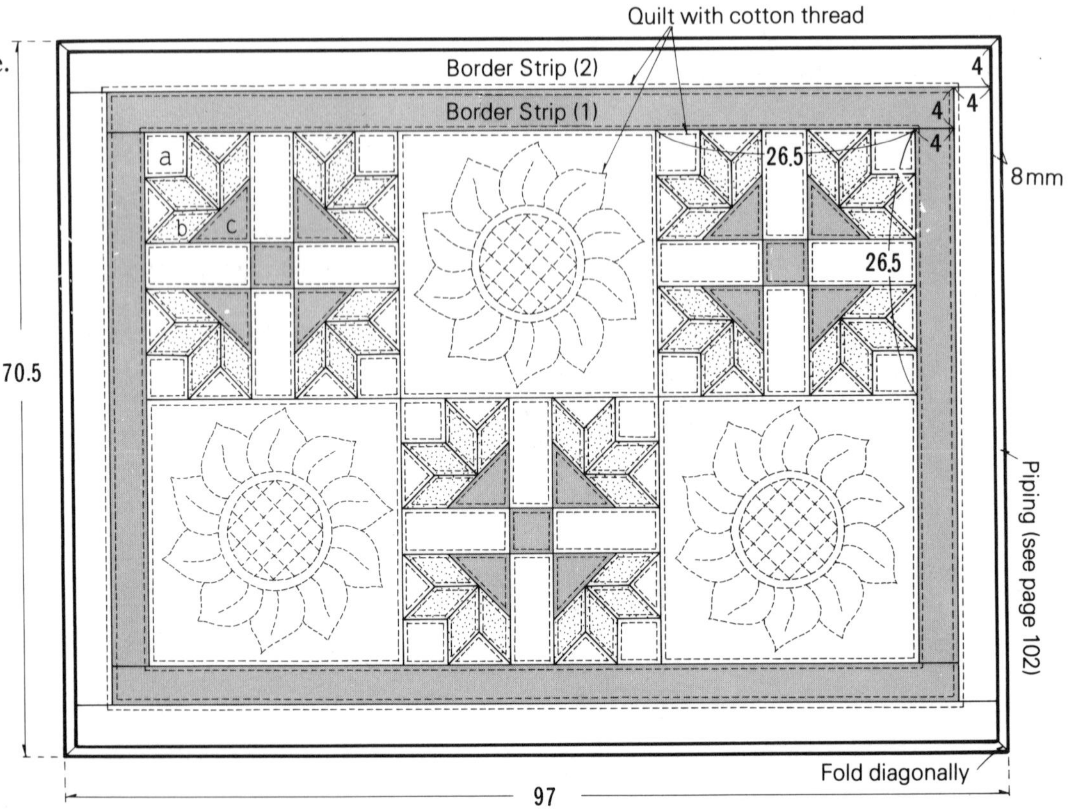

For block B, cut three 28.5 cm squares from fabric (a).

Border strip (1)

Cut 2 of each in (c)

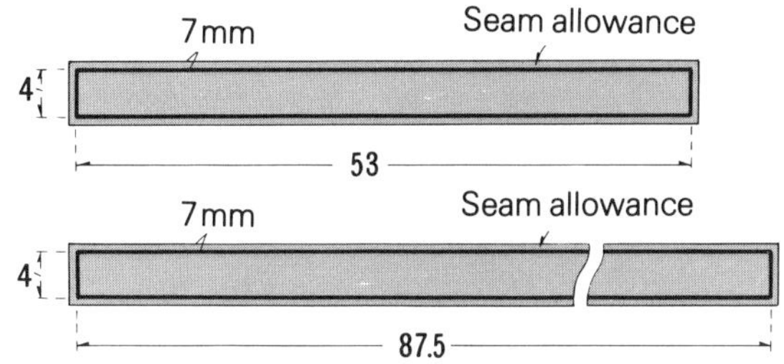
7mm
Seam allowance
4
53
7mm
Seam allowance
4
87.5

Border strip (2)

Cut 2 of each in (a)

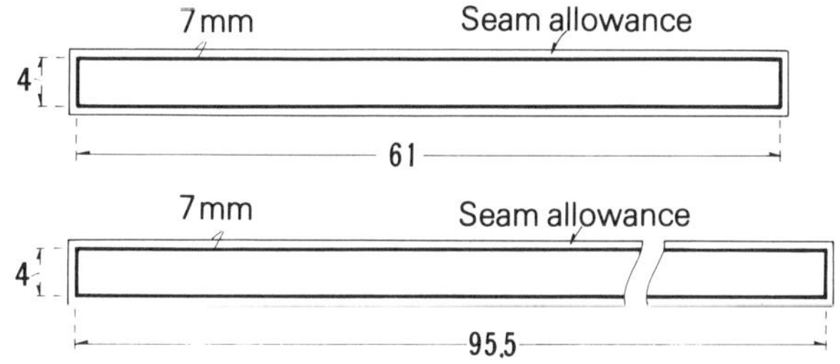
7mm
Seam allowance
4
61
7mm
Seam allowance
4
95.5

Piping strip

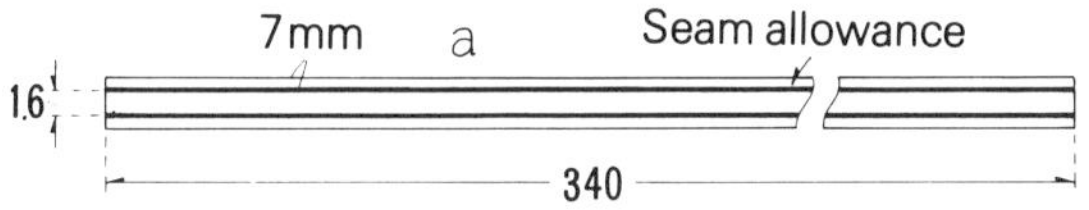
7mm
a
Seam allowance
1.6
340

Quilt Pattern

4cm
Mat
4cm
3cm
Pochette
3cm
Centre

Scale up the design to 1 square = 4cm for mat, and 1 square = 3cm for pochette

Pochette

To make up:

(1) Assemble patches as for the mat.

(2) Place wadding and lining on wrong side of front and back respectively. Quilt and pipe as indicated.

(3) Place front and back wrong sides together. Sew on should strap and loops (see page 90).

Chart of Measurements

Front

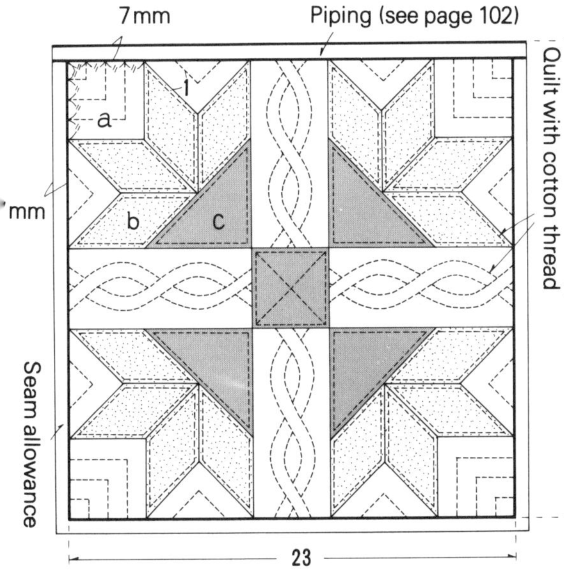
7mm
Piping (see page 102)
1
a
mm
b
c
Quilt with cotton thread
23.7
Seam allowance
23

Cut lining and wadding same size as top piece

Back

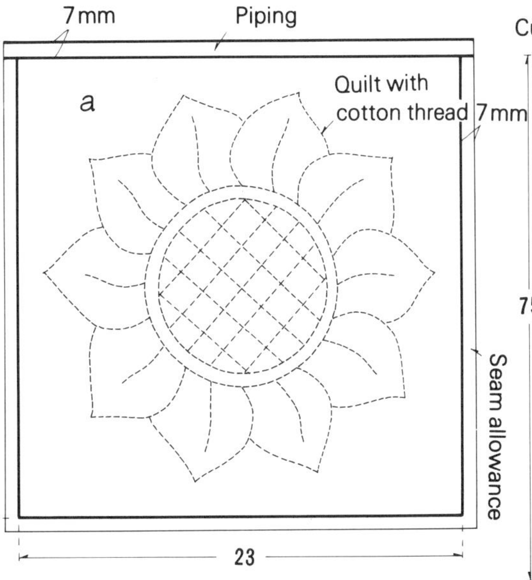
7mm
Piping
a
Quilt with
cotton thread
7mm
Seam allowance
23

Piping strips

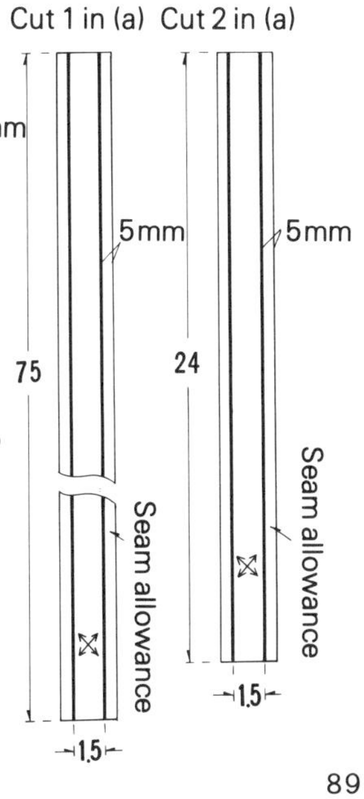
Cut 1 in (a)
Cut 2 in (a)
5mm
5mm
75
24
Seam allowance
Seam allowance
1.5
1.5

Shoulder Strap
Cut 3 in (a)

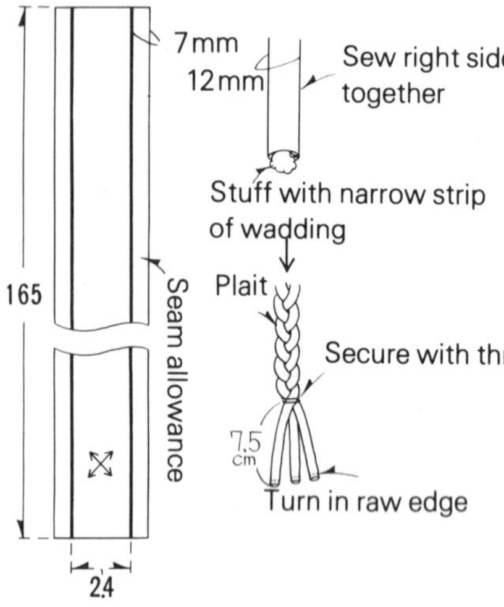

7mm
12mm
Sew right sides together
Stuff with narrow strip of wadding
Plait
Secure with thread
7.5 cm
Turn in raw edge
165
Seam allowance
2.4

Securing loop
Cut 2 in (c)

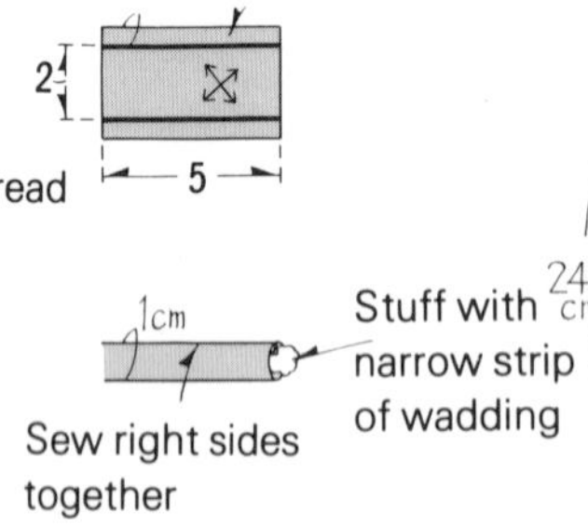

5mm seam allowance
2
5
1cm
Stuff with narrow strip of wadding
Sew right sides together

To finish

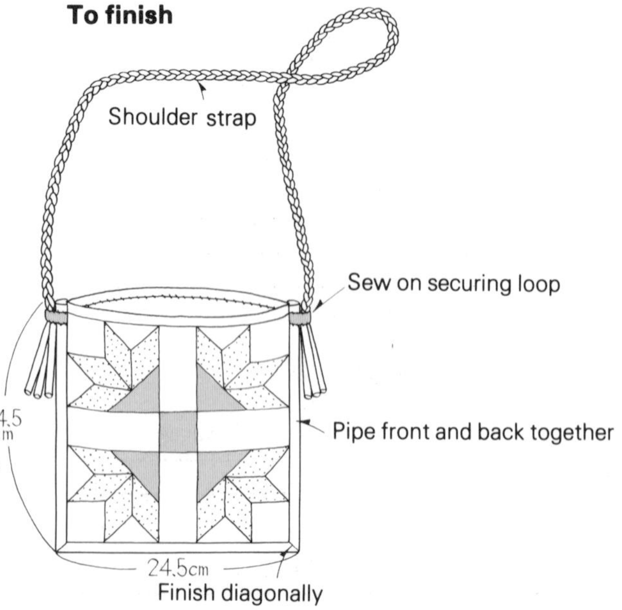

Shoulder strap
Sew on securing loop
24.5 cm
Pipe front and back together
24.5cm
Finish diagonally

SPECTACLE CASES

As shown on page 49

To make up the blue-and-red case:

(1) Cut out patch pieces, adding 7 mm seam allowance. Join as shown on the chart.

(2) Appliqué patchwork to foundation fabric. Lay wadding between top piece and lining. Quilt along grain of fabric as shown.

(3) Right sides facing, stitch top piece at centre back. Turn in seam allowance on lining and slipstitch together. Pipe bottom edge and top opening.

Chart of Measurements

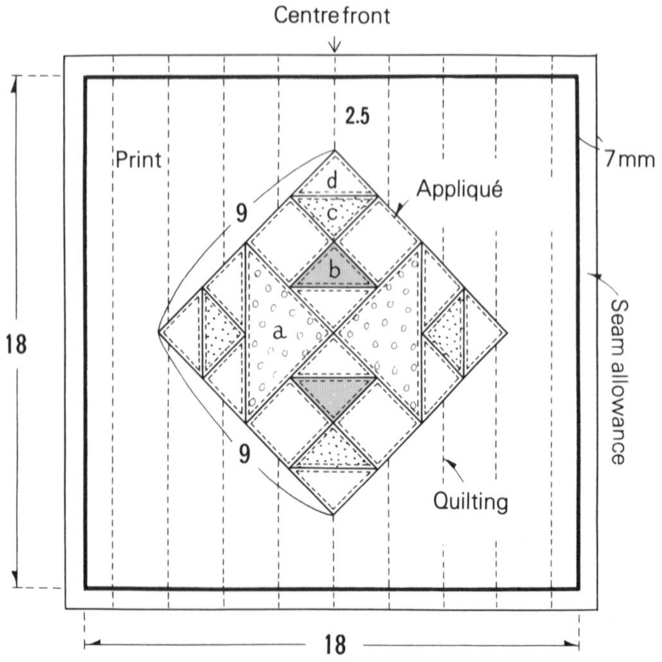

Centre front
2.5
Print
7mm
d
c
Appliqué
9
b
a
18
Seam allowance
9
Quilting
18

Cut 19.5cm square from print for lining

Sizes of Fabric

Fabrics	Sizes
Navy print	40cm × 20cm
a	9cm × 7cm
b	7cm × 5cm
c	15cm × 5cm
d	20cm × 15cm
Red	20cm × 5cm

To finish

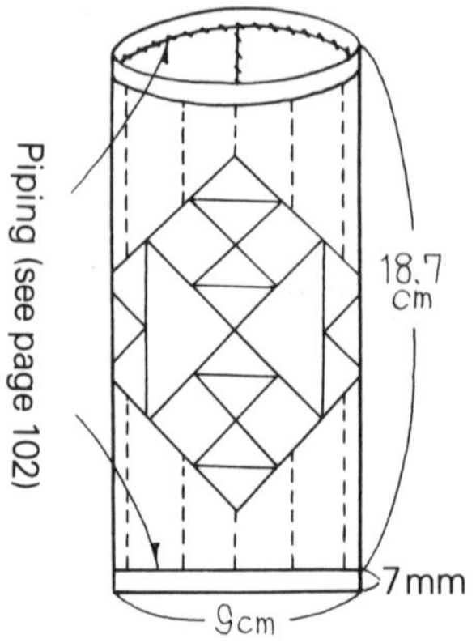

Piping (see page 102)
18.7 cm
7mm
9cm

Piping strips
Cut 1 each in red

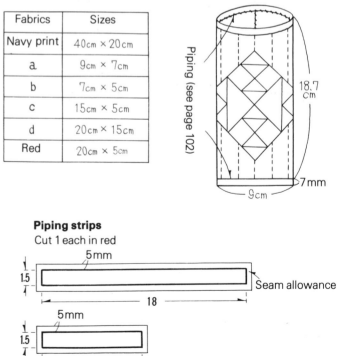

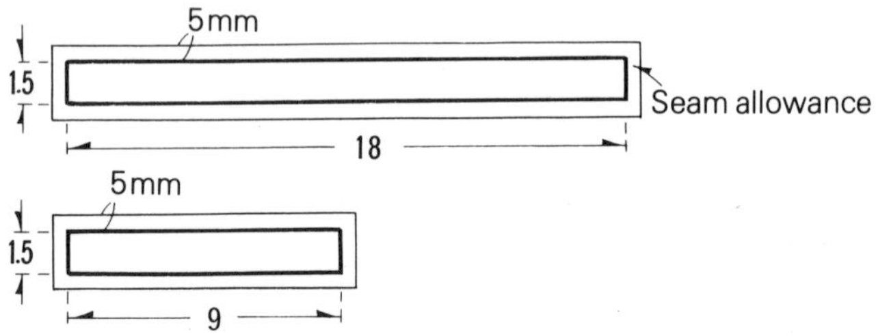

5mm
1.5
Seam allowance
18
5mm
1.5
9

To make up the green-and-purple case:
(1) Make up blocks as for the previous case.
(2) Join purple and green squares as shown. Lay wadding between top piece and lining. Quilt with matching thread.
(3) Right sides facing, stitch top piece at centre back. Turn in seam allowance on lining and slipstitch together. Sew bottom edge and pipe top opening.

Chart of Measurements

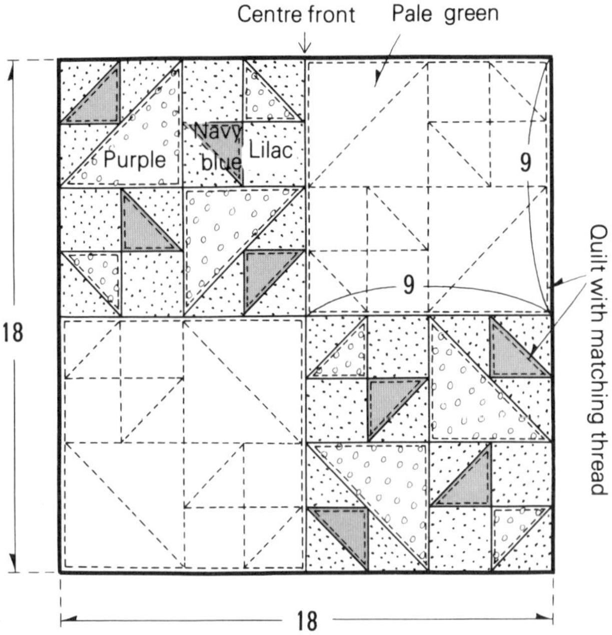

Centre front
Pale green
Navy blue
Lilac
Purple
9
9
Quilt with matching thread
18
18

Cut out 19.5cm square from pale green cotton for lining

Sizes of Fabric

Fabric	Sizes
Pale green	42cm × 20cm
Purple	18cm × 7cm
Navy blue	15cm × 10cm
Lilac	20cm × 30cm

To finish

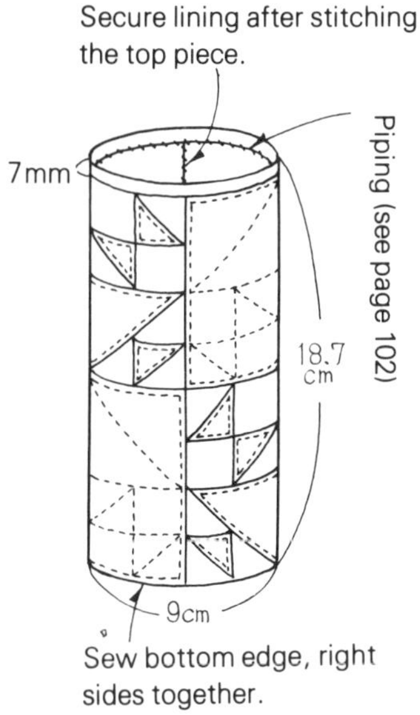

Secure lining after stitching the top piece.
7mm
Piping (see page 102)
18.7 cm
9cm
Sew bottom edge, right sides together.

Piping strips

Cut 1 in pale green

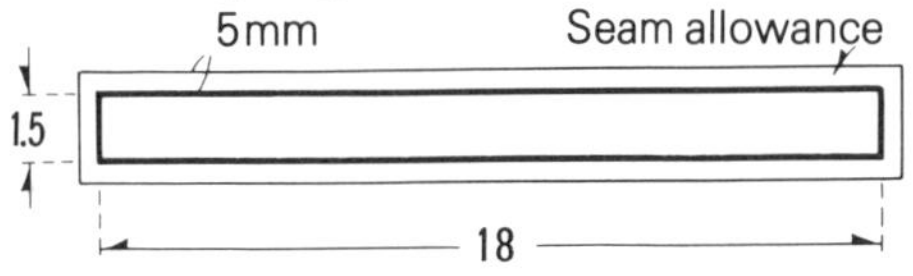

5mm
Seam allowance
1.5
18

RUNNER & PLACEMATS

As shown on page 55

Placemat

To make up:

(1) Cut out patch pieces and join as shown on the chart.
(2) Right sides together, sew border strips to sides. Press flat. Iron interlining to wrong side of lining. Right sides facing, stitch lining to top and bottom across ends of border strips. Press, leaving 2.5cm border.

Chart of Measurements

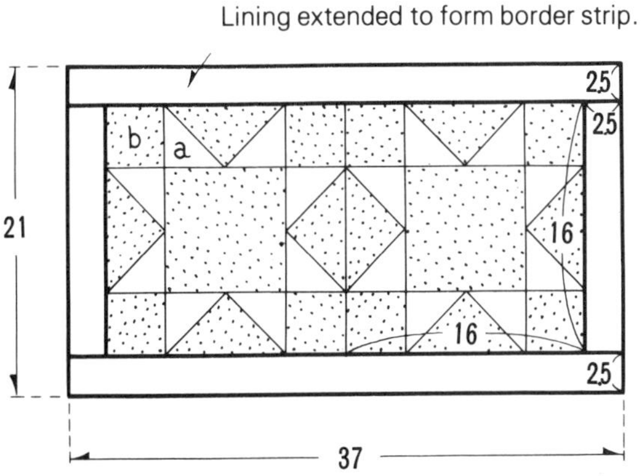

Lining extended to form border strip.
2.5
2.5
2.5
b
a
16
16
21
37

Cut lining in fabric (a), 38.5cm x 27.5cm

Border strips

Cut 2 in (a)

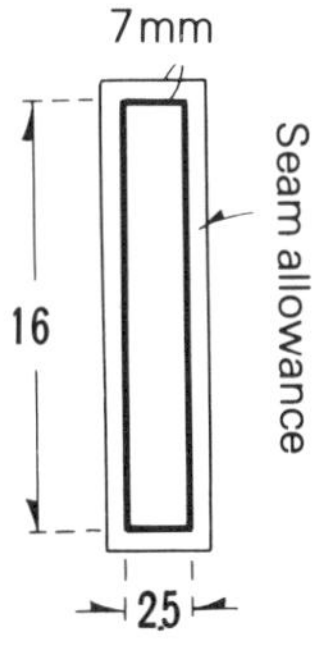

7mm
Seam allowance
16
2.5

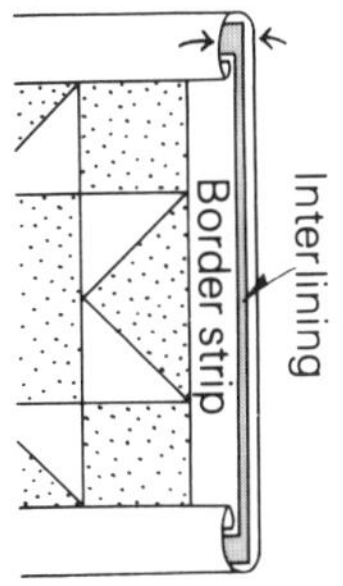

Border strip
Interlining

(3) Turn in seam allowances on sides. Slipstitch border strip to lining.

Table Runner

To make up:

Work in the same way as for the placemat (page 91).

Chart of Measurements

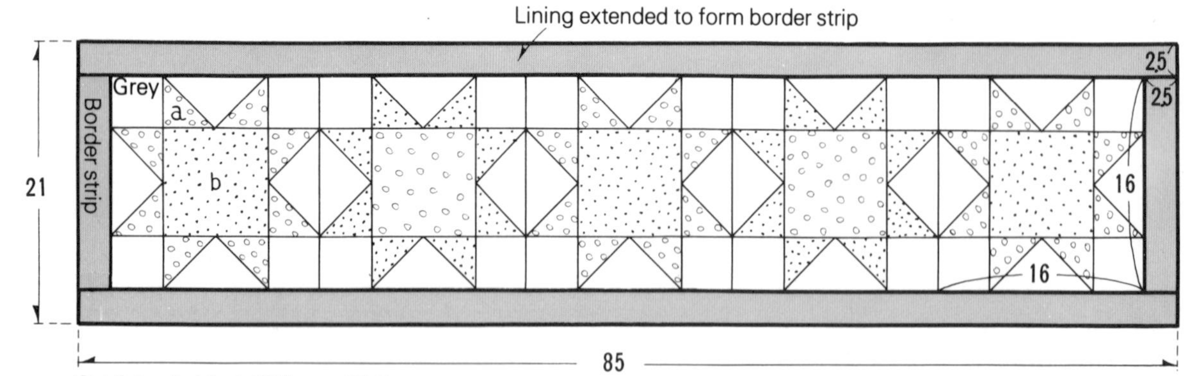

Lining extended to form border strip
2.5
2.5
Grey
a
b
Border strip
21
16
16
85

Border strips

Cut 2 in black

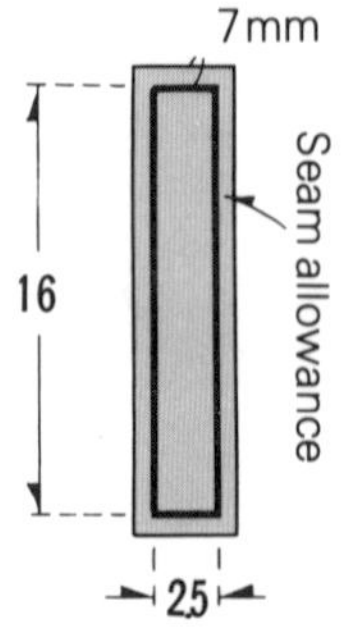

7mm
16
Seam allowance
2.5

Cut lining in black 86.5cm x 27.5cm

POT HOLDER & TABLE RUNNER

As shown on page 57

Table Runner

To make up:

Work in the same way as for the placemat (page 91)

Chart of Measurements

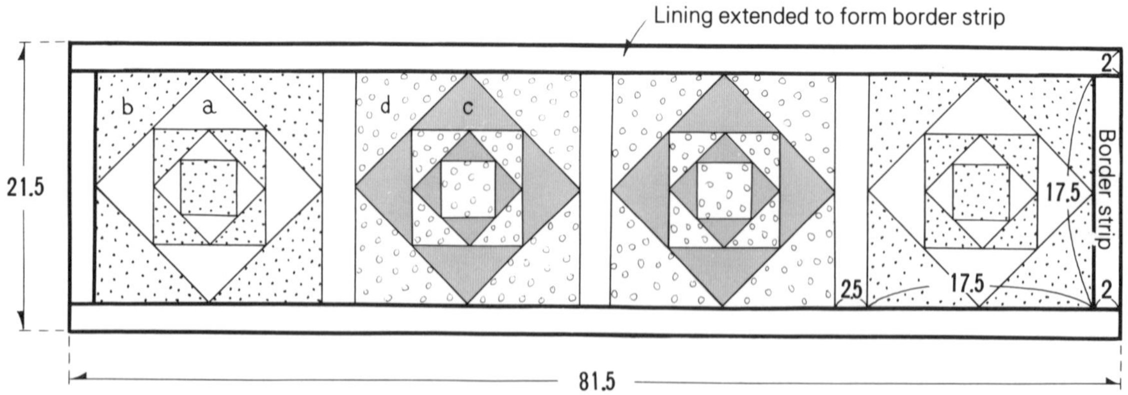

Lining extended to form border strip
2
b
a
d
c
21.5
17.5
Border strip
2.5
17.5
2
81.5

Border strips

Cut 2 in (a), 3 in (a)

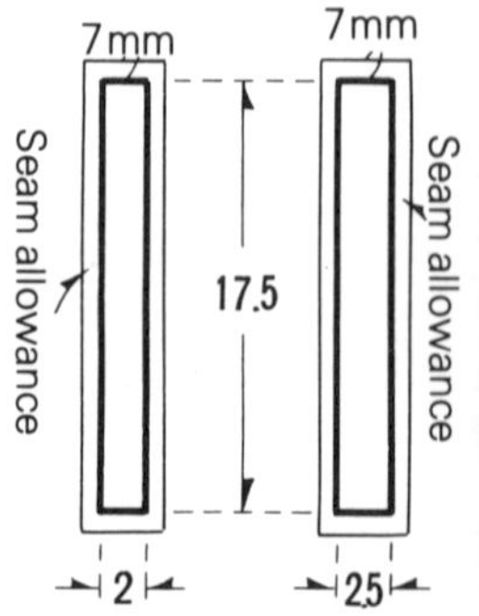

7mm
7mm
Seam allowance
17.5
Seam allowance
2
2.5

Cut lining in fabric (a), 83cm x 27cm

Pot Holder

To make up:

Work in the same way as for the placemat (page 91), placing wadding on wrong side of lining when sewing to front. Attach loop as indicated.

Chart of Measurements

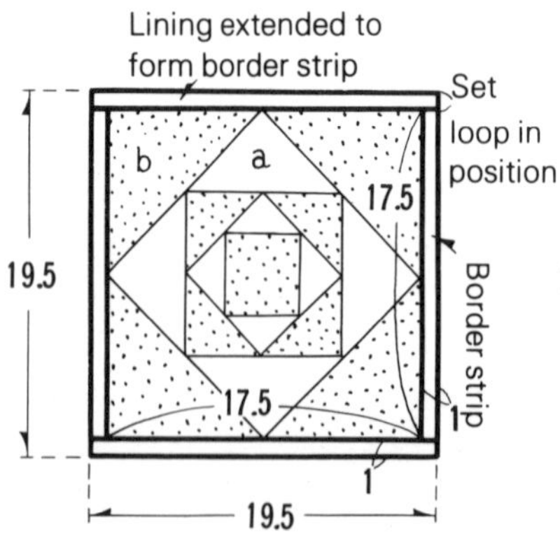

Lining extended to form border strip
Set loop in position
b
a
17.5
19.5
Border strip
17.5
1
1
19.5

Border strips

Cut 2 in (a)

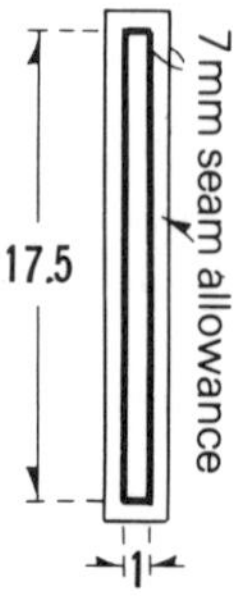

17.5
7mm seam allowance
1

Loop Cut 1 in (a)

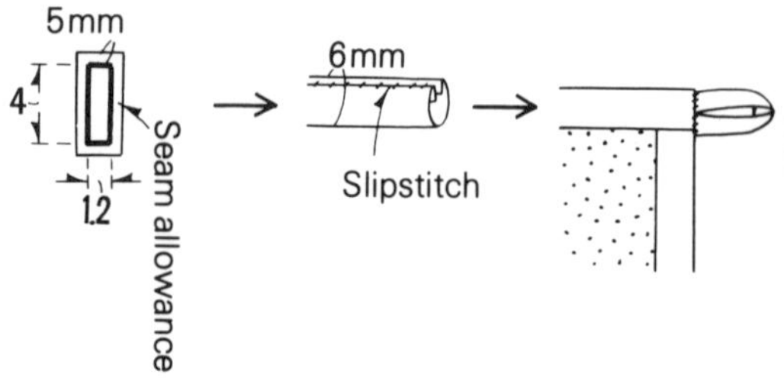

5mm
4
1.2
Seam allowance
6mm
Slipstitch

Cut lining in fabric (a) 21cm x 23cm

QUILT
As shown on page 43

To make up:
(1) Cut out patch pieces, adding 7 mm seam allowance. Join as shown on the chart.
(2) Lay wadding between top piece and lining. Quilt together. Pipe edges crosswise then lengthwise.

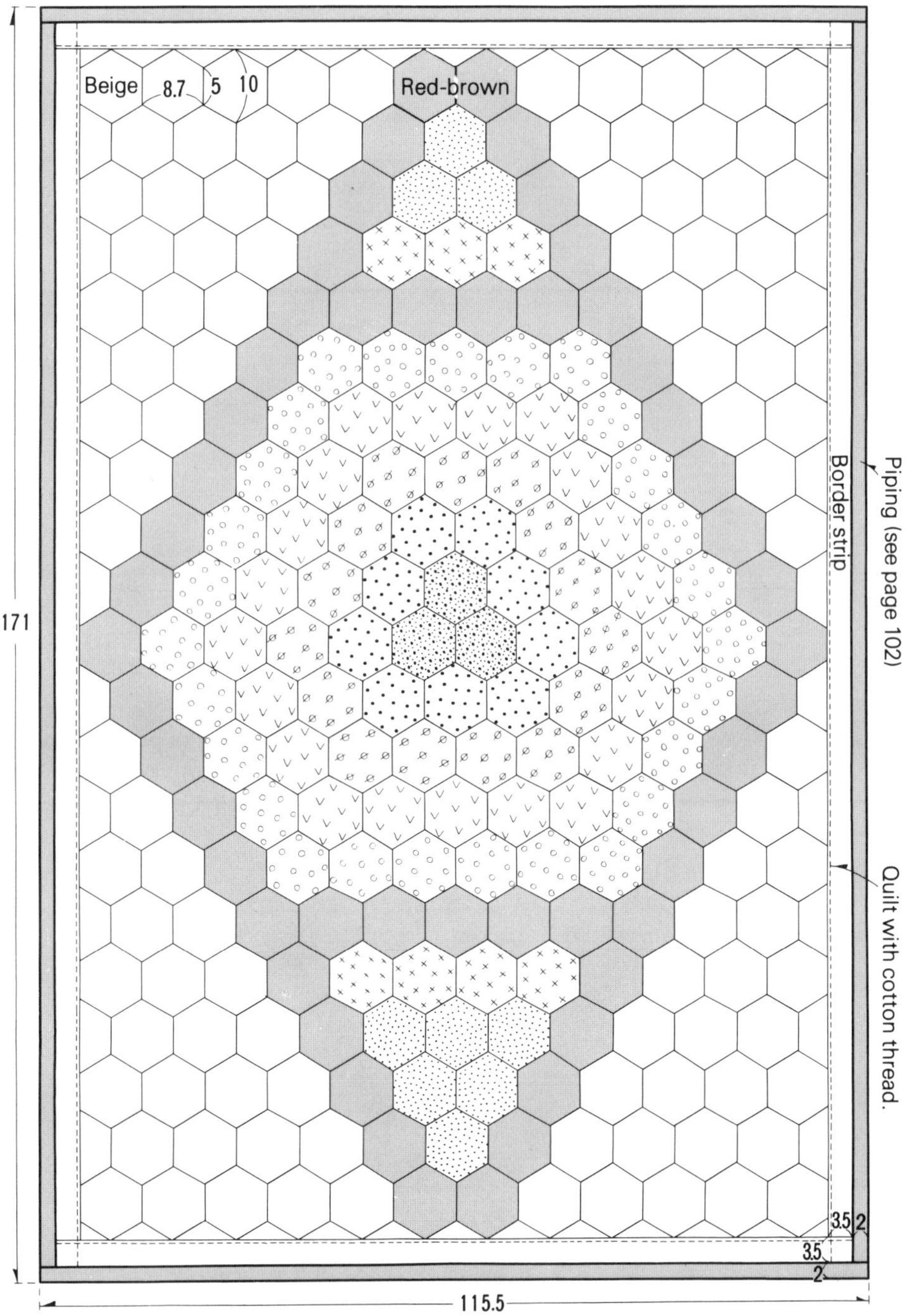

Beige
8.7
5
10
Red-brown
171
Border strip
Piping (see page 102)
Quilt with cotton thread.
3.5
2
3.5
2
115.5

Cut lining in pale pink and wadding 115.5 cm x 171 cm

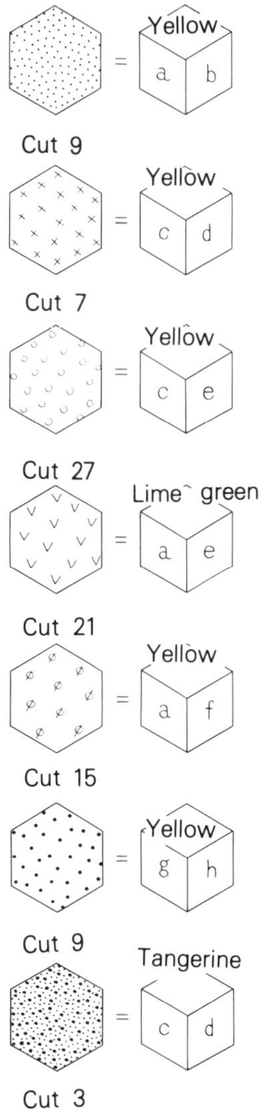

Yellow
a b
Cut 9
Yellow
c d
Cut 7
Yellow
c e
Cut 27
Lime green
a e
Cut 21
Yellow
a f
Cut 15
Yellow
g h
Cut 9
Tangerine
c d
Cut 3

Border strips

Cut 2 of each in pale pink

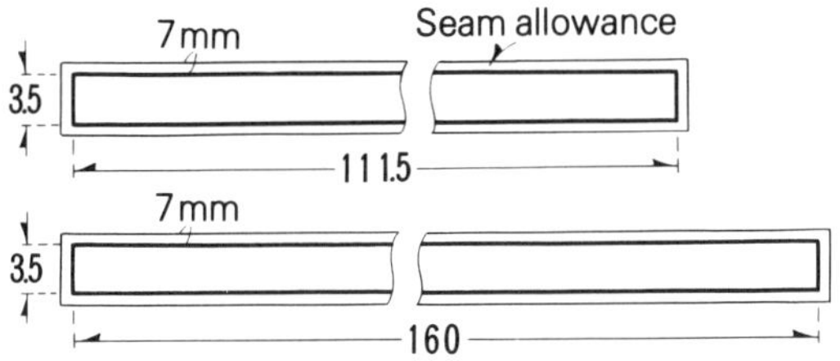

Piping strips

Cut 2 of each in red-brown

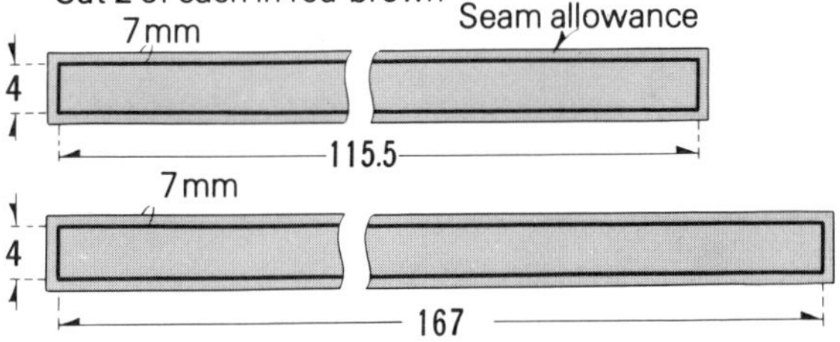

To finish piping

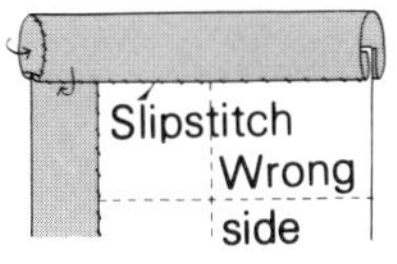

Slipstitch
Wrong side

WALL HANGING & BAGS

As shown on page 59

Wall Hanging

To make up:

(1) Cut out patch pieces adding 7 mm seam allowance. Join as shown on the chart.
(2) Lay wadding between top piece and lining. Turn in hem and bring lining to front. Slipstitch to patchwork. Quilt.
(3) Make a loop and stitch to back. Sew button in place.

Chart of measurements

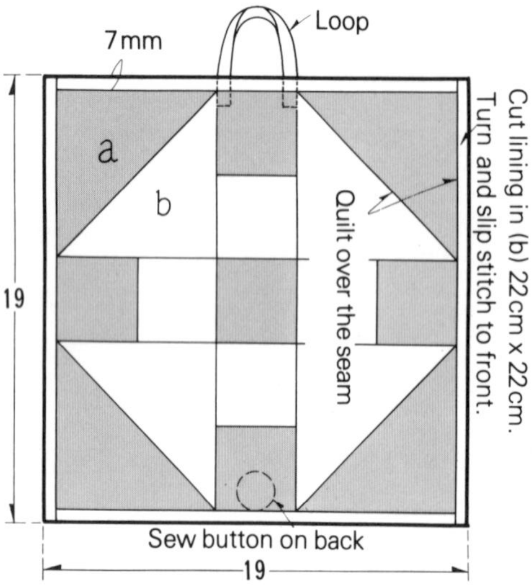

7mm
Loop
a
b
Quilt over the seam
Cut lining in (b) 22cm x 22cm.
Turn and slip stitch to front.
19
Sew button on back
19

Loop (b)

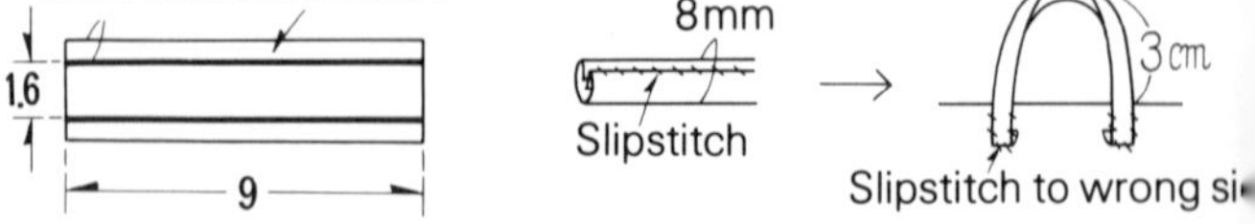

5mm seam allowance
1.6
9
8mm
Slipstitch
3cm
Slipstitch to wrong si

To finish corner

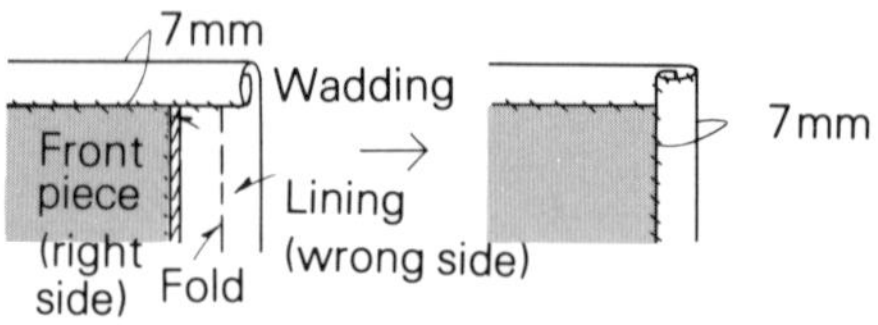

7mm
Wadding
Front piece (right side)
Fold
Lining (wrong side)
7mm

Bags

To make up:

(1) Assemble patches as for the wall hanging.
(2) Cut out pieces in (e) as specified and join to patchwork centre. Cut (a) 25 cm square of wadding and lining and lay on back of the patchwork. Quilt as shown.
(3) Cut yoke and strap pieces. Make up straps and sew to yoke pieces. Stitch yoke pieces to back and front respective then machine side seams and base. To line, make up inner bag and slipstitch to top as shown. Finish corners.

Chart of measurements

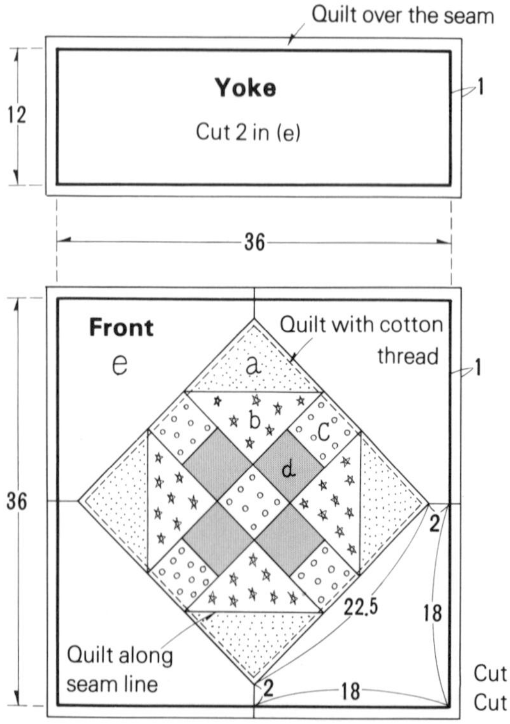

Quilt over the seam
Yoke
Cut 2 in (e)
1
12
36
Front
e
Quilt with cotton thread
1
a
b
c
d
36
2
22.5
18
Quilt along seam line
2
18

Strap

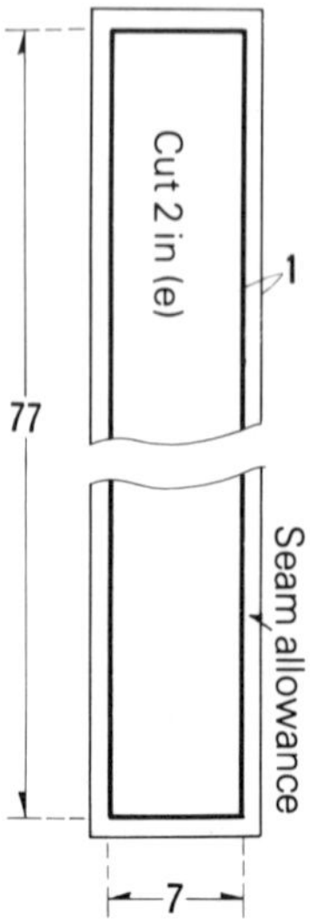

Cut 2 in (e)
1
77
Seam allowance
7

Cut back 38 cm square in fabric (e)
Cut 2 pieces 38 cm x 50 cm for inner bag

To finish

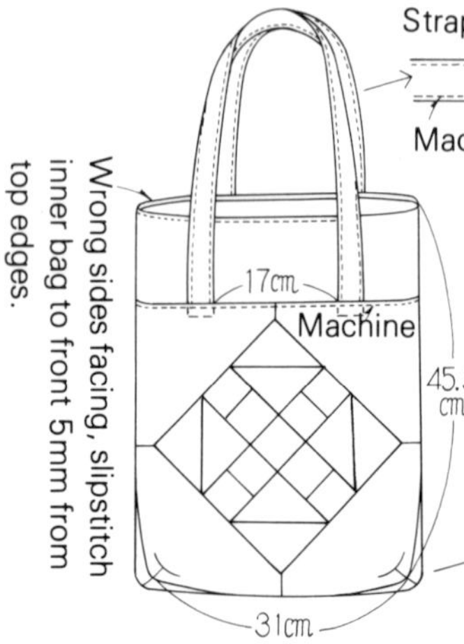

Strap
3.5cm
Machine
Wrong sides facing, slipstitch inner bag to front 5mm from top edges.
17cm
Machine
45.5 cm
31cm

To finish corners

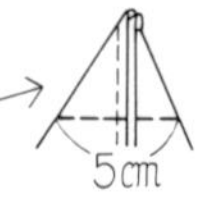

5cm

Fold right sides together as shown, stitch 5cm across

QUILT & POCHETTE

As shown on page 51

Quilt

To make up:

(1) Cut out patch pieces adding 7 mm seam allowance. Join as shown on page 50.

(2) Slipstitch the daisy motif to blue fabric to make block A. Working in rows across the quilt, stitch A and B to dividing block C. Join blocks C and D into strips as shown and stitch to assembled blocks. Repeat for length of quilt. Tack wadding to wrong side. Quilt design on block B and along seamlines.

(3) Right sides facing join border strips to edge lengthwise then crosswise. Turn in seam allowance on lining and 1 cm plus seam allowance on borders. Slipstitch lining to back of border strip 1 cm from edge. Quilt as shown.

Chart of Measurements

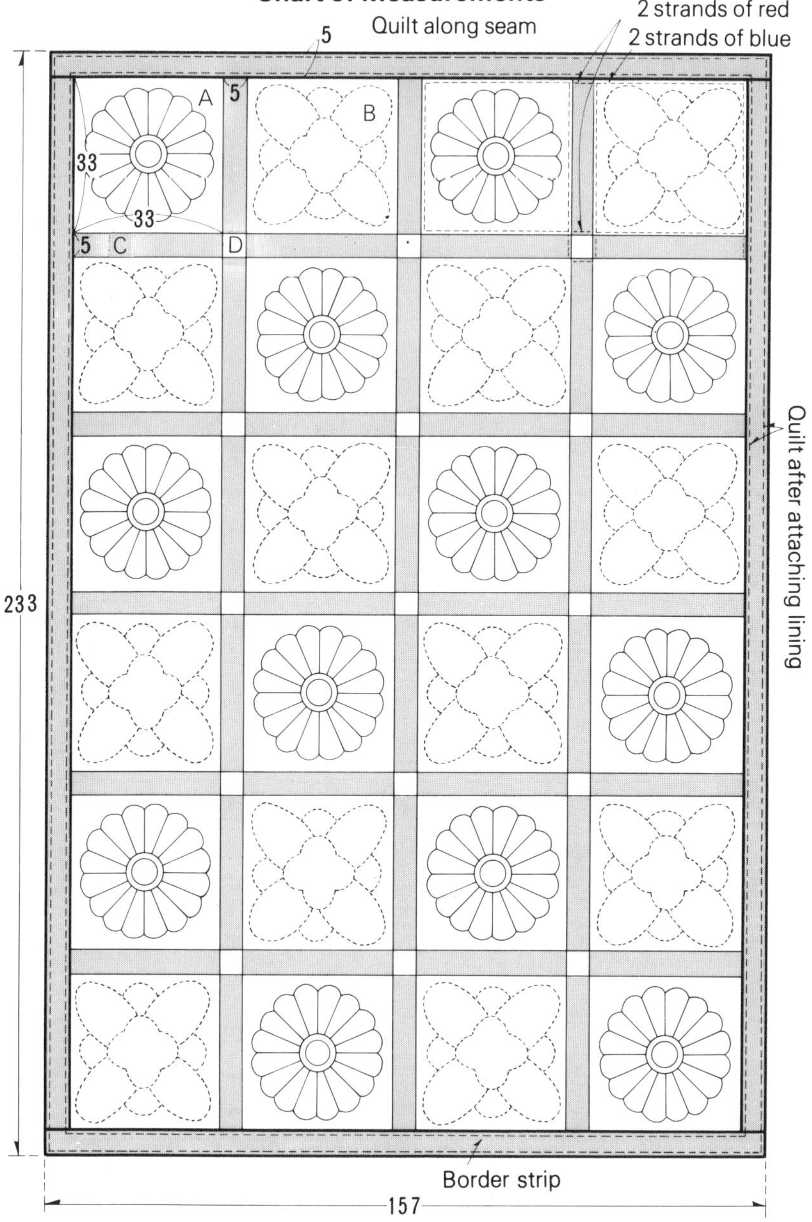

Quilt along seam
2 strands of red
2 strands of blue
5
A
B
5
33
33
5
C
D
Quilt after attaching lining
233
Border strip
157

Cut lining and wadding 157 cm x 233 cm

Block A (make 12)

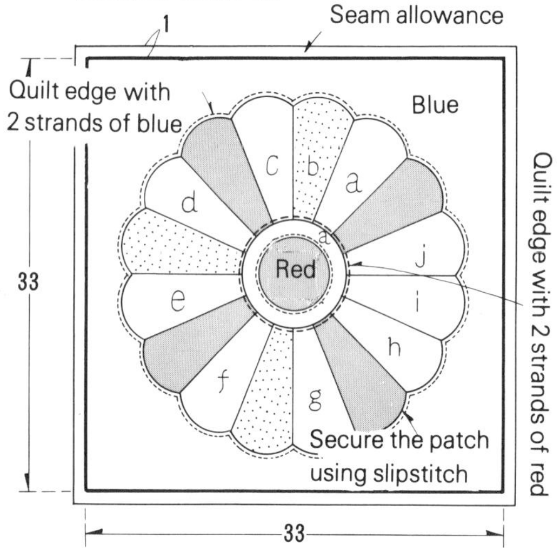

1
Seam allowance
Quilt edge with
2 strands of blue
Blue
c
b
a
d
a
Red
j
e
i
h
f
g
Secure the patch
using slipstitch
Quilt edge with 2 strands of red
33
33

Cut 12 of block B

Block C (cut 38)

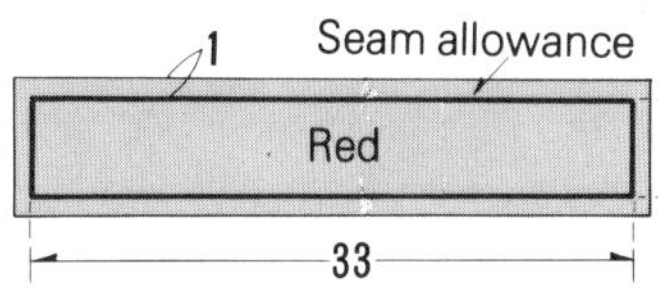

Block D (cut 15)

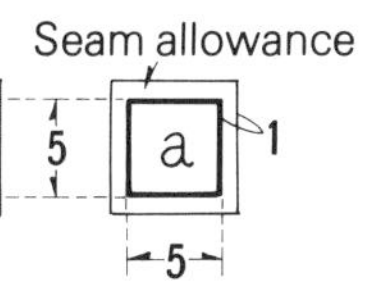

Seam allowance
5
a
1
5

Border strips (cut 2 of each)

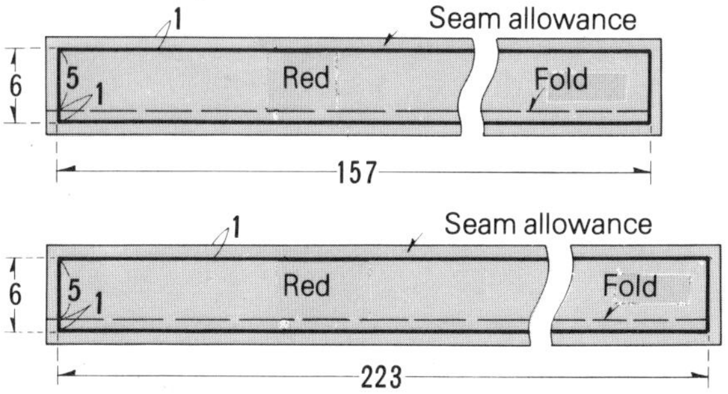

1
Seam allowance
6
5
1
Red
Fold
157
1
Seam allowance
6
5
1
Red
Fold
223

Quilt Design for Block B (actual size)

2 strands of blue

Pochette

To make up:

(1) Assemble patches as for the quilt.

(2) Slipstitch patchwork to front. Quilt front and back respectively, with wadding and lining on wrong side. Pipe as indicated.

(3) Place front and back wrong sides together. Pipe edge, extending one end of piping strip for loop, the other for shoulder strap. Machine strap and loop in position.

Chart of Measurements

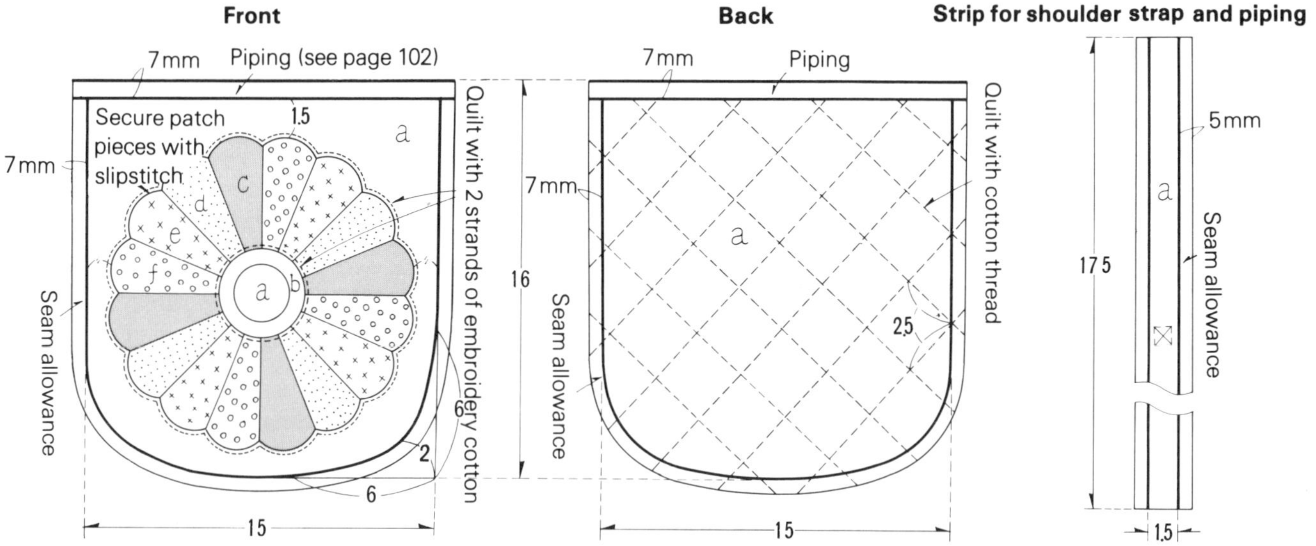
Front
Back
Strip for shoulder strap and piping
7mm
Piping (see page 102)
Secure patch pieces with slipstitch
1.5
a
b
c
d
e
f
7mm
Seam allowance
Quilt with 2 strands of embroidery cotton
6
2
6
15
16
7mm
Piping
7mm
Seam allowance
Quilt with cotton thread
2.5
15
5mm
Seam allowance
17.5
1.5

Cut lining in fabric (a) and wadding same size as top piece.

Piping strips (cut 2)

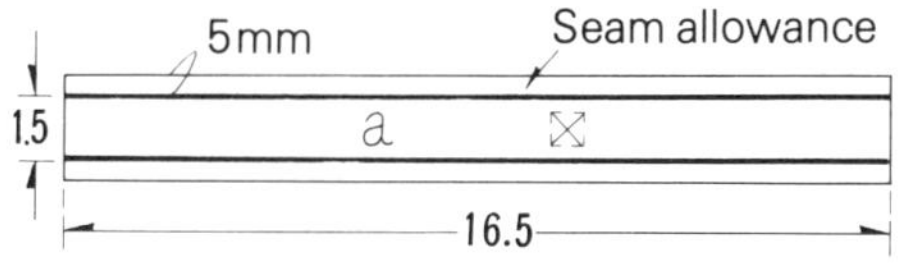
5mm
Seam allowance
1.5
a
16.5

To finish

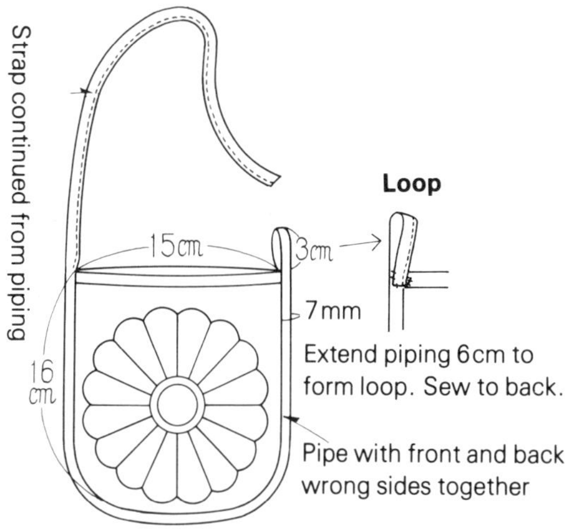
Strap continued from piping
15cm
3cm
Loop
7mm
16 cm
Extend piping 6cm to form loop. Sew to back.
Pipe with front and back wrong sides together

PEN CASE & PHONE SET

As shown on page 61

Phone Set

To make up the phone cover:

(1) Cut out patch pieces adding 7mm seam allowance. Join as shown on the chart.

(2) Place top piece and lining wrong sides together, turn edges of lining over top piece and quilt down.

To make up the mat:

(1) Assemble patches as for phone cover.

(2) Lay wadding between front and lining. Quilt together and finish edges with piping.

Chart of Measurements

Phone cover

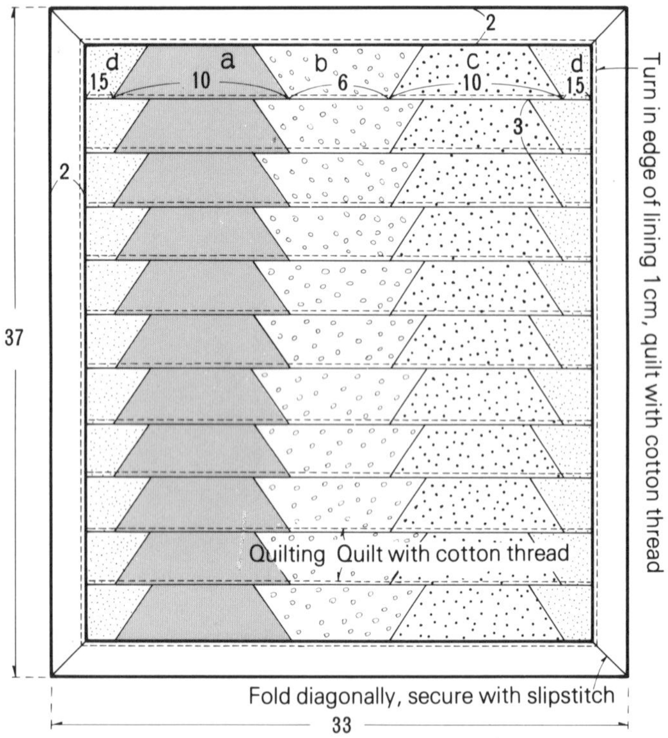

2
d
a
b
c
d
1.5
10
6
10
1.5
3
2
37
Turn in edge of lining 1cm, quilt with cotton thread
Quilting Quilt with cotton thread
Fold diagonally, secure with slipstitch
33

Cut lining 39cm x 43cm in yellow

Mat

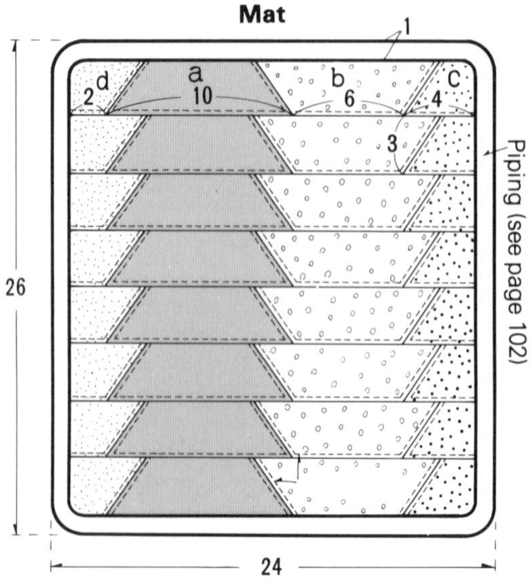

1
d
a
b
c
2
10
6
4
3
26
Piping (see page 102)
24

Piping strip

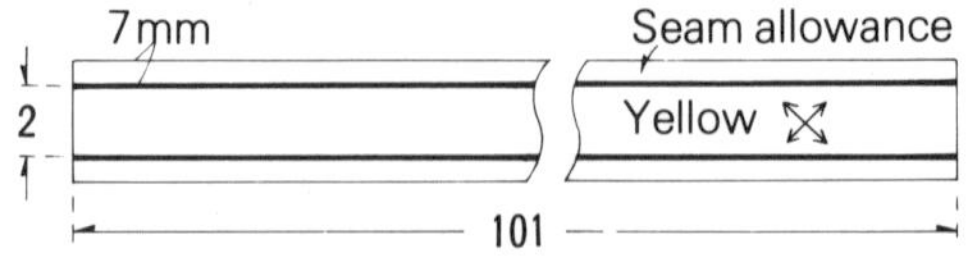

7mm
Seam allowance
2
Yellow
101

Pen Case

To make up:

(1) Assemble patches as for phone cover.

(2) Lay wadding between top piece and lining. Quilt Pipe front as indicated.

(3) Front and back wrong sides together, finish edges with piping. Sew Velcro in position.

Chart of Measurements

Front

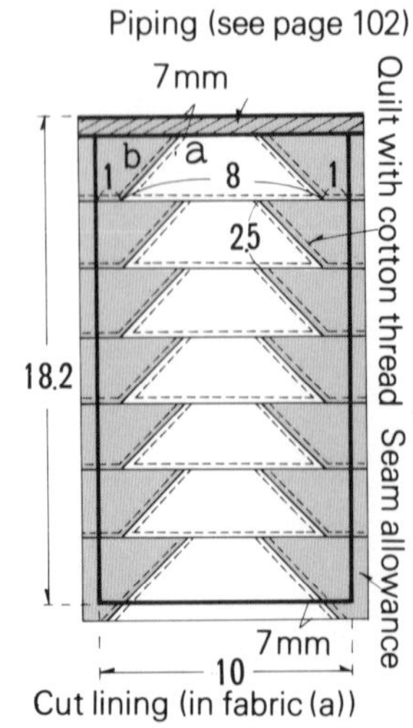

Piping (see page 102)
7mm
b
a
1
8
1
2.5
18.2
Quilt with cotton thread
Seam allowance
7mm
10

Cut lining (in fabric (a)) and wadding 12cm x 19.2cm

Back

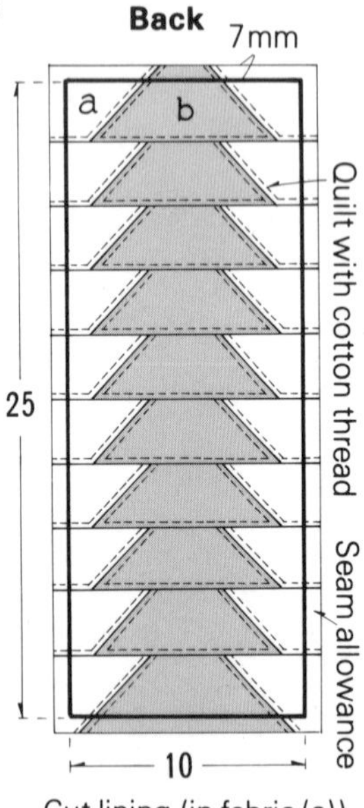

7mm
a
b
Quilt with cotton thread
25
Seam allowance
10

Cut lining (in fabric (a)) and wadding 12cm x 27cm

Piping strips

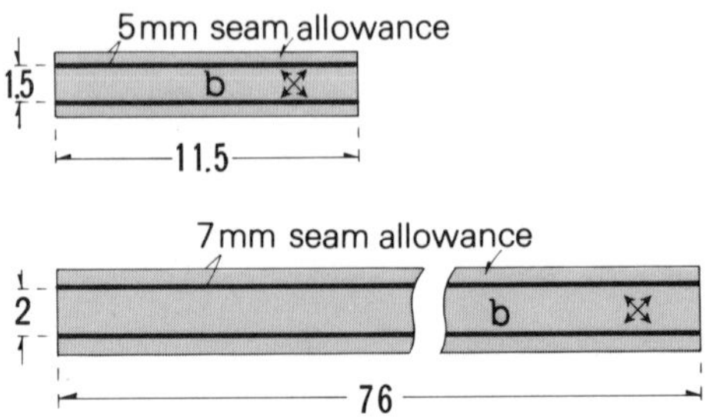

Cut 1 of each
5mm seam allowance
1.5
b
11.5
7mm seam allowance
2
b
76

To finish

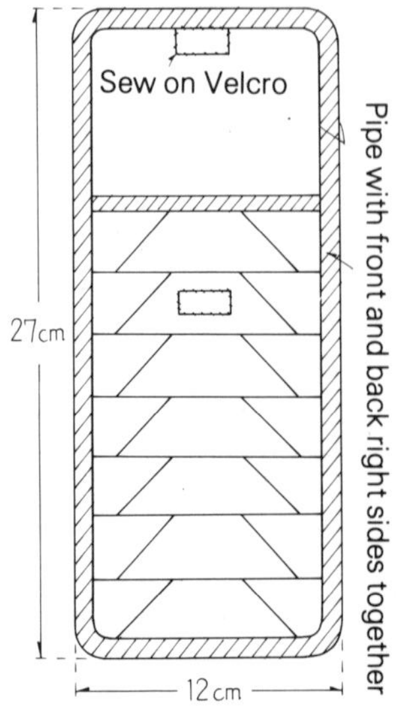

Sew on Velcro
Pipe with front and back right sides together
27cm
12cm

CUSHION & BAGS
As shown on page 63

Cushion
To make up:
(1) Cut out patch pieces adding 7 mm seam allowance. Join as shown on the chart.
(2) Join border strips to front. With wadding to wrong side quilt as shown.
(3) Cut out pieces for back. Sew in zip and stitch back piece to border strips right sides facing. Turn right sides out and insert inner cushion.

Chart of Measurements

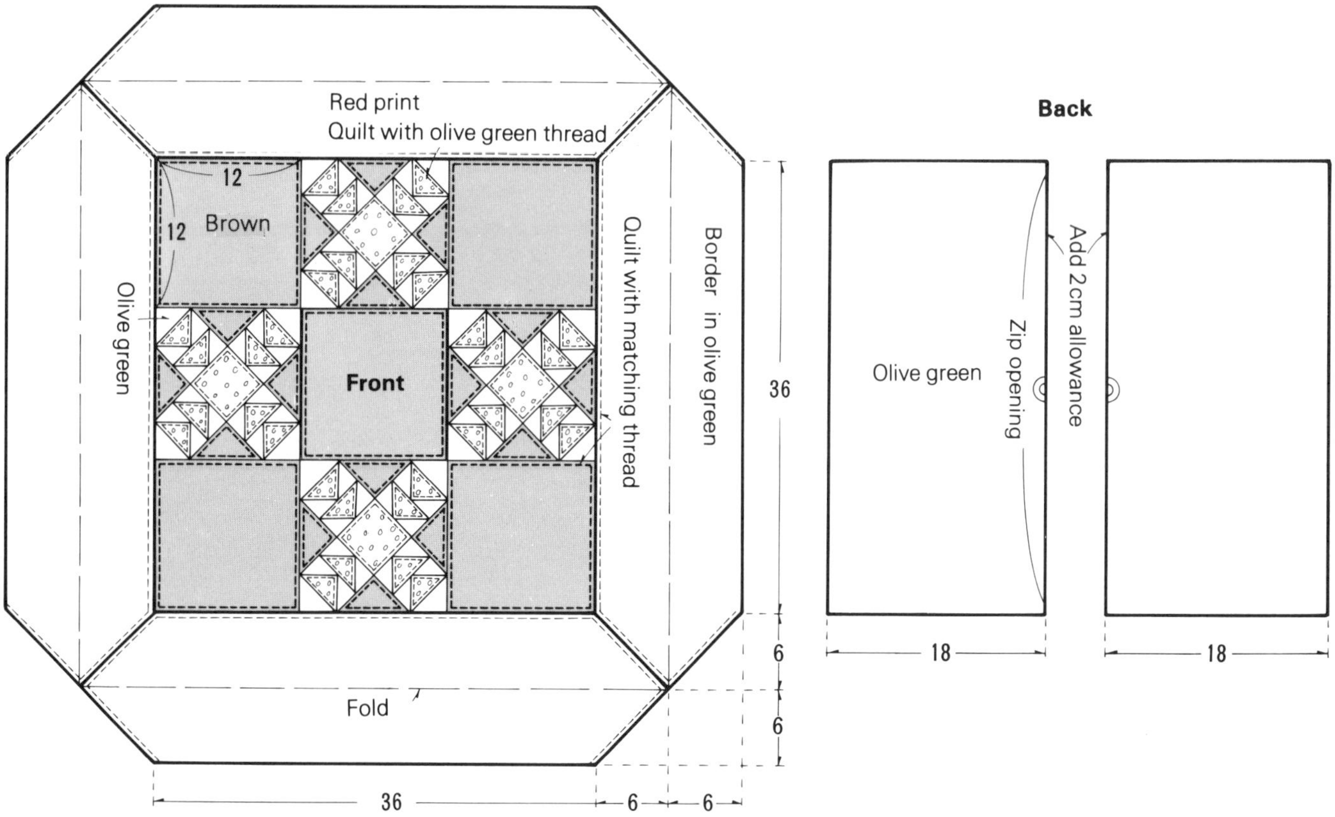

Add 1 cm seam allowance unless specified
Red print
Quilt with olive green thread
12
12
Brown
Olive green
Front
Quilt with matching thread
Border in olive green
36
6
6
Fold
36
6
6
Back
Olive green
Zip opening
Add 2 cm allowance
18
18

Cut out a piece of wadding 62 cm square.
Clip corners as shown

Bag
To make up the blue bag (bottom right)
(1) Assemble blocks as for cushion and join as shown.
(2) Quilt patchwork to backing piece. Cut out pieces for front and back. Set panel in front. Right sides together stitch front to back.
(3) Stitch together 2 lining pieces and line bag, machining top of bag as shown. Sew on handle.

To make up the white bag (top right)
(1) Assemble block as for cushion. Quilt to backing piece.
(2) Right sides facing sew lining to patchwork leaving opening for turning. Turn right sides out and close opening.
(3) Cut out front and back. With wadding to wrong side, quilt at 5 cm intervals. Sew pocket to front.
(4) Sew front to back right sides together. Line and finish as for blue bag.

Blue Bag (bottom right)

Chart of Measurements

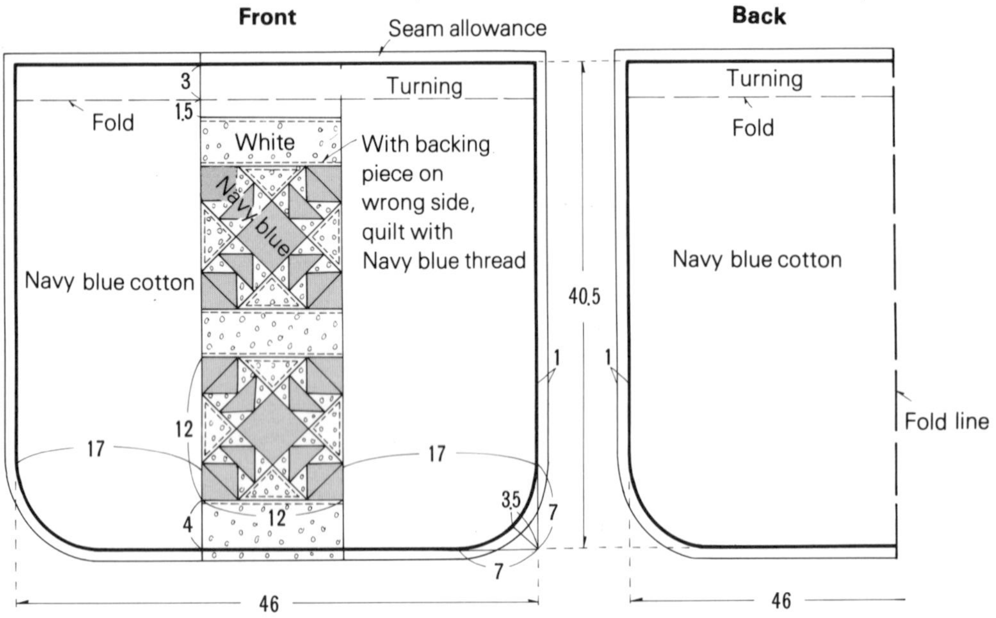
Front
Seam allowance
Turning
Fold
3
1.5
White
With backing piece on wrong side, quilt with Navy blue thread
Navy blue
Navy blue cotton
40.5
1
12
17
17
12
4
3.5
7
7
46
Back
Turning
Fold
Navy blue cotton
1
Fold line
46

Cut 2 pieces of lining 48cm x 38.5cm. Round bottom corners.

To finish

To hem top

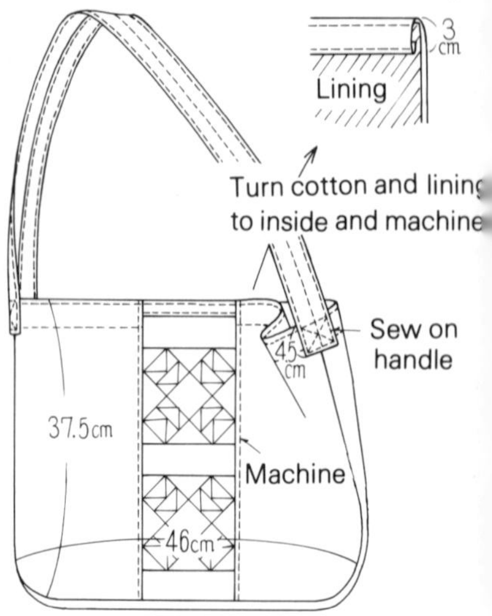

Handle

Cut 1 in navy blue

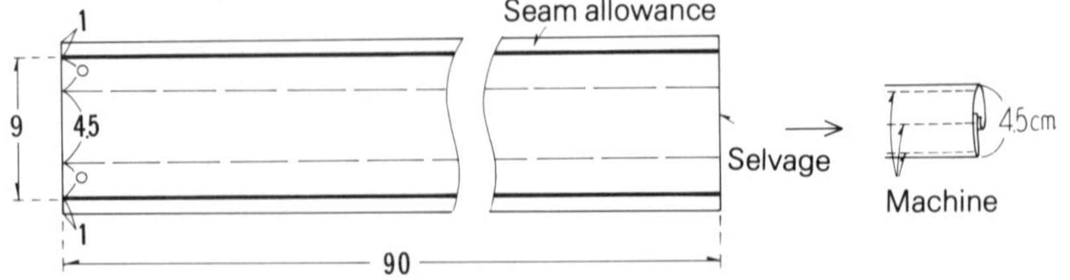
1
Seam allowance
9
4.5
Selvage
1
90
Turn cotton and lining to inside and machine
4.5cm
Machine

White Bag (top right)

Pocket

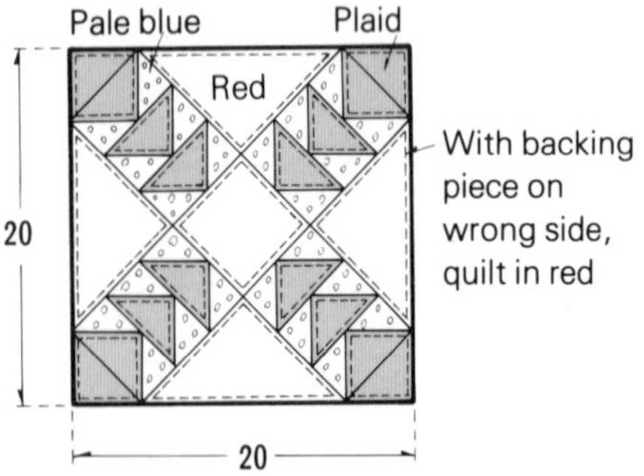
Pale blue
Plaid
Red
With backing piece on wrong side, quilt in red
20
20

Cut lining 22cm square, sew to top piece right sides facing, turn right side out, close the opening for turning.

To finish

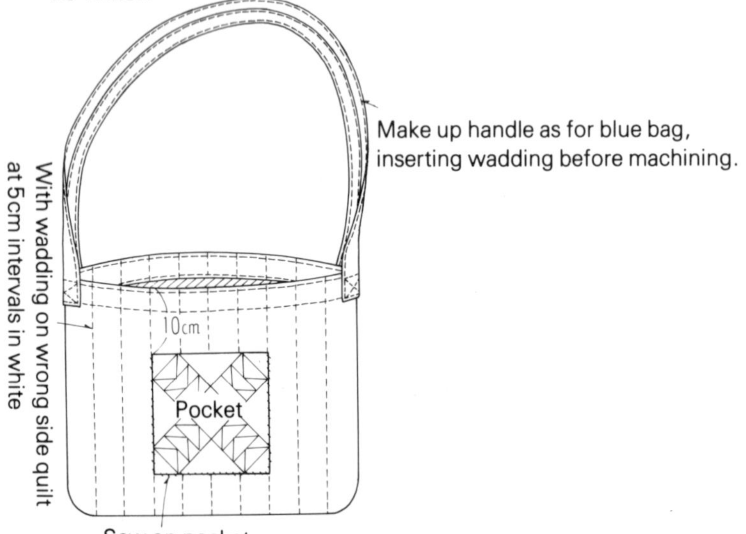
Make up handle as for blue bag, inserting wadding before machining.
With wadding on wrong side quilt at 5cm intervals in white
10cm
Pocket
Sew on pocket

Cut front and back from white cotton as for blue bag. Line as before.

PATCHWORK TECHNIQUES

CUTTING

(1) Cut out the actual size pattern in thick cardboard.

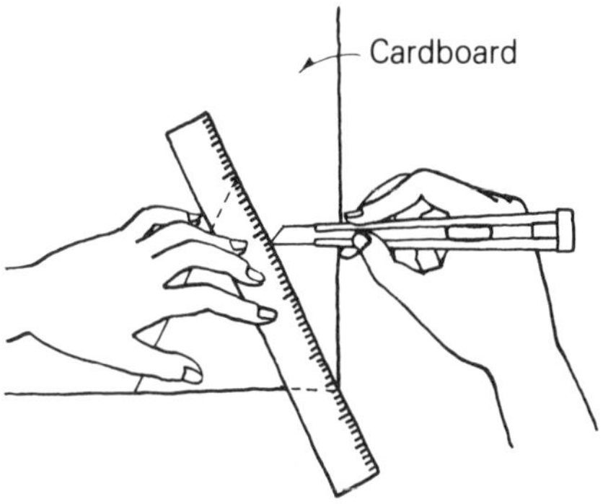
Cardboard

(2) Place the carboard shape (called a template on the fabric and draw around it accurately. Add a 7 mm seam allowance before cutting out. (Accuracy is imperative if a good result is to be achieved.)

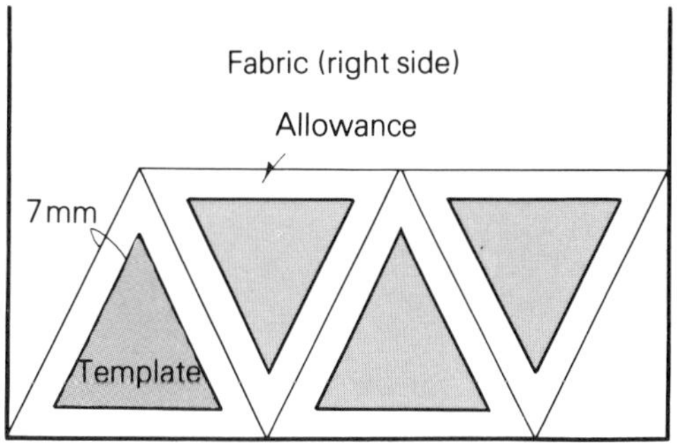
Fabric (right side)
Allowance
7mm
Template

JOINING

Using Paper Linings

Although this traditional method takes time and effort, the result is impressive.

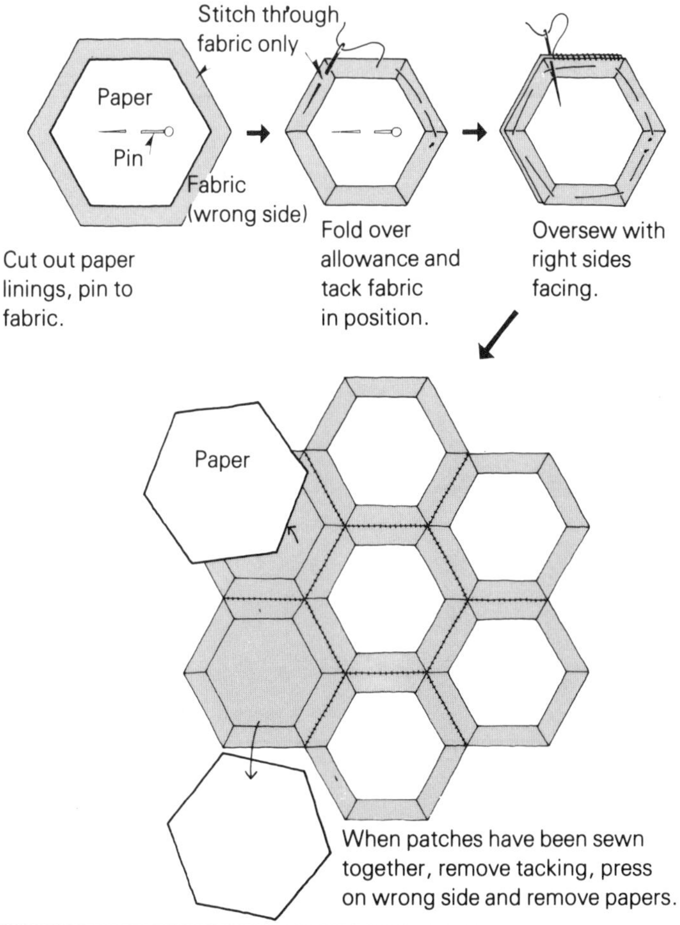
Stitch through fabric only
Paper
Pin
Fabric (wrong side)
Cut out paper linings, pin to fabric.
Fold over allowance and tack fabric in position.
Oversew with right sides facing.
Paper
When patches have been sewn together, remove tacking, press on wrong side and remove papers.

Joining Patches by Hand:

Common method of joining simple patches. Press seam allowances to one side (preferably towards darker colour so that seams are less obvious).

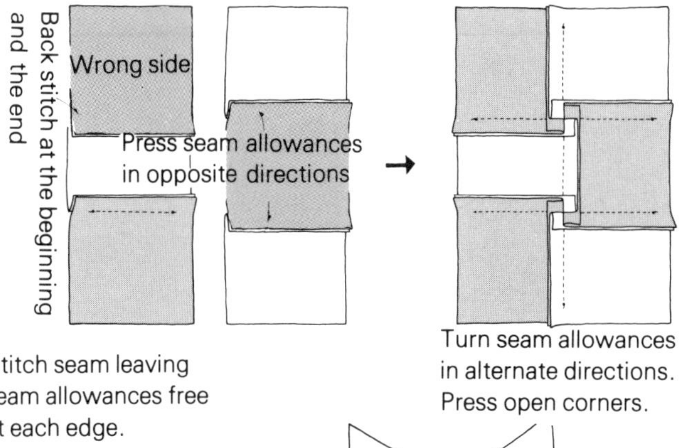
Back stitch at the beginning and the end
Wrong side
Press seam allowances in opposite directions
Stitch seam leaving seam allowances free at each edge.
Turn seam allowances in alternate directions. Press open corners.

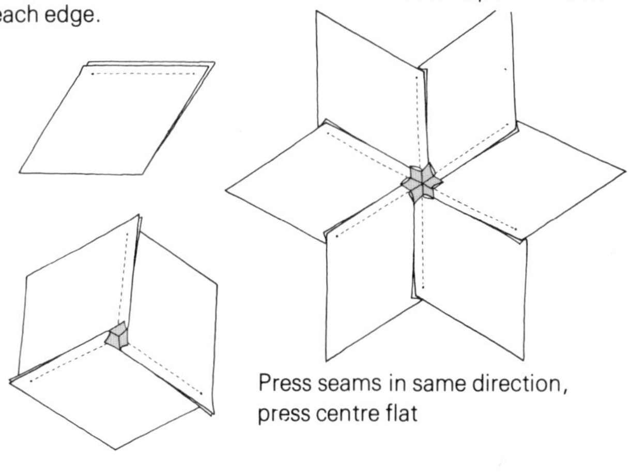
Press seams in same direction, press centre flat

Joining Patches by Machine:
A good way to make up large items. Seams are usually pressed open but sometimes turned to one side so a dark colour does not show through a light one.

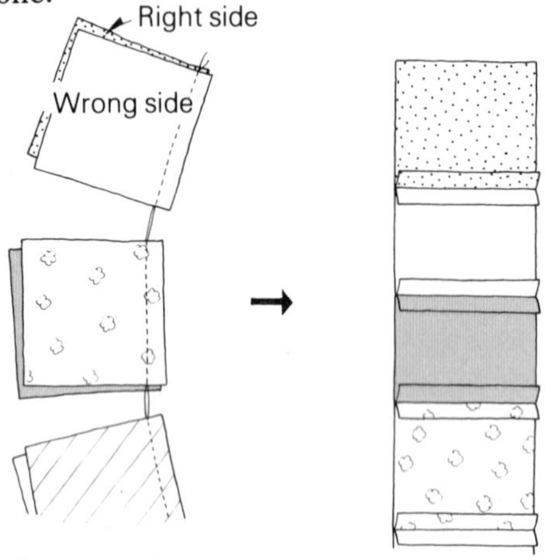
Right side
Wrong side

Machine pieces together without cutting thread, then join pairs to make a row.

QUILTING

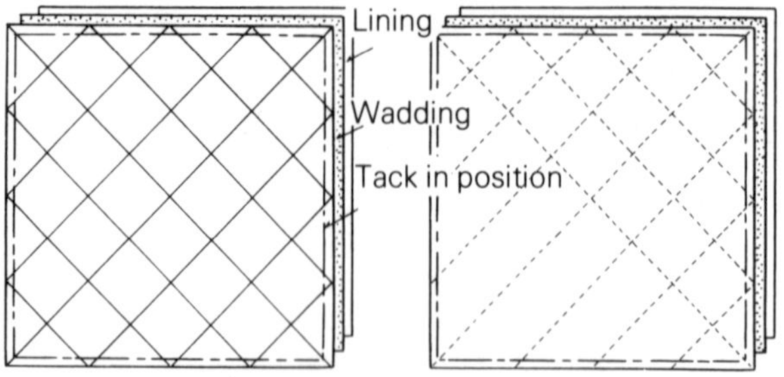

Lay wadding between top fabric and lining, tack in position and quilt with machine or running stitch.

Angle of the Needle

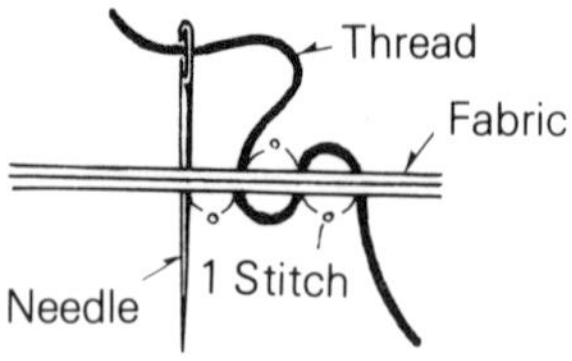

Insert needle at 90° to fabric

PIPING

①

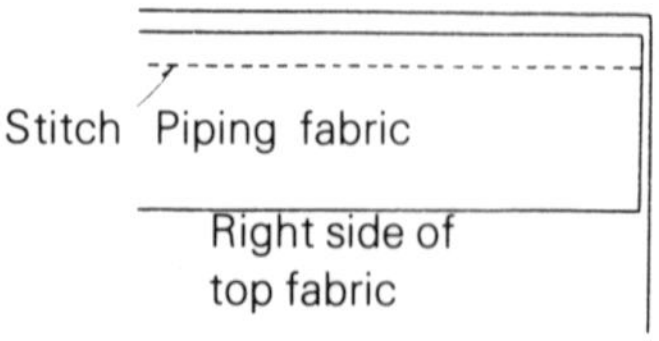
Stitch
Piping fabric
Right side of
top fabric

Position piping strip and stitch

② **Machine sewing**

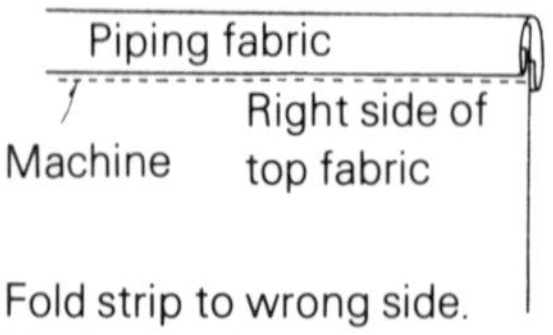
Piping fabric
Machine
Right side of
top fabric

Fold strip to wrong side. Machine right along the hem from right side

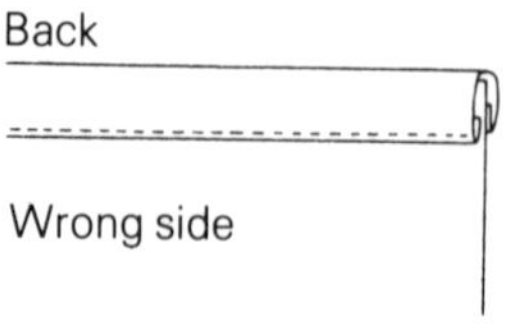
Back
Wrong side

Hand sewing

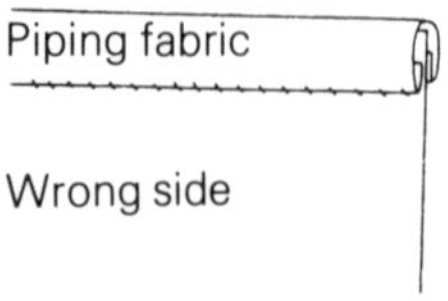
Piping fabric
Wrong side

Fold the piping strip to wrong side, slipstitch

SLIPSTITCH

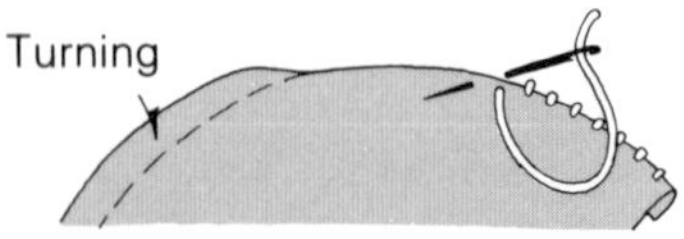
Turning

Make small stitches at right-angles to the seam with matching thread.

MAKING BIAS STRIPS

Method (A)

Cutting

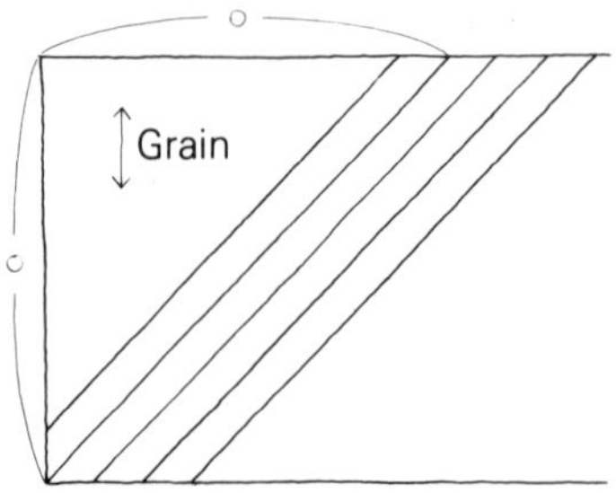
Grain

Joining

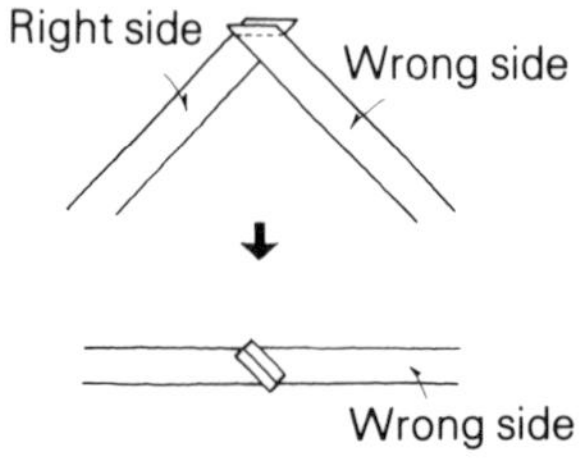

Press seam open

Method (B)

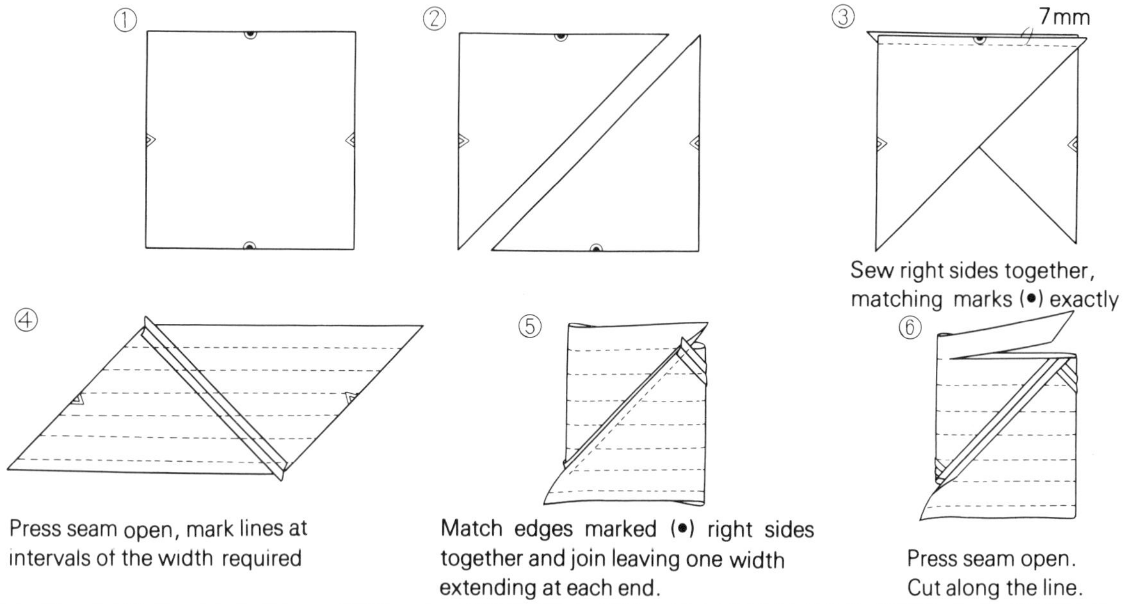
①
②
③
7mm
Sew right sides together, matching marks (•) exactly
④
⑤
⑥
Press seam open, mark lines at intervals of the width required
Match edges marked (•) right sides together and join leaving one width extending at each end.
Press seam open. Cut along the line.

List of Suppliers

John Lewis
Oxford Street
London W1A 1EX

(branches)
Peter Jones
Sloane Square
London SW1W 8EL

John Barnes
Finchley Road
London NW3 6LJ

Jones Brothers
Holloway Road
London N7 6NY

Pratts
Streatham High Road
London SW16 1BD

Caleys
High Street
Windsor SL4 1LL

Heelas
Broad Street
Reading RG1 2BB

Trewin Brothers
Queens Road
Watford WD1 2LQ

Bainbridge
Market Street
Newcastle-upon-Tyne
NE99 1AB

Cole Brothers
Barkers Pool
Sheffield S1 1EP

George Henry Lee
Basnet Street
Liverpool L1 1EA

Jessops
Victoria Centre
Nottingham NG1 3QA

Robert Sayle
St Andrew's Street
Cambridge CB2 3BL

Tyrell and Green
Above Bar
Southampton SO9 5HU

Knight and Lee
Palmerston Road
Southsea PO5 3QE

John Lewis
St James Centre
Edinburgh EH1 3SP

Laura Ashley Limited
40 Sloane Street
London SW1

(branches)
71-73 Lower Sloane Street
London SW3

157 Fulham Road
London SW3

12 New Bond Street
Bath
Avon

1a Queens Circus
Montpelier
Cheltenham
Gloucestershire

17-19 Watergate Row
Chester
Cheshire

10 Spittal Street
Edinburgh
Midlothian

404 Byres Road
Glasgow
Lanarkshire

30 Great Oak Street
Llanidloes
Powys
Wales

58 Bridesmith Gate
Nottingham
Nottinghamshire

26-27 Little Clarendon
Street
Oxford

3-5 Dove Street
Norwich
Norfolk